DATE DUE

JE 23 '94			
MR 31 '95			
MY 26 '95			
JY 6 '9~			
MY 30 '9~			
AP 5 '99			
JE 9 '04			
DE 17 '04			

LEARNING

LEARNING

A Survey of Psychological Interpretations

Fifth Edition

Winfred F. Hill

Northwestern University

HarperCollins*Publishers*

Sponsoring Editor: Laura Pearson
Project Editor: Susan Goldfarb
Art Direction: Heather A. Ziegler
Cover Coordinator: Mary Archondes
Cover Design: Delgado Design Inc.
Production: Willie Lane

Learning: A Survey of Psychological Interpretations, Fifth Edition
Copyright © 1990 by HarperCollins, Publishers, Inc.

Library of Congress Cataloging-in-Publication Data

Hill, Winfred F.
    Learning : a survey of psychological interpretations / Winfred F.
Hill. — 5th ed.
      p. cm.
    Bibliography: p.
    Includes index.
    ISBN 0-06-042809-0
    1. Learning, Psychology of. I. Title.
BF318.H553 1990   89-7631
153.1′5—dc20   CIP

     91 92 9 8 7 6 5 4 3 2

To my father, a devoted educator

And my mother,
whose experience in education
helped her to educate me

Contents

Preface

As in the previous editions of *Learning: A Survey of Psychological Interpretations,* a major focus of the fifth edition is on theories that combine the best features of connectionist and cognitive approaches to learning. In any revision, there is always the feeling that more new or newly popular theories should be added. In the interest of keeping the book manageable for the reader, I have restricted my choices to two: Anderson's ACT theory and the set of network models based on parallel distributed processing. The former begins with cognitive assumptions and moves via response compilation to processes with which a traditional connectionist would be almost comfortable. The latter appropriates the term *connectionism* but proceeds to develop models that might be most pleasing to a gestalt psychologist. Both, therefore, contribute to the search for a theory that will deal optimally with learning across the range, from classical conditioning to logical deduction.

Bandura's social learning theory, which represented a "liberalization" of the behaviorist approach in a cognitive direction, has now moved further in that direction and become social cognitive theory. Treatment of Bandura has been correspondingly expanded. Other topics that receive a little more attention than in the previous edition are Pavlovian theory, biological constraints on learning, and the relationship between behavioral regulation and reinforcement.

The cumulative effect of the three previous revisions has been to increase both the length and the difficulty level of the book. In an effort to stop this trend and to keep the book both short and accessible to a wide range of readers, I have made a number of deletions. The most conspicuous is in mathematical models. One such model of learning is enough to illustrate the approach, and Estes' stimulus-sampling model seemed best to serve that function. I therefore reluctantly made the decision to drop Rescorla and Wagner's conditioning model, along with Estes' single-element model, and not to put any others in their place. In addition, the treatment of Hull and the neo-Hullians has been further reduced, various other deletions and abridgements have been made, and some passages have been rewritten to increase clarity.

As in the previous editions, I have tried to focus more on theories than on data, and on the learning process per se rather than on peripheral issues. The problem, of course, is to decide which peripheral issues are actually important to an understanding of learning. My decision, for a mixture of logical, historical, and personal reasons, has been to give some attention to issues of motivation, memory, problem solving, and development, but little or none to perception, information processing, and language comprehension. In addition, I have occasionally included a topic in order to highlight the contrast between approaches that emphasize learning and related ones that do not, as with Lewin's theory and to some extent with cybernetics.

I am indebted to the following reviewers of the manuscript for their comments and suggestions:

Veronica Dark
Iowa State University

Ken Leask
Aurora University

Thomas Mahan
The Citadel

Stephen Klein
Fort Hays State University

Martin Gipson
University of the Pacific

Horace Marchant
Westfield State College

Wayne Sjoberg
Northern Arizona University

Yoshito Kawahara
San Diego Mesa College

Karen Chapin
University of Detroit

S. David Leonard
University of Georgia

George Marsh
California State University, Dominguez Hills

Scott Brown
University of Connecticut

Julia Wallace
University of Northern Iowa

The goal of this book is to provide a short, broad-spectrum, relatively easy treatment of theories of learning, past and present—a treatment just technical enough to give the flavor of the field, but with substantial emphasis on applications and general-interest implications. The text is designed to be useful either as primary reading in courses on learning or as supplementary reading in learning and memory, history and systems, advanced educational psychology, and other courses in both pure and applied psychology.

WINFRED F. HILL

Chapter
1

How Psychologists Study Learning

*T*heoretical systems for the interpretation of learning have grown up along with the experimental study of learning, and to understand one it is necessary to understand the other. Although the experimental study of learning to a large extent grew out of everyday problems, particularly problems in education, it soon became involved with theoretical issues and with experiments appropriate for dealing with them. This theoretical involvement proceeded to such an extent that the original problems became barely recognizable. It is therefore worthwhile to take a long look at the interrelations between theory, research, and applications in the field of learning before undertaking a detailed survey of different theoretical systems.

The reader should be warned at the outset that psychologists use the term *learning* more broadly than it is used in popular speech. Although it is almost impossible to give an exact definition of learning that will be generally acceptable to psychologists, we can at least note certain phenomena to which the term is or is not applied. In psychological usage, what is learned need not be "correct" or adaptive (we learn bad habits as well as good), need not be conscious or deliberate (one of the advantages of coaching in a skill is that it makes us aware of mistakes we have unconsciously learned to make), and need not involve any overt act (attitudes and emotions can be learned as well as knowledge and skills). Reactions as diverse as driving a car, remembering a pleasant vacation, believing in democracy, and disliking one's boss all represent the results of learning.

How does learning take place? What factors determine what we will learn and how rapidly we will learn it? There are innumerable

1

people in situations in which it would be useful to have answers to these questions. We think at once of students looking for better methods of study, of teachers wanting to improve their classroom techniques, and of people in industry seeking better ways of training new workers. We may also consider the parent looking for the best way of raising children, the counselor trying to improve a client's emotional and social adjustment, the animal trainer preparing seeing-eye dogs for their work, and the advertiser attempting to develop a consumer's preference for a client's product. In all of these cases, knowledge about the learning process represents power.

The above practical needs are not the only reasons for wanting to know more about learning. People have always been curious about themselves, have always wanted to know more about what "makes them tick." Since learning is such an important factor in what we are and do, a greater understanding of the learning process would go far toward increasing self-knowledge. Consequently, people are motivated to study learning, not only by the practical benefits to be gained but also by curiosity about themselves and how they came to be as they are.

LEARNING IN SCHOOL

Let's begin by looking at a setting in which learning is the primary focus: the school. Children in school face a bewilderingly complex learning situation. It is complex from their point of view; it is even more so from the point of view of the psychologist who bravely attempts to analyze it. The children are influenced in countless ways by the varied aspects of the classroom situation. They learn much from the teacher, including many things not prescribed in the curriculum and some things of which neither teacher nor pupils are aware. They also learn from books, from fellow students, and from the physical arrangements of the school. Part of what they learn is measurable as specific knowledge and skills, while another part involves changes, some very subtle but a few quite dramatic, in attitudes, emotions, social behavior, and a variety of other reactions. The psychologist's job is to analyze such complex situations into their component parts and to try to understand the principles of learning and motivation involved.

Let us consider some incidents in the school day of a particular sixth-grader, Alex B. We meet Alex first as he is studying a vocabulary list in his reading book. His teacher (a trifle old-fashioned) has instructed the class to learn to spell these words. He is thus confronted with a list of 12 words for which he must learn to give the correct written form when presented with the spoken form. However, in studying from his book he faces a slightly different task, since only the written form is before him and he must provide the spoken version (subvocally) himself. He goes through the list, pronouncing and spelling the words to himself, but finds his attention wandering. He looks out the window and remembers how much he enjoyed the previous weekend. Snapping back to the spelling book, he continues dutifully to the end of the list. Then he tries covering all but the first letter of each word with his hand in an attempt to spell the word to himself. At *r* he proceeds cautiously, trying to remember the rule for *i* and *e*. Finally he decides on "receive," moves his hand away, and relaxes a bit as he finds his guess confirmed. At *s* he spells to himself, without hesitation, "seperate," then frowns as he sees his mistake. He stares for a moment at the *ar*, trying to fix it in his memory, then continues through the list. Halfway through, he finds himself unable to remember a word from the first letter.

Annoyed, he looks at the word and then concentrates heavily on trying to remember it. Two words later, the same thing happens again. He looks at the word, wonders why it should be hard to remember, and begins to feel discouraged. He stares at the picture on the wall of Washington crossing the Delaware, and imagines himself leading such an expedition. Catching the teacher's eye, he returns quickly to his book and finishes the list. He spells the last word confidently as "cematary," only to find "cemetery" staring back at him from the page. Puzzled, he looks back and forth from "separate" to "cemetery" and thinks, "I hate spelling."

We see Alex next at recess running excitedly out to join a softball game. He begins the game in the outfield. As the batter hits a ground ball in his direction, he starts running, his speed and direction adjusted to make his path intercept that of the ball. As he nears the ball he bends over, puts his hands in front of it, and closes them at just the right moment to catch the ball. He then looks up, notes the position of the runner, and throws the ball in the direction of first base, his arm motion just forceful enough to carry the ball to the first baseman. This whole sequence of coordinated, purposeful behavior occurs rapidly, almost automatically, with no evidence of thought or verbal self-instruction. Watching him, the teacher is impressed by how much Alex has improved at softball since she has known him.

During the game, Alex calls frequently, "Wait'll I get to bat!" and "When am I up?" Finally his turn comes. He pounds the plate and shouts, "Put it over!" When the pitcher throws the ball, Alex takes a mighty swing at it, and misses. He looks chagrined, but shouts, "Let's have another!" Again he swings and misses. This time he frowns and says nothing. He stands more rigidly at the plate, his teeth clenched. His swing at the third pitch is more tense, less free, and again he misses. He throws the bat down and stalks away. At his next turn in the outfield, he does no shouting, and his fielding is less coordinated. When recess ends, he returns quietly to the classroom, ignoring the chatter around him. He seems relieved that recess is over.

Later we see Alex during his math lesson. The class has been learning how to find the areas of rectangles. Now the teacher raises the problem of how to find the area of a triangle. She draws a right triangle with a 4-inch side and a 3-inch side on the blackboard and asks the students what the area is. Alex likes math and enjoys learning how to solve new problems, so he eagerly tries to figure this one out. He tries to apply the rule for rectangles, but cannot see how to do it. Then the teacher draws two more lines, making a rectangle with the hypotenuse of the triangle as its diagonal. Alex stares at this for a moment, then grins and excitedly holds up his hand. "The area is 6. The whole rectangle is 12, and there are two triangles, and each triangle is half of the rectangle!" The teacher smiles. "Very good. The area is half of 4 times 3. Math makes a lot of sense when you figure it out like that." Alex basks in his success, pleased both with the teacher's approval and with his triumph over the impersonal challenge of the problem.

We leave Alex now, happy that a rather frustrating day for him has ended with success. However, the challenge to a psychologist to analyze Alex's experiences lasts long after the incidents are over. In fact, the narrative of Alex's day might be used as a hidden-picture puzzle: "How many aspects of learning can you find illustrated in these incidents?" Consider, for example, the similarities and differences among the three situations in which we saw Alex. All involved learning, motivation, goal-directed behavior, and success or failure. All could be analyzed in terms of the responses that Alex made to various stimuli in his environment, and also in terms of the way he perceived the environment. All occurred in social situations and against a background of norms and values shared (though not completely) by Alex, his teacher, and his fellow students. However, the three situations differed in the principal kinds of learning involved (verbal memorization of the spelling list, motor skill on the softball field, and logical insight in the math problem). The situations also differed in the emotional learning that occurred and in some of the subsidiary principles. In each situation we may ask what factors contributed to Alex's successes and failures. How much did his difficulty in spelling *cemetery,* for example, depend on the word itself, on its position in the list, on the fact that *separate* came earlier in the same lesson, on distractions in the room at that moment, or on a variety of other facts about Alex, the lesson, and the general situation? There are endless possibilities for the psychologist to analyze in these three everyday situations.

However, such analysis assumes that we already know a great deal about the principles of learning. In cases where a number of factors might have influenced Alex's behavior, we cannot make worthwhile guesses about how important each was unless we have information about how important each has been in other similar situations. For example, we cannot judge whether the word *cemetery* itself or the situation in which Alex encountered it contributed more to his error unless we know something about the relative importance of words and their context in other cases of memorization. It is to provide such information about the regularities in behavior that psychologists do experimental studies. If we learn from such studies that certain situations cause special difficulty in memorizing, we are in a much better position both to explain Alex's errors and to find ways of helping him.

LEARNING IN THE LABORATORY

Let us now look at some typical laboratory learning situations. As compared with Alex's experiences, some of these may appear artificial or trivial. This difference is the price we pay in order to have situations in which we can manipulate certain variables, hold others constant, and measure precisely the resultant changes in behavior. We will see many relations between the complex situations in which Alex learned and these simpler, better-controlled laboratory learning situations.

Two Complex Learning Situations

In the first laboratory situation, as in Alex's math lesson, the learner (commonly called the subject) is presented with a problem for which he must find a solution. A traditional problem for use with college students requires the subject to tie together two strings hanging from the ceiling. The strings are so far apart that when one is held, the student cannot reach the other, which is why this otherwise easy task constitutes a problem. The only equipment available to help with the job is a pair of pliers. Can the student find a way of tying the strings together? (There need not be an actual room with two strings; problem and solution can all be worked with pencil and paper.)

What commonly happens in this situation is that the subject tries a variety of approaches, all unsuccessful. The pliers might be used as an extension of the arm to reach the second string, but they are too short. It might be possible to cut a piece off one of the strings with the pliers and tie it to the other, but the two strings could still not be brought together. Finally the thought of swinging the strings occurs to most people. Given this lead, the solution usually comes quickly: tie the pliers to one of the strings, start the string swinging as a pendulum, then run over to the other string, bring it as close as possible to the one that is swinging, and catch the swinging one at the closest point of its arc. Since the subject is now holding both strings, he or she can easily tie them together.

How does this laboratory problem differ from the geometric problem that Alex solved in the classroom? In principle, there is very little difference. Both have simple solutions drawing on the solver's past experience, but both are difficult because they require the use of this past experience in new ways. The solution in each case usually involves a period of futile search followed by a flash of insight. A hint, such as the two extra lines the teacher drew, or the word *pendulum* in the two-string problem, often results in quick solution of the problem. The ability to tie the strings or compute the area of the triangle not only appears suddenly but is also very well retained as compared with most other learned material.

The important difference is not between the two problems but between the classroom and the laboratory. In the classroom case, we do not know how soon (if at all) Alex would have solved the problem without the teacher's hint, or why Alex rather than another student solved it first, or how many other students would have found the solution if Alex had not beaten them to it, or how the presence of other students helped or hindered him. In the laboratory, on the other hand, all of these questions can be systematically studied. The problem can be presented to subjects singly or in groups, with hints at predetermined points, and each person's time to solution (and mistaken "solutions") can be recorded. This laboratory situation makes it possible to investigate two sets of factors—those in the situation and those in the individual—that contribute to this learning.

Another laboratory example, closer to the popular image of a learning situation, involves rote memorization. The items to be memorized are commonly either words or *trigrams* (three-letter sequences that do not make a word), but they may be sentences or longer passages of connected material. The task may be to learn a series of them in order (as would be the case in learning a series of instructions), or to remember as many items as possible regardless of order (as for remembering a number of jobs that need to be done), or to learn a number of pairs of items with one member of the pair always given as the response to the other (comparable to learning a foreign language vocabulary), or any of various other possibilities. Usually the rate at which the items are delivered to the learner is controlled by the experimenter, such as by presenting them on the screen of a computer terminal.

The contrast between such a learning task and Alex's spelling lesson again lies largely in the precision of control that the laboratory setup permits. Alex could approach the words to be learned in any order and divide his time among them in any way he chose. Moreover, he had to study from a book, even though the test of his mastery would consist of writing the words in response to oral dictation. This difference forced him to devise techniques of practice that would as nearly as possible match the test procedure. Finally, he was subjected to the distractions of the classroom situation. The laboratory subject, on the other hand, commonly sees the items in a predetermined order and for constant amounts of time in a small room with a minimum of distractions. Often the subject is automatically tested on each item each time through the list, so there is a continuous record of mastery of each item at each stage in the learning process. This record makes possible separate analyses of different stages of learning, different parts of the list, and different individual items.

Three Simpler Learning Situations

Both the problem-solving and the rote-learning situations in the laboratory represent refinements of learning situations found in the classroom and elsewhere in everyday life outside the laboratory. However, many psychological experimenters analyze these and other examples of learning (e.g., Alex's learning of the motor skills involved in fielding a softball) into simpler components and then study these components separately. Rather than working with complex patterns of responses such as Alex learned, they study changes in the frequency or magnitude or speed of a single response. Their object is not to study everyday kinds of learning under better-controlled conditions, but to study the underlying components of everyday learning in order to get a better understanding of what learning is. Such understanding, it is hoped, can then be used to predict learning in a great variety of more complex situations. This approach is comparable to that in other sciences, in which complex chemical substances are analyzed into their component elements or the speed of a falling object is studied as a function of the distance it has fallen, without regard to whether the object is a mailbag, a skydiver before the parachute opens, or a hydrogen bomb.

Since research of this sort attempts to reduce learning to its assumed simplest essentials, animals have often been found to be more satisfactory subjects than humans. Animals lack the complexities of language and cultural traditions, their background of previous experience is both simpler and (at least if they are reared in the laboratory) less variable than that of humans, and their heredity as well as their rearing can to a considerable extent be controlled. All these factors make it easier to study one aspect of the animal's learning processes at a time while holding others constant. For example, if we want to study the rate at which a dog learns to flex its leg to avoid an electric shock, we probably do not have to worry about the dog's interpretation of the purpose of the experiment or about its concern with behaving bravely, politely, or rationally, all of which would be factors if we were studying the same behavior in humans. This is not to say that humans cannot usefully be studied in such situations, for they often are; but it points out why for certain purposes animals often are preferred.

The above discussion implies that it does not make much difference what species we study—that the basic laws of learning are the same in rats, dogs, pigeons, monkeys, and humans. Learning theorists have indeed commonly made that assumption. The emphasis here is on the word *basic*. No one doubts that there are differences in the way different species learn, but it is often assumed that there are common underlying principles that apply to a wide range of species, principles from which we can deduce the detailed patterns of learning in different species. More is said about this assumption in Chapter 17, but for the present it is enough to note how important the assumption has been in learning theory over the years. We will see many examples of its application in the chapters that follow.

One simple animal response that has been extensively studied is the pecking response in pigeons. A lighted disk is displayed on the side of the box in which the pigeon is confined. The disk is referred to as a *key*, since like a telegraph key it closes an electrical circuit to record the pigeon's response, and the whole apparatus is known as a Skinner box, in honor of the theorist we will consider in Chapter 6. If a hungry pigeon is occasionally rewarded with food for pecking the key, it will peck it at a high rate. This pecking rate is quite sensitive to changes in level of hunger, frequency of food reward, and other variables. It can thus be used to investigate many of the phenomena of simple learning.

The low rate at which the pigeon pecks before food is introduced is called the *operant* (or *baseline*) *rate*. When food is first presented as soon as the pigeon pecks the key, the rate of pecking rises. In technical terms, this change indicates that the food reinforces the pecking, or that it is a *reinforcer*. If some but not all pecks are followed by food, the particular pattern used (e.g., food after every tenth peck, or after one peck each minute) is known as the *schedule of reinforcement*. If pecking is no longer followed by food, the rate drops. This decline in rate resulting from the removal of the reinforcer is known as *extinction*. If after extinction takes place there is an interval of time during which the pigeon does not have access to the key, and then the key is presented again, the pecking rate is likely to be higher than it was at the end of extinction. This increase in rate is called, naturally enough, *spontaneous recovery*. If a key that the pigeon has been reinforced for pecking is replaced by another key of a different color, the pigeon will peck at this key also, though not as much as at the original one. This tendency to respond to stimuli other than the one used in training is known as *generalization*. If, however, the two keys are presented alternately, with pecking at one reinforced and pecking at the other nonreinforced (extinguished), the pigeon will learn to peck the reinforced key at a high rate and the nonreinforced key very little. We then say that a *discrimination* between the keys has been formed.

Many aspects of the above learning phenomena have been studied experimentally. How does the rate of pecking vary with the amount of food given, the schedule of reinforcement, or the delay between peck and food? How does spontaneous recovery vary with the time interval between extinction and test, or generalization vary with the difference in color between the two keys? Will making a pigeon more hungry increase or decrease its ability to form a discrimination? Questions like this may be studied, not only with regard to the rate of key pecking in pigeons, but also with regard to many other forms of behavior in a variety of species.

These learning phenomena, established in experimental studies, can be applied (though often with some modification) to complex learning in everyday life. Though we did not see Alex over a long enough period of time to observe the effects of reinforcement and extinction in his behavior, we can note a number of cases in which these processes were probably occurring for him. His statement about the area of the triangle was reinforced by the teacher's praise, his techniques of fielding the softball by the approval of his fellow players, and his correct spellings by seeing those spellings confirmed by the printed words. On the other hand, his incorrect spellings, his batting techniques, and his confident manner with regard to batting were not reinforced and hence presumably underwent some extinction. The disappearance of his confident shouting after he struck out might be taken as evidence of extinction. If the shouting reappeared at his next softball game, this renewal could be interpreted as spontaneous recovery. The problem of spelling *separate* with an *ar* and *cemetery* with an *er* clearly involved making a discrimination between two similar situations, and it might also be interpreted as extinguishing the tendency to spell phonetically.

Not only can we identify these learning processes operating in everyday life; we can also make predictions from learning experiments to everyday learning situations. For example, it is commonly found in experiments that a delay between the response and the reinforcer results in poorer performance of the learned response. From this finding we could make predictions about the efficacy of different teaching methods. If Alex had taken a spelling quiz on one day but had not found out which words he got right until the papers were handed back the next day, he probably would have learned less spelling than he did with his book, because of the delay in reinforcement. However, it is possible that the opposite might be true, either because correctness on a graded test is more reinforcing than correctness on a private self-test, or because writing from dictation is a better way of studying spelling, or for a variety of other reasons. This example thus points up both the usefulness of laboratory study in making suggestions about everyday learning and the danger in taking such suggestions uncritically.

A fourth example of laboratory learning, and one even less like the ordinary picture of a learning situation, occurs in experiments on *classical conditioning*. The first of these, and still the most famous, were those in which the Russian physiologist Ivan Pavlov, who will be considered in Chapter 3, used the procedure to train dogs to salivate to a new stimulus. Another version of this procedure (less famous than Pavlov's salivating dogs, but more popular in American labs) is the conditioning of the eyeblink reflex in humans and in rabbits. If people who are watching a dim light see the light grow somewhat brighter, they ordinarily do not blink their eyes in response to this stimulus. If, however, they are hit in the eye by a mild puff of air, they do blink. The conditioning procedure consists in pairing these two stimuli, with the brightening of the light coming a fraction of a second before the puff of air. Each time this sequence occurs, the subject blinks in response to the air puff. Presently, however, the subject begins to blink as soon as the light changes, before the puff comes. Since the changing light now produces a blinking response which it formerly did not produce, learning is said to have taken place. In this setup the puff, which already produced blinking, is called the *unconditioned stimulus,* and blinking to the puff is the *unconditioned response.* The increase in brightness of the light is called the *conditioned stimulus,* and the learned response of blinking to it is the *conditioned response.* The whole learning sequence is known as *conditioning.* The same principles of reinforcement, extinction, spontaneous recovery, generalization, and discrimination that were illustrated by the pigeon pecking a key can also be demonstrated in classical conditioning situations.

The distinctive characteristic of this kind of learning is that the conditioned stimulus elicits a response after the learning experience that only the unconditioned stimulus elicited before. (Because some authorities use the term *conditioning* rather broadly, this specific kind is often referred to as either classical conditioning or Pavlovian conditioning.) Since classical conditioning does not involve learning new responses, solving problems, or carrying out goal-directed activity, it seems at first glance to be of little importance compared with the other forms of learning discussed so far. Some theorists have concurred in this judgment, regarding classical conditioning as nothing more than a laboratory curiosity. Others, as we shall see, have regarded it as being of central importance. One viewpoint is that its importance is mainly for understanding the learning of emotional reactions. When Alex experienced failures at spelling and at batting, he reacted with discouragement and anger. These can be considered unconditioned responses to the unconditioned stimulus of failure. When he said, "I hate spelling," this opinion may have indicated that conditioning was taking place, with the spelling lesson as the conditioned stimulus and discouragement and anger as the conditioned response. This interpretation makes classical conditioning of emotional responses crucial to our learning of attitudes toward all the people, objects, and situations we encounter in our lives.

A fifth and final laboratory example of learning is the *maze.* The principles involved in maze learning are similar to those in the key-pecking experiments already mentioned, but the maze has been used so widely in learning experiments that it deserves separate mention. The original mazes were modeled after the Hampton Court maze in England, where tall hedges formed an intricate pattern of winding pathways through which visitors tried to find their way. Miniature versions of this maze were used to study the ways in which both humans and animals learned to avoid the many blind alleys and find the correct path from the starting point to the goal. In earlier years mazes became simpler and simpler as psychologists tried to find the basic principles involved in learning them. The winding pathways of the Hampton Court maze were replaced by alleys with a simple series of left and right turns. Even these, however, came to be considered too complicated, and were largely replaced with "mazes" that offered only a single choice, between a right and a left turn. Because of their shape, these are known as T-mazes. They are too easy to be useful with humans, but have been widely used with animals, particularly well-domesticated white rats. Even the one choice point may be eliminated, leaving only a straight runway. Here one can study only how fast the animal runs and whether it runs at all. Simple as it is, the runway has proved valuable for studying many aspects of reinforcement, extinction, and even discrimination. More recently, mazes have grown more complicated again. A popular example is the *radial maze,* with eight arms radiating out from a central platform, in which rats scurry from arm to arm finding food. The radial maze has proved useful in studying animals' memories for where food is located.

Advantages of Laboratory Study

The preceding examples should have helped to indicate the relationships between the sorts of learning situations studied in the laboratory and those of most interest to educators and to others directly concerned with the problems of learning in everyday life. However, it may be well to discuss certain aspects of the relationships more explicitly. Two main points need to be considered: (1) what psychologists gain by studying learning under the somewhat artificial conditions of the laboratory, and (2) what difficulties are involved in applying the results to other, nonlaboratory situations.

There are two main ways in which psychologists gain by taking questions about learning into the laboratory. One of these pertains to measurement. The laboratory situation permits experimenters to measure the subject's behavior more adequately than is usually possible outside the laboratory. They can keep an accurate record of how long it takes a subject to memorize certain material or to solve a given problem, of how many and what kinds of errors a subject makes, and of the successive stages by which mastery is reached. This improved measurement is valuable for three reasons. First, it gives a more complete picture of the learning process. Details are recorded that otherwise would be overlooked or quickly forgotten. Second, it protects researchers from the mistake of noticing and remembering only what they expect. Thus a teacher who is convinced that a certain new method of teaching long division will work better than the old method may clearly remember striking successes with the new method, while overlooking the failures as unimportant exceptions. It is possible, of course, that in this case the failures *are* unimportant exceptions, but whether or not they are should be decided by careful consideration, not by spur-of-the-moment intuition. If both successes and failures are recorded as they occur, and if extenuating circumstances are noted for the successes as well as for the failures, the effect of teaching with the new method can be more objectively evaluated. Third, apart from such systematic biases as this teacher has, careful measurement also protects researchers against all the unsystematic errors of observation and memory that are likely to occur when research is carried on as part of everyday work. Thus measurement in the laboratory will probably be more thorough, more precise, and more objective than measurement in comparable situations elsewhere. Although in principle it is possible to achieve equally good measurement outside the laboratory, in practice it is usually much harder to do so.

The other gain from studying learning in the lab is control. Essentially, this gain is associated with our ability to study one thing at a time. When we control a variable, we hold it constant so that it will not interfere with our studying another variable. Suppose, for example, that we want to find out whether it is easier to learn spelling when words that are likely to cause confusion because of similar letter sequences (e.g., *separate* and *cemetery*) are in the same lesson or in different lessons. We can study this problem by preparing two sets of lessons, one according to each principle, and using them with two sets of students. However, we must see to it that the two sets of students do not differ in intelligence, interest in spelling, previous experience with these words, or motivation to do well in their studies. We must also see that the groups are taught by teachers who do not differ in teaching ability or in enthusiasm. In other words, we must control intelligence, motivation, and all other variables except arrangement of the words in the spelling lessons. Only then can we be confident that any difference we find in mastery of the spelling lessons is due to arrangement of the words rather than to some other difference between the two sets of students. Because the practical demands of the classroom make it difficult to obtain such control, or even to know whether one has obtained it, it is valuable to have laboratories specially arranged for doing well-controlled experiments.

Though laboratory studies of learning provide great advantages in measurement and in control, we must not suppose that they provide easy answers to questions about the practical management of learning. Because they typically study single variables out of their usual context, laboratory experiments can seldom give direct answers to questions about how these variables work together in that context. For example, it has been established in a number of experiments that larger reinforcers lead to better performance in a learning situation. Does it follow that the more lavishly a teacher praises students for their successes, the better the students will do their work? Perhaps, but there are various reasons that this result might not follow. The students might become so used to this effusive praise that it would soon be no more reinforcing to them than mild praise would be to other students. Or, perhaps, those who failed to win the praise might be all the more frustrated because the praise they missed was so desirable, a consequence that might result in more disappointment and anger becoming conditioned as responses to the stimuli of the whole situation. Moreover, neither the reinforcers nor the learning tasks used in the laboratory are likely to be the same ones used in the classroom (in fact, many of the studies on reinforcement magnitude were done with animals); this kind of difference will probably make the outcomes different in degree, and possibly in kind. Finally, even if the subjects, tasks, and reinforcers are all similar in the laboratory and in the classroom, the difference between working alone in an unfamiliar situation (the laboratory) and working in a familiar group situation (the classroom) may produce considerable differences in behavior. For all these reasons we would be rash to generalize directly and confidently from the laboratory studies to the classroom application. However, the laboratory studies, in addition to providing basic knowledge about the processes of learning, suggest many possible applications to the classroom and to other applied settings.

Chapter
2

The Nature of Learning Theories

*R*esearchers in the field of learning, like those in any other branch of science, are concerned with discovering scientific *laws*. All the experimental procedures we have examined are directed toward such discovery. A law is a statement about the conditions under which certain things occur. Some laws are highly precise and accurate, as in the physicist's statement that the period of a pendulum is proportional to the square root of its length. Other laws are much less precise and much more subject to error, as when the amateur weather prophet maintains, "Red sky at night, sailor's delight; red sky in the morning, sailor take warning." In both cases, however, we are being told that certain events occur under certain conditions. Given those conditions, we can predict that these events will occur. The prediction need not always be correct, so long as it is correct often enough to be useful. If bad weather occurs 75 percent of the time when the morning sky is red and only 20 percent of the time when the morning sky is gray, the amateur weather prophet has a useful law, even though not a wholly accurate one, for predicting the weather.

VARIABLES AND LAWS

All laws state a relationship between a *dependent variable* and one or more *independent variables*. A variable is any measurable characteristic, whether of a person, a situation, or anything else. A dependent variable is one about which we make a prediction; an independent variable is one we use to make the prediction. In the above examples, the length of the pendulum and the color of the sky were independent variables, while the period of the pendulum (the time it takes to make its complete swing) and the weather were dependent variables. In a study of learning, the dependent variable is some aspect of the learner's performance, while the independent variables may be any characteristics of the learner, the task, or the situation.

In some cases these variables and the laws relating them to one another involve merely the presence or absence of something. This is true with the weather prediction law. Red in the evening indicates good weather and red in the morning bad weather; that is all we are told. Does it matter whether the red is pale or deep? Will the bad weather be a drizzle or a hurricane? The law does not tell us. In other words, it deals with *qualitative* information only, information about the *kinds* of events that occur. In other cases, however, degrees of the independent variable are related to degrees of the dependent variable. The physicist's law tells us how much of a change in pendulum length will produce how much of a change in period. This, then, is a *quantitative* law, one that gives information about *amounts* of things, about the degree to which certain events occur. In learning, the statement that removal of a reinforcer produces extinction is a qualitative law, since it refers only to whether or not reinforcement is removed and whether or not extinction occurs. On the other hand, the statement that a larger reward results in a higher level of performance is quantitative, since it deals with different amounts of reward and different levels of performance. Both qualitative and quantitative laws are found in all branches of science, but in general the more highly developed sciences tend to have more quantitative laws, resulting in more precise predictions.

Independent variables also differ in another respect. Some independent variables can be directly varied by an experimenter, who can arrange the independent variable in a certain way and then see what happens to the dependent variable. For example, a physicist can change the length of a pendulum in order to see how this difference affects the rate at which the pendulum swings. Likewise, a psychologist can stop reinforcing a pigeon for pecking a key and watch what happens to the rate of pecking. Such a study, in which the independent variable is manipulated by the researcher, is called an *experiment*. If the experiment is properly controlled, we can conclude definitely that the changes in the independent variable caused the changes in the dependent variable.

There are other independent variables, however, that cannot be manipulated by an experimenter. The weather prophet cannot make the sky red in order to see what will happen to the weather. One has to wait until the sky gets red by itself and then watch for changes in the weather. This is still a perfectly valid scientific study, but it is not an experiment, for the researcher does not manipulate the independent variable. A similar example in learning would be a study of memorization rate in people of varying IQs. Here IQ would be the independent variable and rate of learning the dependent variable. The researchers could not change a person's IQ; they could only choose subjects who already had different IQs and then compare learning rates. A difficulty with this kind of nonexperimental study is that we can seldom be sure just what is causing what. We would not be likely to say that red in the evening sky caused good weather; presumably some atmospheric condition caused both. The red sky was merely an indicator of good weather, not its cause. We might say that high IQ caused faster memorizing (if we found such a relationship, as we quite likely would not), but perhaps it would be just as reasonable to say that high memorizing ability was responsible, over a lifetime, for the development of a high IQ. These nonexperimental studies do give us laws that are valuable for prediction, but for telling us what causes what, they are definitely inferior. For this and other reasons, experimental studies are preferable whenever it is possible to do them, and the great majority of psychological studies of learning are experiments.

As we have seen, scientific laws may differ in several ways. They may indicate simply that when something happens, something else will happen, or they may relate the amount of something to the amount of something else. They may be based on experiments or on nonexperimental observations. They may be very precise or they may allow for a large amount of error. In all cases, however, they state a relationship between an independent and a dependent variable in such a way as to make possible prediction from the independent to the dependent variable. These laws are the primary focus of science in general and hence of the psychology of learning in particular.

ABSTRACTION

Scientific laws are statements about the way the world operates, and like all statements they involve abstractions. Whenever we apply words to things and events, we ignore a great deal of what is there in order to focus attention on what this particular thing or event has in common with others. For example, when we call something a car, we are ignoring its make, model, year, and color in order to emphasize the features it has in common with other cars. In other words, we are abstracting its "car-ness" from all the other characteristics of the particular battered brown 8-year-old two-door Ford. The same is true when we use the term *discrimination* to describe the behavior both of a rat learning whether to turn right or left in a T-maze and of a pupil learning whether to use *ar* or *er* in spelling a word. Again, we are dealing with an abstract concept, ignoring most aspects of the two situations in order to concentrate on one thing that they have in common.

Since some degree of abstraction is inescapable, any statement, however concretely "factual," is an abstract formulation that tells only a part of the truth. To say "Columbus crossed the ocean blue in 1492" is to give only the barest outline of that momentous event. Even to say "Jane Doe dropped a copy of *A Tale of Two Cities* from her school desk to the floor in the middle of an arithmetic lesson in Room 6 on the morning of March 17" is to give only a minute fraction of the detail that could have been observed. For all their tremendous value, words are only pale shadows of the things they represent.

This process of abstraction goes on in all description and in all thought. Every intellectual activity involves the organization and simplification of "reality" as it is presented to our senses. This statement is true whether we consider simple perceptions or complex thoughts, and whether we look at science, art, sports, business, or any other area of human interest. Imagine, for example, what the radio broadcast of a football game would sound like if it were presented by a society editor, or by the proud parent of one of the players, or by a foreigner studying American customs. The society editor might concentrate on the uniforms and the family backgrounds of the players; the proud parent might report only what his or her own son was doing; and the foreigner might be much more interested in the cheers and card stunts than in the progress of the game. Each of these three descriptions could be perfectly true and valid as far as it went, but what football fan would accept it as an adequate report of the game? Any description, including that of the professional sportscaster, deals with only some aspects of the "real game," reflecting not only what "really happened" but also the interests and biases and vocabulary of the reporter.

In effect, there is no such thing as pure reality; there is only reality as described or interpreted or reacted to by someone. Some descriptions are more accurate or more detailed than others, but no description is complete. Even if someone were ambitious enough to collect descriptions of a football game from everyone who was there, check them with other kinds of evidence, spend years sifting and combining these accounts, and give a final report of the game many volumes long, there would still be details that were omitted. The report would still be only an abstract, even though a very detailed one, of what happened at the game. In any case, no one would read the report, since each possible reader would be interested in those aspects of the game that the reader considered interesting or important, not in the most detailed account that human patience and ingenuity could devise. Hence any useful report of the game would involve far more abstraction and organization and simplification than our imaginary multivolume monstrosity of a description.

This process of abstraction is carried even further in scientific laws than in many other kinds of statements. In history, biography, and literature, as well as in everyday speech, we are often concerned with describing an event in as much rich detail as time and the limitations of language permit. Our several imaginary broadcasts of the football game, different as they were, were nevertheless all trying for such completeness within the limits of the reporters' interests. In science, however, we always are concerned with picking out certain aspects of the situation to be related to other aspects. In relating the period of a pendulum to its length, the physicist need not be concerned with what the pendulum is made of or with whether it is a clock pendulum, a plumb bob, or a museum display. Similarly, the psychologist's statement that removal of the reinforcer reduces the frequency of the response applies whether the reinforcer is food or praise and whether the response is pecking a key or studying spelling. The laws connecting independent and dependent variables are not descriptions of any particular event—they are statements about the conditions under which certain kinds of events occur. Scientific laws are not concerned specifically with the red sky in Chicago on June 10 or with the pendulum of Mary Jones's grandfather clock, but with all red skies or all pendulums. Some laws may be quite narrow in the range of phenomena to which they refer, but even the narrowest always refers to collections of certain kinds of events, never merely to a single unique event.

The Value of Scientific Laws

Scientific laws serve two main purposes. One purpose is practical—to provide the means of predicting and controlling events. Simply being able to predict what will happen and thus take measures to deal with it is of considerable value. Such prediction is what keeps the weather bureau and the various investment advisory services in business. It is even more useful, however, to be able to control events. An independent variable that we can manipulate gives us some degree of control over the dependent variable. This fact is the meaning of the saying that "knowledge is power." Only if we have a law about the conditions under which certain kinds of events happen can we set up the necessary conditions for one such event to happen when we want it to. It is not necessary, of course, for the law to be formally stated; much of our practical knowledge is very casual. However, the more complete and accurate our formulation of the law is, the better able we are to control the world around us.

 Scientific laws also have a less utilitarian value. Since earliest times, people have sought to understand the world in which they lived. From the child trying to find out what makes the watch tick to the cosmologist trying to find out what makes the universe tick, people constantly are asking, "What is it?" and "How does it work?" and "Why?" No practical benefits are required to justify this curiosity; to gain the knowledge is benefit enough in itself. This benefit is the basis of pure science, the search for fundamental knowledge about the world.

 Both of these purposes of science are exemplified in the study of the psychology of learning. The laws of learning are of crucial importance to education, to industrial, military, and other forms of training, to child rearing, to psychotherapy, and to a variety of other practical areas of work. They are also basic to an understanding of how individuals and societies come to be as they are, of how knowledge is obtained—indeed, of how people acquire their unique humanness. Hence for both reasons an increase in our knowledge of the laws of learning is much to be desired.

WHAT ARE LEARNING THEORIES?

Researchers are rarely satisfied, however, merely to collect more and more laws about learning or anything else. To satisfy our desire for understanding, knowledge must be organized. An encyclopedia full of laws relating each of a vast number of independent variables to each of a vast number of dependent variables might give its owner the emotional satisfaction of having a great deal of knowledge available, but it would not provide the intellectual satisfaction of understanding the topics involved. Such satisfaction requires more general knowledge than that provided by this imaginary encyclopedia of laws. Even for practical purposes, such an encyclopedia would be cumbersome. It would be more convenient to have general principles from which the specific laws could be deduced. So, although the establishing of laws is in one sense the most basic activity of science, it is not the end of scientific activity. Much of the researcher's effort is dedicated toward establishing more general principles or interpretations. This effort takes the researcher into the realm of scientific theory.

We have already seen that description represents some abstraction and organization and simplification of the events being described, and that the statement of laws represents a higher level of abstraction. With theory we come to a still higher level of abstraction. It differs in degree but not in kind from the lower levels. It is a serious mistake to think of a realm of theory that is separate and different from the realm of fact. When people speak of "facts," they are referring sometimes to descriptions of single events ("It is a fact that John W. Hinckley, Jr., shot President Reagan in 1981") and sometimes to laws ("It is a fact that hydrogen and oxygen will combine with each other to form water"). As we have seen, both descriptions and laws represent organizations and simplifications of what is "really there" according to the language and the biases and the objectives of whoever is describing the event or stating the law. Theory exemplifies the same processes, but in still greater degree. It would be reasonable to say either that facts represent one kind of theory or that theories represent one kind of fact, but most reasonable to say that fact and theory represent different degrees of what is basically a single process.

What is a theory? This is not an easy question to answer, partly because there are a number of different opinions about what a theory should be like and what functions it should serve. It is really only through studying different theories—noting their similarities and differences and the purposes their creators had in mind—that we can get a general understanding of what theories are. In a sense, therefore, the rest of this book is an attempt to answer this question. In this chapter we can hope to get only a rough and general overview.

In the broadest sense, a theory is a systematic interpretation of an area of knowledge. In the psychology of learning, *system* or *systematic interpretation* is probably a better term than *theory*, for *theory* sometimes is used in a narrower sense to refer to a kind of formal logical system. However, in this book *theory, system,* and *systematic interpretation* will be treated as synonyms.

Three Functions of Theory

A theory of learning usually consists of three different but closely related functions. First, it is an approach to the area of knowledge, a way of analyzing and talking about and doing research on learning. It represents the researcher's point of view about what aspects of learning are most worth studying, what independent variables should be manipulated and what dependent variables studied, what research techniques should be employed, and what language should be used to describe the findings. It focuses the researcher's attention on certain topics and helps the person to decide which of all the possible abstractions will be most useful. Thus theory serves as a guide and a source of stimulation for research and for scientific thought.

Second, a theory of learning is an attempt to summarize a large amount of knowledge about the laws of learning in a fairly small space. In this process of summarization, some exactness and detail are likely to be lost. In such precise and well-developed sciences as physics and chemistry, theories do quite well in summarizing laws so that the same exact predictions can be made from the theories as from the much more detailed laws. Psychology, to date, has been less successful in finding such theories. Theories of learning, in attempting to summarize large amounts of knowledge, lose completeness and precision. They are simplifications or skeletal outlines of the material with which they deal. As such, they represent a gain in breadth, in organization, and in simplicity, but also a loss in accuracy of detail.

Third, a theory of learning is a creative attempt to explain what learning is and why it works as it does. The laws give us the "how" of learning; the theories attempt to give us the "why." Thus they seek to provide that basic understanding which is one of the goals, not alone of science, but of all forms of scholarship. Theories represent people's best efforts to determine the underlying structure of the world in which they live.

Intervening Variables

In most cases, theorists have sought this underlying structure in entities that were not visible to the observer. Theorists in the field of chemistry, for example, assumed the existence of molecules long before anyone had ever seen a molecule under the microscope. They did so because the laws of chemistry formed a simpler and more logical pattern if all substances were assumed to be made up of molecules. The laws of chemistry did not themselves deal with molecules, but with substances that could be seen and touched and weighed. The molecules were in effect invented by the theorists as an explanation for the laws. This invention was a creative guess that has received more and more support from later evidence and that has contributed immensely to the development of chemistry.

Let us consider a corresponding example, though admittedly a less striking one, from the psychology of learning. A person might be deprived of water for a period of time, or be on a daily ration of water below the normal intake, or have a chance to drink only for a limited time once a day, or have to eat a lot of dry food without water available, or have a hypertonic salt solution pumped directly into the stomach. The extent to which any one of these things happened (e.g., how much the water ration was reduced or how concentrated the salt solution was) would be an independent variable. We would find that each of these independent variables was related in much the same way to each of several dependent variables. As any of these independent variables increased, the subject would probably become more restless, would drink more water when water was available, would work harder to get to a drinking fountain, and would complain more about being thirsty. These relationships constitute 20 laws, relating each of the 5 independent variables to each of the 4 dependent variables. We can, however, reduce this figure to 9 laws by saying that each of the 5 independent variables produces a state of thirst and that this thirst in turn produces changes in the 4 dependent variables. By hypothesizing this state of thirst, we have more than cut in half the number of laws required to describe the relationships involved.

So far this act of theoretical simplification is no more than what the average person does. It is so commonplace, indeed, that it is easy to overlook its importance. No one has ever seen or touched or weighed thirst. We have felt it in ourselves, but in anyone else we can only infer it. We have to infer other people's thirst from what has happened to them (the independent variables) or from what they do (the dependent variables). If they tell us they are thirsty, their statement is only one of the possible dependent variables, and not necessarily the most reliable. When a 3-year-old boy gets out of bed for the fourth time and tells his mother he is thirsty, the mother is understandably more likely to trust other evidence than what the child says. Anyone who thinks it is possible to differentiate sharply between theory and fact should consider how much theory there is in the simple "factual" statement "He is thirsty."

The psychologist's use of the concept *thirst* differs from the layperson's in two respects. One is in precision. The psychologist, not satisfied with saying that certain manipulations will produce thirst and thirst will produce certain behaviors, goes on to determine what degrees of the independent variables are related to what degrees of thirst and what degrees of thirst are related to what increases in the dependent variables. Thus the psychologist's use of the concept *thirst* allows for more complete and accurate detail than the layperson's.

The other difference is that the psychologist is likely to go further in relating this concept to others. Many theorists of learning have been struck with the similarities between hunger, thirst, pain, and a variety of other such hypothetical states (hypothetical because none of them can be directly observed). All of these tend to produce both increases in certain forms of activity and physiological changes characteristic of stress. Moreover, the termination of any of these states is reinforcing. They have therefore often been classified together as *drives*. The concept of drive provides a higher level of theoretical integration, bringing together far more laws than the separate concepts of hunger, thirst, pain, and the like.

Theoretical concepts of the sort we have been discussing are often called *intervening variables*. This name reflects their place in the theoretical structure, coming between the independent and the dependent variables, forming a link that joins them together, and serving to explain how the independent variables produce changes in the dependent variables. These intervening variables are states or conditions of the individual that are inferred from observations. *Habits, beliefs,* and *motives* are examples of intervening variables that are important in various theories of learning.

By this time you are very likely asking, "Are these intervening variables really there, waiting to be discovered, or are they invented by theorists as a matter of convenience?" In other words, is the theorist more like an explorer, discovering hidden truths, or more like an artist, creating views of the world that suit her or his own purposes? If the discussion so far has been vague on this question, it is because theorists are by no means agreed on the matter. Undoubtedly both discovery and creation enter into theory, as indeed into all scientific work. A theory must lead to accurate predictions, must be consistent with well-established laws; otherwise it is worthless. This requirement sets limits on the theorist's creative freedom. However, the same laws can be interpreted in different ways, and these interpretations are not waiting around to be discovered—they must be created by an interpreter. Perhaps the theorist is less like either an explorer or an artist than like an architect, limited by materials and by the demands of the job, but still working with originality and imagination to produce a new, useful, and beautiful structure.

This is admittedly not a very adequate answer to the question of whether the intervening variables are "really there." Some theorists talk as though the variables are really there and others as though it is merely convenient to pretend that they are there. It has been suggested that there should be two different terms, one for those variables that theorists think they have discovered and the other for those that they think they have invented. Fortunately, we can leave this issue to the philosophers and concern ourselves only with the part that intervening variables play in the various theories we will be studying.

In any case, the element of creativity in theory construction explains why there are many theories of learning. All theorists try to find ways of structuring reality that will be useful and meaningful to themselves. The differences among the resulting theories reflect partly the differences in the topics that various theorists find most interesting to work with, and partly the differences in the kinds of systematic structures that different theorists consider worth producing. All, however, reflect the efforts of thoughtful humans to interpret the phenomena of learning in coherent and intellectually satisfying ways.

Kinds of Learning Theories

Theories of learning can be classified in a number of ways. For our purposes, one difference is particularly outstanding: the difference between the *connectionist* and the *cognitive* theories. Connectionist interpretations of learning, however much they may differ among themselves, agree in treating learning as a matter of connections between stimuli and responses. (A response may be any item of behavior, while a stimulus may be any input of energy that tends to affect behavior. Connectionist theorists typically assume that all responses are elicited by stimuli.) These connections, which are a simple kind of intervening variable, are called by a variety of names, such as habits or stimulus-response bonds. Always, however, there is a concentration on the responses that occur, on the stimuli (and perhaps other conditions) that elicit them, and on the ways that these relationships between stimuli and responses change with experience.

Cognitive interpretations are concerned with the cognitions (perceptions or attitudes or beliefs, which are more complex intervening variables) that individuals have about their environment, and with the ways these cognitions determine behavior. In these interpretations, learning is the study of the ways in which cognitions are modified by experience.

Common sense makes use of both kinds of interpretations. When discussing simple reactions or more complex physical skills, we are likely to say, "I guess it's just a bad habit I've learned," or "With all that practice, her reactions have become very fast and smooth." These are connectionist interpretations. When discussing matters that involve words or deliberate decisions, we often say things like "He has acquired a lot of knowledge on that subject," or "You'll have to learn that people don't like to be treated that way," or "Now I really understand geometry!" These interpretations are all cognitive.

Whether a given psychologist will prefer a connectionist or a cognitive theory of learning depends partly on the kind of learning in which that person is most interested. A specialist in the study of conditioning may find a connectionist interpretation better suited to certain needs, while a specialist in problem solving may find a cognitive interpretation more useful. However, specialists tend to believe that the theory they prefer is best, not only for their own field of study, but for the whole psychology of learning. This tendency reflects a desire for unity and simplicity that is one of the reasons theories are developed in the first place. As a result, some people adopt general cognitive theories of learning and others adopt general connectionist ones.

The distinction between connectionist and cognitive theories is not, of course, an all-or-nothing matter; there are numerous middle positions and combinations. Nevertheless, the distinction forms a convenient and useful basis for classifying the interpretations of learning that we will be investigating here. We will look first at a number of connectionist theories, since that is the kind of theory which has traditionally been most popular with psychologists of learning in the United States. Next we will consider some cognitive theories, since this kind of theory has become increasingly popular in recent years. After that we will look at various efforts to combine the best features of both kinds of theory and at some special topics and problems in learning theory. Finally, we will speculate a bit on the possible future of learning theory. It is hoped that this survey will indicate what learning theories are, what they try to accomplish, how successful they are, and what they can contribute to our understanding of the learning process.

Chapter
3

Three Early Connectionist Theorists

*H*uman interest in psychology has a long history. At least since the time of the ancient Greeks, philosophers have been speculating about topics that are now considered part of psychology. How do we think and feel and learn and know and make decisions and act on them? Attempts to answer these questions make up a considerable part of the history of philosophy. It was not until the nineteenth century, however, that attempts were made to study these topics experimentally. The first psychological laboratory was founded by Wilhelm Wundt in Germany at a time traditionally given as 1879. Although research in psychology had been going on before then, this date is widely regarded as marking the point at which modern scientific psychology was placed on a definite institutional footing.

Wundt and his colleagues in early scientific psychology, like the philosophers from whom they drew much of their inspiration, were largely interested in conscious experience. They wanted to understand human sensations and thoughts and feelings. They wanted to take the continuous flux of conscious awareness and analyze it into its basic components. Are memory images the same as sensations? Are feelings a special kind of sensation or are they something really different? How is the intensity of a sensation related to the intensity of the physical stimulus that produces it? These were the sorts of questions that the early experimental psychologists studied.

This kind of psychology, developed in Germany, became to a great extent the standard for the rest of Europe and for America. The research in psychological laboratories and the discussion in psychology textbooks were based principally on this approach. Its acceptance, however, was never complete. In both Russia and the United States there were always strong trends toward the study of objective behavior as well as the study of conscious experience, and interest in what people did as well as in what they thought and felt. These trends gave rise to two major traditions of studying behavior, one Russian and one American, to which we now turn.

PAVLOVIAN CONDITIONING

In 1904, Ivan P. Pavlov (1849–1936) won the Nobel Prize in physiology and medicine for his work on digestion. To do this research, he had to perform a difficult operation, opening a fistula in the wall of a dog's stomach. He noticed that the stomach secretions he was studying were first triggered not by food reaching the stomach but by the chewing or even just the sight of food, and he began to find this anticipatory secretion the most interesting aspect of the digestive process. To study it, he focused on a different part of digestion, the secretions of the salivary glands, which could be measured through a much simpler operation: placing a duct in a dog's salivary gland. When Pavlov presented food to a dog with such a duct in its cheek, drops of saliva fell into a beaker, where they could easily be counted. Soon these drops of saliva began to appear in response not only to food but also to a variety of other stimuli in the lab. At the time, the standard way of explaining this extra salivation was to say merely that these other stimuli had become associated with food. Pavlov decided that this was not an exact enough answer, and devoted the rest of his long life to studying the process in precise detail. Through this new line of research (Pavlov 1960), he became even more famous as the father of conditioning.

We saw the basic elements of conditioning in Chapter 1. The experimenter starts with a stimulus (the unconditioned stimulus) that will reliably elicit a specific response (the unconditioned response). In Pavlov's research, the unconditioned stimulus was meat and the unconditioned response salivation. What was to become the conditioned stimulus could be any of a great variety of stimuli: a bell, a ticking metronome, a triangle drawn on a large card, and so on. If this stimulus was presented repeatedly just before the meat, it too came to elicit salivation, the conditioned response, and it thus became a conditioned stimulus. Since the term *conditioning* came to be applied quite broadly, this particular kind of conditioning, being the first studied, came to be called *classical conditioning* (Hilgard & Marquis 1940). More recently, as it has become increasingly common to name everything from diseases to measuring units after people, classical conditioning has come to be often called Pavlovian conditioning. Though Pavlov should share some of the credit with such other Russian pioneer researchers as I. M. Sechenov and V. M. Bekhterev, his work was clearly of central importance and deserving of the tribute.

The terms *unconditioned stimulus* and *conditioned stimulus* may seem a bit odd, considering what they mean. It is now generally agreed that these terms are poor translations of the Russian words that Pavlov used. What is meant is that the meat is an unconditional stimulus (not conditional on any previous training), while the bell (or whatever stimulus precedes the meat) is a conditional stimulus for salivation—conditional on having been paired with the meat. By a clumsiness in translation, then, generations of English-speaking psychologists have been saddled with the strange terms *conditioned* and *unconditioned.* Though a few writers now use *conditional* and *unconditional,* most writers stick with long-standing tradition and use the less appropriate but more familiar terms.

Excitation and Inhibition

Since Pavlov was a physiologist, it was natural that he should try to explain conditioning in physiological terms. He suggested that the laws of conditioning could be explained by the joint action of two main processes in the brain: excitation and inhibition. *Excitation* is a process of arousal, one that tends to make responses happen, whereas *inhibition* is a process of suppression, one that tends to prevent responses from occurring. Excitation and inhibition therefore operate in opposition to each other. Of the two, excitation plays a much greater part in producing conditioning, but inhibition is needed to explain many of the specific ways in which conditioning works.

Let us consider a specific example of conditioning, in which a bell as the conditioned stimulus is presented to the dog just before meat powder is presented as the unconditioned stimulus. Both of these stimuli produce excitation in the cerebral cortex of the brain, each at a particular spot in the cortex appropriate to that stimulus. Since the food is something important to the dog's survival, whereas the bell is a biologically less important stimulus, the excitation produced by the food is the stronger of the two. Excitation is then drawn from the location on the cortex where the bell is represented to the location where the food is represented. This effect occurs because of two general tendencies. One is the tendency for weaker excitation to be drawn toward the location of stronger excitation. The other is the tendency for excitation that occurs first to be drawn toward the location of excitation that occurs slightly later. With repeated presentations of the bell just before the food, the excitation from the conditioned stimulus is drawn more and more to the location of the excitation from the unconditioned stimulus.

Once this movement on the cortex has occurred, what will happen whenever the bell is sounded? Excitation will occur not only at the place on the cortex appropriate for the conditioned stimulus, but also at the place where the unconditioned stimulus is represented. This excitation, in turn, will produce a response similar to the unconditioned response, even if the unconditioned stimulus is not presented on that trial. However, since the excitation at that point on the cortex is weaker than if it had been produced directly by the unconditioned stimulus, the response is also weaker than the unconditioned response would have been. This weaker version of the unconditioned response, produced by the conditioned stimulus rather than by the unconditioned stimulus, is of course the conditioned response.

The process by which excitation from the conditioned stimulus is drawn to the location of the unconditioned stimulus is not the only way in which excitation moves around on the cortex. Excitation also has an automatic tendency to *irradiate*—that is, to spread out from its original focus in all directions over the surface of the cortex. The closer any spot on the cortex is to the center of excitation from the conditioned stimulus, the more quickly and strongly the excitation from the conditioned stimulus will irradiate to that point. When it does, that point also shares in the conditioning, forming a connection (though to a lesser degree) with the cortical site for the unconditioned stimulus.

Because of the way the cortex is organized, points that are close together on the cortex are typically the sites for similar stimuli. For example, a bell of similar tone to the conditioned stimulus will be represented closest to the conditioned stimulus on the cortex; a bell of a different tone will be represented farther away, and a buzzer still farther. The similar bell therefore receives the most irradiated excitation from the conditioned stimulus, the different bell less, and the buzzer still less. As a result, the similar bell has the greatest tendency to produce the same effect as the conditioned stimulus (namely, the conditioned response), whereas the other stimuli do so to progressively lesser degrees. This results in the phenomenon of generalization described in Chapter 1.

Though inhibition and excitation produce opposite effects, the two processes are alike in various other respects. For example, inhibition as well as excitation irradiates over the surface of the cortex. According to Pavlov, the interaction between the two processes explains most of what goes on in conditioning.

Inhibition typically appears in situations where excitation by itself would produce excessive or inappropriate effects. One example is *extinction*. If the bell continued to be presented repeatedly without ever again being followed by the food, inhibition would build up at the cortical site of the conditioned stimulus and weaken the conditioned response. Another example is *inhibition of delay,* which builds up when there is a substantial delay between the beginning of the conditioned stimulus and the beginning of the unconditioned stimulus. At first, the conditioned response tends to occur as soon as the conditioned stimulus is presented, but after a good deal of training it does not come until shortly before the unconditioned stimulus is due to arrive. This increasing delay in the conditioned response is attributed by Pavlov to the gradual buildup of inhibition of delay. A third example involves *discrimination training*. If the original bell continued to be followed by food, but the similar bell was also repeatedly sounded without being followed by food, the generalized response to the similar bell would become less and less, indicating that a discrimination between the two bells had been formed. This would result from a buildup of inhibition at the cortical site of the bell not followed by food.

We should note that none of these ideas of Pavlov's was based on direct physiological information. The irradiation of excitation and inhibition over the surface of the cortex and the drawing of excitation or inhibition from one place on the cortex to another were speculations based on studies of conditioning. Physiologists now know a good deal more than Pavlov did about the ways in which individual neurons excite and inhibit one another; this knowledge has not confirmed Pavlov in detail. The particular excitatory and inhibitory processes that he described remain as they were then: speculations about physiology based only on observations of behavior.

Applications and Implications

Pavlov believed that the principles of conditioning could be used to explain a variety of phenomena. In particular, he related these principles to personality, considering that one of the most fundamental differences among dogs—and among humans—is the balance between excitation and inhibition. Excitatory personalities tend toward too much unrestrained activity ("When in doubt, do something, do anything!"), whereas inhibitory personalities tend toward unresponsiveness ("When in doubt, the safest thing to do is nothing"). Finally, Pavlov considered conflict between excitation and inhibition to be the basis of neurosis. He found that when a dog learned a discrimination between a circle and an ellipse and then the ellipse was gradually changed in shape to resemble more and more closely a circle, the dog would eventually reach a point where discrimination broke down completely. Excitatory dogs would respond to both stimuli, inhibitory dogs to neither. This failure to discriminate was not just a calm adoption of the same response to both stimuli. Rather, the dogs barked, tried to leave the experimental room, and generally appeared anxious, frustrated, and upset. These symptoms seemed so similar to those of humans in difficult conflict situations that Pavlov labeled the syndrome "experimental neurosis."

Pavlov's work earned him tremendous prestige in Russia. Remarkably, this prestige held during both the czarist regime in which he began his work and the Communist regime that followed it, even though his own reaction to the new Soviet government was far from enthusiastic. Various aspects of Pavlov's system probably helped to make him popular with the Soviet government: his emphasis on reducing "higher mental processes" to conditioning appealed to Communist materialism, and his emphasis on learning was consistent with the Communist philosophy of environmental determinism. Pavlov's system became so much a "state system" that citation of Pavlov in an article became almost as much a symbol of loyalty as citation of Karl Marx. Though a good deal has been added to Pavlov's system by other eastern European psychologists and physiologists, his basic ideas remain unchanged.

Many of the later additions to Pavlov's system have involved discoveries as to what can serve as unconditioned and conditioned stimuli and responses. One example is interoceptive conditioning, in which either the conditioned or the unconditioned stimulus, or both, is presented directly to one of the internal organs. The responses that get conditioned by such interoceptive stimulation are also responses of the internal organs or their blood supplies. For example, cold water as the unconditioned stimulus can make the blood vessels in the wall of the stomach constrict, and this unconditioned response can then be trained as a conditioned response to some conditioned stimulus. Such conditioning brings unconscious bodily processes, such as changes in the blood supply to the stomach, under the control of a conditioned stimulus. Sometimes the conditioned stimulus is a word spoken by the person. In that case the person can, by saying that word, bring the response under voluntary control. Interoceptive conditioning thus offers a way of making various unconscious bodily processes voluntary.

The use of words as stimuli introduces another application: semantic conditioning. Later in his career Pavlov noted the importance of words as conditioned stimuli. Whereas bells and lights and other such conditioned stimuli make up a first signaling system, language, he said, becomes a second signaling system. It is, of course, a complicated system, but it is based on semantic conditioning, in which words serve as conditioned stimuli. The relationship of language to conditioning has been demonstrated by a simple experiment (Razran 1961). A boy was conditioned to salivate when he heard the Russian word for "good" or "well" as the conditioned stimulus (S+), while the word for "bad" or "badly" was nonreinforced (an S−). The boy was then tested with a variety of sentences that did not contain either word but that had definite positive or negative connotations, and was found to salivate much more to the positive than to the negative ones. He produced the most drops of saliva to "The enemy army was defeated and annihilated" and the fewest to "The pupil was fresh to the teacher." In addition to what this experiment tells us about conditioning, it gives us an interesting look at the value system of the Soviet Union!

In the Western world, Pavlov's work was received with a good deal of enthusiasm. Americans, in particular, were ready for the idea of conditioning. However, it was primarily the idea that Americans adopted, rather than the details of either research or theory. The empirical findings of Pavlov's research were widely quoted but little studied: some Americans studied the conditioning of the eye-blink reflex or the galvanic skin response, but not of salivation, and the majority of researchers on animal learning did not study classical conditioning at all. As for Pavlov's theory, even those Westerners who admired Pavlov's pioneering research tended to dismiss it. The irradiation of excitation and inhibition was inferred almost entirely from behavior, rather than from any direct study of the brain, and did not seem to most Westerners to be very useful theory anyway. Thus, outside of eastern Europe, Pavlov was widely admired as a pioneer, widely cited, and widely followed in general outline, but many of the details of his system were largely neglected nonetheless. Only fairly recently have psychologists in the West begun to look more carefully at the details of his system. They have since confirmed some of his findings, challenged others, and found still others hard to check because the research reports were so brief and so casually written. Though Pavlov's theories are still not much admired in the West, those of some of his followers have turned out to resemble those of some Westerners, developed independently. Pavlov's influence has, however, survived the mixture of adulation, contradiction, and partial neglect that he has received, so that he remains one of the great pioneers in the psychology of learning.

WATSON'S BEHAVIORISM

About the same time that Pavlov was working in Russia, the trend toward the study of objective behavior in American psychology was bringing it more and more into conflict with the German tradition. Pressure increased to break the traditional mold and to develop a psychology that was frankly oriented toward objective behavior and practical usefulness. To varying degrees, psychologists were taking up the cry "Enough of studying what people think and feel; let's begin studying what people do!" This movement found its most vocal spokesperson in John B. Watson (1878–1958). It was through his vigorous attacks on traditional psychology and his attempts to build a radically different system that American theoretical psychology came into its own.

In 1903 Watson received the first Ph.D. in psychology granted by the University of Chicago. His dissertation was a study of maze learning by rats, and this concern with animal behavior was typical of his early interests. He was impressed by the fact that in studying animal behavior it is possible to dispense with consciousness and simply study what the animal does. Why, he asked, can't we do the same with humans? Behavior is real and objective and practical, while consciousness belongs to a realm of vague subjectivity. Let us abolish consciousness from our discussions and study behavior! Watson's professors at Chicago agreed with many of his objections to traditional psychology, but considered his solution too radical. Perhaps they thought that, like many young rebels, he would become more conservative with age and responsibility. In Watson's case, however, this change did not occur. After joining the faculty at Johns Hopkins University in 1908, he became all the more convinced that his extreme position was the answer to psychology's problems. A few years later (1913), Watson published the first formal statement of his position, an article entitled "Psychology as the Behaviorist Views It," and the psychological revolution known as behaviorism was under way.

The reason for the label *behaviorism* is clear enough. Watson was interested only in behavior, not in conscious experience. Human behavior was to be studied as objectively as was the behavior of machines. Consciousness was not objective; therefore it was not scientifically valid and could not be meaningfully studied. And by *behavior* Watson meant nothing more abstruse than the movements of muscles. What is speech? Movements of the muscles of the throat. What is thought? Subvocal speech, talking silently to oneself. What are feeling and emotion? Movements of the muscles of the gut. Thus did Watson dispose of mentalism in favor of a purely objective science of behavior.

It is easy to satirize such a position. (Estes, for example, has suggested that a behaviorist might change the familiar motto from "Think!" to "Behave!" and finally to "Twitch!") But we must not overlook the tremendous importance of this position for the development of modern psychological science. Though much objective study of behavior antedated Watson, he stands out as the great popularizer, the man who turned this sort of study into a national movement and philosophy.

Watson's opposition to admitting anything subjective into psychology led him to reject much more than the study of consciousness. Another of his targets was the analysis of motivation in terms of instincts. At the time Watson's career began, it was common to explain almost any form of behavior as the result of a particular instinct. Sociability was attributed to an instinct of gregariousness, fighting to an instinct of pugnacity, and so forth. These were assumed to be innate and to determine in considerable measure what behavior people would show. But instincts were too mentalistic for Watson. He asserted that behavior is, on the contrary, a matter of conditioned reflexes—that is, of responses learned by what is now called classical conditioning. We show sociability or aggression not because we are born with an instinct to do so, but because we have learned to do so through conditioning.

Watson's demolition of theories extended not only to instincts but to other supposedly innate mental characteristics of humans. He denied that we are born with any particular mental abilities or traits or predispositions. All we inherit is our bodies and a few reflexes; differences in ability and in personality are simply differences in learned behavior. Thus Watson was in several respects a strong exponent of environment as against heredity in the familiar nature-nurture controversy. What we are (except for clearly anatomical differences) depends entirely on what we have learned. And since what has been learned can be unlearned, this contention meant that human nature, either in general or in a particular person, was greatly subject to change. There was practically no limit to what a person, properly conditioned, might become. As Watson expressed it in his most famous quote:

Give me a dozen healthy infants, well-formed, and my own specified world to bring them up in and I'll guarantee to take any one at random and train him to become any type of specialist I might select—doctor, lawyer, artist, merchant-chief and, yes, even beggar-man and thief, regardless of his talents, penchants, tendencies, abilities, vocations, and race of his ancestors [Watson 1966, p. 104].

This blending of objectivity with faith in the power of learning swept American psychology and captured the popular imagination. Combined with some more specific ideas about learning, it had great implications for child rearing, education, advertising, and social organization. When we consider how well Watson's ideas fitted in with the American belief in equality of opportunity, emphasis on unemotional practicality, and faith in progress, it is no surprise that behaviorism came to occupy the center of the American psychological stage.

We cannot, of course, picture Watson as suddenly presenting behaviorism and having it promptly and universally adopted. When Watson published "Psychology as the Behaviorist Views It," the trends to objectivity and to environmentalism were already under way. The demolition of instinct doctrine was more the work of L. L. Bernard and of Z. Y. Kuo than of Watson. Moreover, Watson owed many of his ideas to sources as diverse as the philosophy of John Locke in England and the new physiological psychology of Ivan Pavlov in Russia. Finally, alternative points of view continued to be defended, and Watson faced much opposition. Nevertheless, there was a marked change in American psychology during this period, and Watson was the keynote speaker around whom any discussion of the change is likely to center. He gave behaviorism its name, its loudest voice, and its sense of mission.

Watson's Interpretation of Learning

What, then, was Watson's interpretation of learning? We have already seen that he regarded all learning as classical conditioning. We are born with certain stimulus-response connections called reflexes. Examples are sneezing in response to an irritation of the nose and the knee-jerk reflex in response to a sharp tap on the knee. These reflexes, according to Watson, are the entire behavioral repertoire that we inherit. However, we can build a multiplicity of new stimulus-response connections by the process of conditioning. If a new stimulus occurs along with the stimulus for the reflex response, after several such pairings the new stimulus alone will produce the response. This conditioning process, first described by Pavlov, makes it possible for each response in the original repertoire of reflexes to be elicited by a great variety of new stimuli in addition to the ones that originally elicited it. This, according to Watson, is how we learn to respond to new situations.

Such conditioning, however, is only part of the learning process. We must not only learn to respond to new situations; we must also learn new responses. Sneezes, knee jerks, and the like would not carry us very far in dealing with complex situations. How can complex new habits be learned? The answer, according to Watson, is by building up a series of reflexes. Walking, for example, is a sequence of many responses: putting the weight on one foot, swinging the other foot forward, bringing it down, thrusting the weight forward from one foot to the other, and so forth. All these responses occurring in proper order constitute the skilled performance of walking. The building up of such a sequence is possible because each response produces muscular sensations that become stimuli for the next response. Thus new and complex behavior is acquired through the serial combination of simple reflexes.

Let us look at this kind of learning in more detail. Consider one response in the sequence, such as swinging the leg forward. Originally the stimulus for this response is, perhaps, the sight of the place toward which we are walking. However, we can swing our leg forward only if our weight is on the other foot. Hence, whenever we swing our leg forward, we do so in the presence of those sensations from our own body that result from having our weight on the other foot. Those sensations thus are paired with the response of swinging the leg, and through repeated pairings they come to elicit leg swinging. Hence, in the well-learned habit of walking, the sensation of having weight on one foot automatically elicits the conditioned response of swinging the other leg forward. This response merges with the others in the sequence, each providing the stimulus for the next response. The sequence eventually becomes so well integrated that for practical purposes we can speak of the whole process of walking from one place to another as a single response, even though it is actually a complex sequence of stimulus-response connections.

After reading the above discussion, you may well be dissatisfied with Watson's explanation of complex learning. What, you may fairly ask, determines that this particular sequence of stimulus-response connections will be formed? Why does the sensation of weight on one foot elicit the response of swinging the other leg forward? Reading between the lines in Watson's last book (*Behaviorism*, first published in 1924 and revised in 1930) leads to the feeling that he was still seeking the answer to this problem. He had two different answers, neither completely adequate, and the relation between the two was still unclear. One answer was to say that the stimulus-response connections that make up the skilled act are conditioned reflexes. Each response produces sensations that become conditioned stimuli for the next response, and thus the whole sequence of conditioned stimulus-response connections is formed. This formulation gave Watson the satisfaction of having reduced complex habits to their simple building blocks—conditioned reflexes. Now, he said, we can turn to the physiologists to explain why conditioning occurs; we as behaviorists have done our job. However, Watson never really carried the analysis through in detail. If feeling weight on the left foot is the conditioned stimulus and swinging the right leg forward is the response, what is the unconditioned stimulus which always guarantees that the response will occur so that conditioning can take place? To this crucial question, Watson had no answer. As a result, his reduction of complex behavior patterns to sequences of conditioned reflexes is more apparent than real.

Watson's other explanation of this form of learning relies on two principles: *frequency* and *recency*. The principle of frequency states that the more frequently we have made a given response to a given stimulus, the more likely we are to make that response to that stimulus again. Similarly, the principle of recency states that the more recently we have made a given response to a given stimulus, the more likely we are to make it again.

Watson illustrates these principles with the example of a 3-year-old boy learning to open a puzzle box with candy inside. The boy turns the box around, pounds it on the floor, and makes a variety of other useless responses. Finally, by chance, he presses a button on the box, which is the one response that will release the lid so he can open the box and obtain the candy. Since the box is now open and the candy obtained, the child is no longer in the presence of the stimuli that kept him working at the box. The last response made in the presence of those stimuli was the response of pressing the button. The next time his father or mother puts candy in the box and closes the lid, the child will go through much the same sequence of trial and error as before. However, by chance, he will try some new responses and leave out some of those from last time. Again, however, the last response he makes will be that of pressing the button, since that is the one which changes the stimulus situation. Every time he works with the box, pressing the button occurs, whereas other responses may or may not. Thus, in the long run, button pushing gains a lead in frequency. Since it is always the last response, it always has a lead in recency. As a result, button pushing occurs sooner and sooner on successive experiences with the box. Since button pushing solves the problem, other responses have less and less chance to occur on successive experiences with the box. Button pushing as a response to the stimulus of the closed box has been learned.

This illustration shows only how a single response, pressing a button, is learned. The problem might, however, have required the child to make a series of several successive responses to open the box, with each response changing the situation so that the next response could be made. Pressing the button, for example, might have opened an outer lid and revealed a lever that had to be moved sideways in order to open the inner lid. In this case, both button pushing and lever moving would be learned in the same way, since each would change the stimulus and thus become the last response to the old stimulus. Such a series of responses could be extended indefinitely.

Why, then, does one particular response rather than others occur to the stimulus at a given place in a complex sequence? Watson's answer is that during learning many different responses occur to the stimulus, but that through the process described above, most of them drop out. The response that changes the situation gains in frequency and recency until it comes to occur as soon as the stimulus is presented. That particular stimulus-response unit in the sequence is then complete.

All these statements about the learning of new responses are left rather undeveloped in Watson's treatment. How are conditioning, the principle of frequency, and the principle of recency related? How does the fact that the learner may at first make some wrong response much more often than the right one, yet still eventually learn the right one, fit in with the principle of frequency? Watson does not tell us. He was confident that complex learning could be explained by simple principles, but his attempted explanations were tentative and were never organized into a clear and consistent theory.

One thing that is clear, however, is Watson's lack of interest in reinforcement, in reward and punishment as causes of learning. Indeed, he regards such concepts as too subjective for a really behavioristic interpretation of learning. Instead, he maintains, we learn a connection between a stimulus and a response simply because the two occur together, in *contiguity*. Watson is therefore referred to as a *contiguity theorist*—that is, one who believes that contiguity alone, without reinforcement, is sufficient to produce learning.

Special Kinds of Learning

What about the learning of emotional reactions? Here Watson makes a concession to heredity, beyond what he has already made by recognizing the existence of innate reflexes, since he recognizes three innate patterns of emotional reaction. In principle, these reaction patterns are the same as reflexes, for we can state what movements (including those of the internal organs) they involve and what stimuli will produce them. However, they are more complicated than what is usually meant by a reflex. The three emotional reaction patterns may for convenience be labeled as fear, rage, and love. We must note, however, says Watson, that these labels refer to patterns of movement, not to conscious feelings. If we bang a gong close to a child, and she starts to cry, we may describe this event by saying that the stimulus of a loud noise has produced the emotion of fear. However, we are simply giving a name to the behavior we see, not commenting on the child's feelings.

Emotional learning involves the conditioning of these three patterns of emotional response to new stimuli. The above example of innate fear was taken from a famous experiment of Watson's, one that can also be used to illustrate conditioned fear. Little Albert, aged 11 months, was permitted to play with a white rat, which he did happily and with no sign of fear. A metal bar was then hit with a hammer close behind him. He started and fell sideways. This sudden loud noise was repeated a number of times just as the rat was presented to him, and each time he reacted in the same way, sometimes also whimpering. These responses indicate that the noise was an unconditioned stimulus for fear. After this training, the rat was presented without the noise. Albert fell over, cried, and crawled away from the rat as fast as he could. This change indicates that through the training procedure the rat had become a conditioned stimulus for fear. According to Watson, such conditioned and unconditioned responses account for all our emotions.

What about the acquisition of knowledge? Can conditioning be used to explain how we learn, for example, the facts of history? Certainly, says Watson, for this knowledge consists simply of saying certain words, aloud or to ourselves. The response sequence involved in saying "William the Conqueror defeated Harold the Saxon at Hastings in 1066" is in principle no different from that involved in walking across a room. A question such as "How did the Norman Conquest occur?" elicits the statement, which is itself a sequence of words with each word a conditioned stimulus for the next one. Acquiring knowledge is a process of learning to give the proper sequence of words in response to a question or other conditioned stimulus.

All of our behavior, says Watson, tends to involve the whole body. When we think, we may pace the floor or furrow our brows. We announce our opinions with smiles or waves of the arm as well as with words. We cannot therefore really say that emotions are responses of the gut or that thinking is made up of vocal responses. These are the dominant but by no means the only responses involved. Everything we think, feel, say, or do involves, to varying degrees, the activity of the entire body. This is probably the most fundamental credo of behaviorism.

Evaluation of Watson

Watson's great contribution to the development of psychology was his rejection of the distinction between body and mind and his emphasis on the study of objective behavior. This battle was so effectively won that most of the learning theory in America, at least through the 1950s, was behavioristic in the broad sense of the term. Since then more of the field has gone in directions that are no longer commonly called behavioristic, but that still reflect the legacy of behaviorism.

In this book we will see a number of theoretical systems that represent different variations on the behaviorist theme. All of them have in common a concern with objective behavior, a strong interest in animal studies, a preference for stimulus-response analysis, and a concentration on learning as the central topic in psychology. This fact makes Watson in some ways the intellectual father or grandfather of a large portion of the systems we will be considering here.

Watson, however, was much less thorough than he might have been in dealing with the detailed problems of learning. We have already seen the incompleteness and inconsistency in his treatment of complex learning. In his eagerness to build an objective psychology, he was somewhat cavalier with the matter of logical thoroughness. Perhaps if he had worked on his theory longer he would have extended his system to deal with some of these problems. More likely, however, his zeal for freeing psychology from subjectivism and belief in innate tendencies was incompatible with laborious theoretical completeness. In any case, he left the academic world in 1920 as a result of a sensational (for its day) divorce scandal and, though continuing to write about behaviorism for a short time afterward, devoted most of his later life to the applied psychology of advertising. Watson is now admired mainly for his philosophical trail blazing rather than for his detailed system building. It has remained for others to try to build, within the behavioristic framework, a more complete theory of learning.

THORNDIKE'S EARLY CONNECTIONISM

One idea that is noticeably absent from Watson's theory is the concept of reinforcement. The tendency of rewards to increase a given response, and of nonrewards to produce extinction, is not part of his thinking (or, should we say, of his verbal behavior?). However, many of those who agreed with his emphasis on the objective analysis of behavior disagreed with that omission. They felt that the question of which responses will be learned could best be answered by looking at the rewarding or punishing consequences that each response produced.

The idea that pleasure and pain as consequences of our acts are important determiners of behavior has a distinguished history in psychology. It forms the basis of the theory of psychological hedonism that was developed by Jeremy Bentham in the eighteenth century and adopted by a number of other British philosophers. According to this view, we all do those things that give us pleasure and avoid those that give us pain. However, it remained for Edward L. Thorndike (1874–1949) to make a similar, more behavioristic view central to the psychology of learning.

Thorndike was a pioneer in experimental animal psychology. Instead of relying on stories about the intelligent feats of this or that animal, he took animals into the laboratory, presented them with standardized problems, and made careful observations of how they solved the problems. His monograph "Animal Intelligence" (1898) is one of the classics in the field. His most widely quoted studies involved cats in a problem box. A hungry cat was confined in a cage with a tempting morsel of fish outside. The cat could open the door by pulling a loop of string hanging inside the cage. Usually a cat went through a long process of walking around, clawing the sides of the cage, and other responses before it pulled the loop of string and was able to leave the cage. On successive tests in the cage, the cats took shorter and shorter times to pull the string. However, this improvement was very gradual. Even after several experiences of opening the door by pulling the string, on a given trial a cat would still spend considerable time in other behavior before pulling the string. This led Thorndike to conclude that the cat's learning to pull the string involved not an "intelligent" understanding of a relation between string pulling and door opening but a gradual "stamping in" of the stimulus-response connection between seeing the string and pulling it.

At the time Thorndike published these studies, they were radical in two respects: their careful observation of animal behavior under controlled conditions and their concern with the gradual strengthening of stimulus-response bonds. They were Thorndike's answer to the argument about whether animals solve problems by reasoning or by instinct. By neither, said Thorndike, but rather by the gradual learning of the correct response.

The most noteworthy point is that, whereas Watson was a contiguity theorist, Thorndike was a reinforcement theorist. Watson's laws of frequency and recency state that stimulus-response bonds are strengthened simply by the response occurring in the presence of the stimulus. Thorndike did not completely reject this view, which he summarized as the *law of exercise.* His primary law of learning, however, was the *law of effect.* This stated that the stamping in of stimulus-response connections depended not simply on the fact that the stimulus and response occurred together but on the effects that followed the response. If a stimulus was followed by a response and then by a *satisfier,* the stimulus-response connection was strengthened. If, however, a stimulus was followed by a response and then by an *annoyer,* the stimulus-response connection was weakened. Thus satisfying and annoying effects of responses determined whether the stimulus-response connections would be stamped in or stamped out.

The terms *satisfier* and *annoyer* sound startlingly subjective for a theory concerned with the mechanical stamping in and stamping out of stimulus-response bonds. This language is much more like that of the hedonistic philosophers than that of the behaviorist psychologists. Thorndike was indeed criticized by behaviorists for this way of talking about learning. Actually, however, he defined the two terms in a quite objective way:

> By a satisfying state of affairs is meant one which the animal does nothing to avoid, often doing things which maintain or renew it. By an annoying state of affairs is meant one which the animal does nothing to preserve, often doing things which put an end to it [Thorndike 1913, p. 2].

Thorndike says nothing here about the animal's feelings, only about what the animal does. Thus he adheres to the concern of behaviorism with what organisms do. His language may sound subjective, but his meaning is as objective as Watson's. Working at the height of the behaviorist movement, Thorndike had his disagreements with its extreme supporters, but actually he and they were close together in interests and objectives. In the broader sense of the term, Thorndike was certainly himself a behaviorist.

Later in his career, Thorndike modified the law of effect to make satisfiers much more important than annoyers. Reward, he decided, strengthens connections, but punishment does not directly weaken them. If punishment is effective in weakening the tendency to do something, it is because it produces variable behavior and thus gives some new response a chance to be rewarded. With this modification, the law of effect became the now familiar statement (but not at all familiar when Thorndike presented it) that satisfying consequences serve to reinforce stimulus-response bonds.

Thorndike was a man of practical interests, and he took a special interest in the psychology of education. For many years he served on the faculty of Teachers College, Columbia University. Throughout his professional life, his studies on the "pure" psychology of learning with both human and animal subjects were interspersed with studies on the applied psychology of education. His emphasis on specificity in learning and on the mechanical stamping in of stimulus-response connections has been both praised and condemned by educators over the years. (It is to him, indeed, that we owe the term *connectionism.*) For our purposes, however, these aspects of Thorndike's work are too similar to Watson's to require further comment here. Thorndike was no less a pioneer of objective psychology than Watson; indeed, his original contributions were quite likely more important than Watson's. However, our concern here is that he incorporated within his objective psychology of learning the law of effect, and thus became the first real reinforcement theorist.

Thorndike's view of learning—that it involves the formation of stimulus-response bonds through the operation of reinforcement—became the dominant view in American learning theory. Not only did the majority of learning theorists hold some version of this view until well beyond the middle of the twentieth century; even those who held other views found that much of their energy went into disagreeing with Thorndike's approach. As Edward Tolman later wrote (1938), one might agree with Thorndike or disagree with him or try to improve on him in various ways, but he remained the starting point for any discussion of learning. As we will see, much of Chapters 5, 6, and 7 is concerned with attempts by other theorists to improve on Thorndike's work while maintaining its basic ideas.

Chapter
4

Guthrie's Contiguity Interpretation of Learning

Of those who continued in the behaviorist tradition, the one who remained closest to Watson's original position was Edwin R. Guthrie (1886–1959). From 1914 until his retirement in 1956, Guthrie was a professor at the University of Washington. He never studied with Watson, and his graduate education was more in philosophy than in psychology. Nevertheless, his interpretation of learning sounds much like what Watson's might have been if he had had another decade to work on the topic. His definitive work, *The Psychology of Learning*, was published in 1935 and revised in 1952, and his final theoretical statement was published in 1959. Thus, though his university teaching career began only 10 years later than Watson's, Guthrie was of an intellectually younger generation. He belongs, not with the pioneers of American learning theory, but with the generation that came next and followed up on those pioneering ideas.

Among theories of learning, Guthrie's is one of the easiest to read but nonetheless hardest to discuss. It is easy to read because he wrote in an informal style, making his points with homely anecdotes rather than with technical terms and mathematical equations. It is hard to discuss or write about because his casual presentation contains the germ of a highly technical deductive theory of learning. Reading Guthrie is like reading an exciting novel that contains a difficult allegory. That is, he can be read on an easy or a hard level. At the heart of his system is one basic principle of learning. Interpreted loosely, this principle is a source both of entertaining interpretations of learning and of valuable advice about the management of learning situations. Interpreted rigorously, it becomes the basis of a profound theory. This theory, so deceptively simple at first glance but so maddeningly complex on closer investigation, stands as a challenge to students of learning. Has Guthrie actually succeeded in summing up the whole field of learning in one key statement?

ONE BASIC PRINCIPLE OF LEARNING

Guthrie's basic principle of learning is similar to the conditioning principle that was basic for Watson, but it is stated in a still more general form. Guthrie says: "A combination of stimuli which has accompanied a movement will on its recurrence tend to be followed by that movement" (1960, p. 23). The principle may be paraphrased as, "If you do something in a given situation, the next time you are in that situation you will tend to do the same thing again." This principle is more general than the principle of classical conditioning, in that it says nothing about an unconditioned stimulus. It says only that if a response accompanies a given stimulus once, it is likely to follow that stimulus again. In classical conditioning, the response occurs with the (conditioned) stimulus during training because the unconditioned stimulus elicits it. This sequence of course fulfills Guthrie's conditions for learning. However, it does not matter to Guthrie whether the response is elicited during training by an unconditioned stimulus or in some other way. As long as the (conditioned) stimulus and the response occur together, learning will occur.

In claiming to sum up the whole field of learning in that one statement, Guthrie was inevitably challenging others to find inadequacies in the summary, and psychologists were quick to answer the challenge. The first difficulty with this principle is that a person often does many different things in the same situation. Which one will occur next time? This challenge is no problem for Guthrie; he simply replies, "The last one." A man struggling with a mechanical puzzle tries many responses. If he finally makes the correct response, he will tend to make this same response when next confronted with the puzzle. We say, then, that he has learned how to do the puzzle. Suppose, however, that he finally gives up and puts the puzzle aside unsolved. The next time he sees the puzzle he will tend to do what he did last—namely, put it aside. In that case we do not say that he has learned how to do the puzzle, but he has still learned something. In both cases he was presented with a combination of stimuli from the puzzle. In each case there was a movement that removed the stimuli. To the observer, one of these movements represented success and the other failure, but to Guthrie they both represented responses that removed the stimuli of the unsolved puzzle and that therefore became more likely to occur again. In both cases a response was learned, and in both cases the last response that the learner made to the stimuli was the one that was learned.

This aspect of Guthrie's system sounds much like Watson's principle of recency, since the last thing that occurred in a situation is the one that will occur again. However, Guthrie does not use Watson's other principle, frequency. Whereas for Watson a stimulus-response connection is something that varies in strength and grows stronger with practice, for Guthrie it is an all-or-nothing bond. The connection is either present or absent, with no intermediate variation in strength. Hence the conditioning of a movement to a combination of stimuli takes place completely in one experience, and further practice adds nothing to the strength of the connection.

At first glance this assumption seems contrary to well-known laws of learning. While practice may not make perfect, it usually does produce gradual improvement. How can Guthrie say that all the improvement takes place in a single experience? We must beware, replies Guthrie, of treating a "movement" as the same thing as an act or an accomplishment. Guthrie is referring in his principle of learning to specific small movements of particular muscles. It takes many such movements working together to make up a skilled act. Moreover, competent performance involves not just one but many skilled acts, each in response to a particular combination of stimuli. Hence learning how to do something involves learning an enormous number of specific stimulus-movement connections. Improvement in the skill is gradual even though the learning of each minute part occurs suddenly.

Consider a particular skill, such as riding a bicycle. For each possible position of the bicycle, a different motion is required in order to keep it upright. Each of these motions, in turn, is made up of movements of the arms, torso, and legs. A particular movement of the left arm to help correct a particular kind and degree of tilt may be learned in one experience, but it certainly does not follow that the whole skill of balancing the bicycle will be learned so quickly. If we also consider all the other aspects of bicycle riding, the distinction between learning a movement and gradually mastering a skill becomes evident. This illustration does not show that Guthrie is necessarily correct when he says that a movement is learned in one trial, but it does make his interpretation more plausible.

This explanation, however, introduces some ambiguity into Guthrie's theory. In many cases "the last thing one did in a situation" refers to an act, such as lighting a cigarette or making a remark. These, however, are skilled performances made up of many specific movements. Why does Guthrie treat them as if they were single movements that could be conditioned in one trial? Presumably what is needed here is an analysis in terms of hierarchies of complexity. Lighting a match is a skill made up of many stimulus-movement connections that must be conditioned. However, once learned, this whole act may behave like a single movement in that it can be conditioned as such to combinations of stimuli. Guthrie does not concern himself with this relationship, but applies his principle of learning sometimes to movements and sometimes to acts, depending on the point he wants to make. Fortunately, this ambiguity is unimportant in most situations.

The aspect of Guthrie's theory that has been most attacked is his lack of concern with success and failure, with learning to do the "right" thing. Whatever one did last in the situation, right or wrong, is what one will do again. Guthrie makes no use of the concept of reinforcement. He does not say that we learn to make those responses that work, or that obtain reward. Whether or not something we do becomes learned as a response to the situation depends only on whether it changes the situation into a different situation, so that it becomes the last thing done in the old situation. Success has this result, since a solution changes a problem situation into a situation without a problem. Thus the successful act is the last one that occurs in the problem situation, and it will tend to occur if the problem is presented again. However, if we can somehow escape from the situation without solving the problem, the escape response will be learned. Inefficient methods may be learned and retained as well as efficient ones, since both get us out of the situation. Mistakes may be repeated over and over again. We learn, not by success or by reinforcement, but simply by doing.

A number of testable predictions follow from this position. As an example, consider a hungry rat that can obtain food by pressing a lever. The rat learns to press the lever more and more rapidly. According to Guthrie, the rat learns because the food changes the situation through its effect on hunger and on the sensations in the mouth. Thus pressing the lever becomes the last thing the animal did in the old situation, and it becomes increasingly likely to occur. Suppose instead of getting food after each pressing of the lever the rat was simply taken out of the box as soon as it pressed the lever. This would change the situation even more than food did, so the rat should be even more likely to press the lever at the next opportunity than if it had been fed. This experiment has been done, and the results did not confirm the prediction (Seward 1942). The rats receiving food showed far more lever pressing than those removed from the box, contrary to what would be expected from Guthrie's theory. This experiment and others like it cast doubt on Guthrie's view that reward has nothing to do with learning.

It may be, however, that our interpretation of this experiment is not altogether fair to Guthrie. Although the food produced less change in the total stimulus combination than did removal from the box, the food did produce a marked change in certain particularly important stimuli. These were the *maintaining stimuli*—those stimuli that kept the rat active in the situation. In this particular case the maintaining stimuli were those resulting from food deprivation—in other words, the stimuli of hunger. In other situations they might be the stimuli of thirst or pain or sexual arousal or anger or fear. At some places in his writings Guthrie suggests that it is changes in the maintaining stimuli that are crucial for learning. If a response removes the maintaining stimuli, by definition it solves the problem and thus becomes the last response in the problem situation. If it fails to remove the maintaining stimuli, then no matter what other changes it may produce it cannot be the last response in the problem situation. By this interpretation, we can see why food might be expected in Guthrie's theory to produce more learning than removal from the box.

However, this interpretation also raises other problems. In some cases responses are learned that do not remove the maintaining stimuli. A softball player learns those responses that produce successful batting and fielding, even though a base hit or a good catch does not reduce the competitive excitement that provides the maintaining stimuli for playing. A rat in a maze learns the correct turn at each choice point, even though only the last turn is followed by any change in the maintaining stimuli. In both cases, however, the response does change the overall stimulus combination, so that it is in one sense the last response in the situation. Thus we are faced with the problem that sometimes only changes in the maintaining stimuli are crucial, while at other times changes in other stimuli are important. How do we know which times are which? Guthrie does not tell us. By sometimes considering all stimuli and sometimes considering only maintaining stimuli, Guthrie can explain any case of learning after it has occurred, but he cannot do so well at predicting what learning will take place.

By now it should be clear why Guthrie's system is difficult to treat as a formal logical theory. When are we talking about movements and when about acts? When should we look at all stimulus changes and when only at changes in the maintaining stimuli? Because he concentrates on presenting simple, entertaining interpretations of learning, Guthrie never gives clear answers to these awkward questions. As a result, his theory, which at first glance seemed so direct and precise, turns out to be discouragingly vague. His attempt to reduce all learning to one basic principle is, in any precise sense, inadequate.

His loose, anecdotal approach reflects the fact that Guthrie was interested more in the undergraduate teaching of psychology than in detailed research. He himself produced only one major experiment bearing on his theory, a demonstration of the stereotyped behavior of cats in escaping from a cage (Guthrie & Horton 1946), which we will encounter again in Chapter 17. Perhaps because of this lack of emphasis on research he has had many sympathizers but few active followers. There has never been a long and active tradition of research within the framework of Guthrie's theory (though various of his followers did make some starts toward one, and we will see his influence on Estes in Chapter 12). However, many psychologists have found that, once they stop treating Guthrie's system as a formal theory and concentrate on its informal implications, its basic principle of learning turns out to be quite useful. In any situation, says Guthrie, if you want to know what an individual will learn, look at what he or she does. What the person does, right or wrong, is what he or she will learn. As an informal source of advice, this suggestion turns our attention to aspects of learning that we would otherwise be very likely to neglect. We can best appreciate Guthrie's contribution by looking at his discussions of some practical learning situations.

BREAKING HABITS

Perhaps the best known of Guthrie's applications are his three methods for changing a bad habit. All three methods depend on finding out what stimuli evoke the undesirable response and then finding a way of making some other response occur in the presence of those stimuli. This other response should then occur again the next time the stimuli are presented. The emphasis is on the exact stimulus and the exact response that are connected. Guthrie gives the example of a 10-year-old girl who, whenever she came in the door of her house, threw her hat and coat on the floor. Time and again her mother scolded her and made her go back and hang them up, but to no avail. Finally the mother realized that the stimulus for the girl to hang up her wraps was the mother's nagging. The next time the girl threw down her wraps, her mother insisted that she put them on again, go outside, come in the door again, and hang up her coat and hat at once. After a few trials of this procedure the girl learned to hang up her wraps. The desired response had been attached to the stimuli of coming in the door, and the habit of throwing down the wraps had thus been replaced by the habit of hanging them up. This procedure worked where the previous nagging had failed because this time the mother saw to it that the girl hung up her wraps in the presence of the particular stimuli (those resulting from having just come through the door) that had previously led to the response of throwing the wraps down.

How does one get the desired response to occur in the presence of those stimuli that have been eliciting only an undesired response? The first method, which may be called the *threshold* method, involves presenting the stimuli so faintly or weakly that the undesirable response does not occur. (The stimuli are said to be below the threshold intensity for the response, hence the name.) The stimuli are then increased in strength so gradually on successive occasions that the response never occurs. These repeated experiences with the weak stimuli raise the threshold so that stronger stimuli will also be below threshold. Eventually the stimuli can be presented at full strength without eliciting the undesired response, since the individual has been making some other response repeatedly in the presence of the stimuli. This method is useful mainly for emotional responses involving anger, fear, and the like. Guthrie gives the example of the old cavalry method of training saddle horses. If an untrained horse is saddled and ridden, it will buck wildly. This reaction can be avoided by employing the method of thresholds to replace the bucking response with a response of standing quietly. First a blanket is put on the horse's back. This pressure on its back is the sort of stimulus that induces bucking, but the blanket alone is too weak a stimulus to have this effect. After some experience with the blanket the horse is saddled. Prior to experience with the blanket, the saddle might have produced bucking, but now it does not. Eventually, after the horse's experience with the saddle, a rider can mount without producing bucking, though the horse would certainly have bucked if it had been mounted before the training with blanket and saddle. The experience of not bucking while successively heavier weights were placed on its back has eventually resulted in the horse's standing still even for the weight of a rider.

The second method may be called the method of *fatigue*. The response to be eliminated is elicited again and again, until the individual is so tired that he or she stops making the response and does something else (if only resting) instead. This other response is then the one likely to occur when the stimuli are presented again. Here too Guthrie used an example of a disobedient girl, though we are not told whether it is the same one who would not hang up her clothes. This girl had a habit of lighting matches. After scolding and punishment failed, her worried mother finally eliminated the habit by making the girl light a whole box of matches in quick succession. Long after the girl was thoroughly tired of lighting matches, her mother insisted that she continue. Eventually the girl began actively resisting, throwing the box of matches down and pushing it away. At this point new responses, incompatible with match lighting, had been attached to the stimuli from the match box. The next time she had a chance to light matches, the girl showed no inclination to do so. This method illustrates in extreme degree Guthrie's reliance on his version of Watson's law of recency (doing again what one did last in a given situation) and his rejection of Watson's law of frequency. The girl had lighted matches more frequently at the end of this experience than at the beginning, but the last thing she did was to push the match box away. Pushing it away was therefore what she tended to do when she next encountered a match box.

In the third method, which we may call the method of *incompatible stimuli*, the stimuli for the undesired response are presented along with other stimuli that can be counted on to produce a different, incompatible response. The original stimuli then become attached to the new response. Guthrie illustrated this method with the case of a college student who could not study because of distracting noises. She solved this problem by spending a period of time reading absorbing mystery novels instead of studying. These stories held her attention so well that she ignored the distracting noises. The stimuli of noise thus occurred along with the responses of reading and became attached to these responses. When she then changed back (however reluctantly) from reading mysteries to reading textbooks, she found that the noises no longer distracted her, for they were now attached to reading responses instead of listening responses.

It is noteworthy that there is no reference to punishment in any of these methods. Someone might suggest that it was punishing for the one disobedient girl to go out of the house, come in again, and hang up her clothes, and also punishing for the other girl to light so many matches at once. True, says Guthrie, but remember that other forms of punishment had previously failed. The important question is not whether these experiences were punishing but what they led the individuals to do. Inflicting pain on someone, says Guthrie, cannot be expected to change bad habits if the pain does not occur in the presence of the stimuli that produce the behavior. Scolding the one girl after her clothes were already on the floor, or slapping the other girl after she had finished with the matches, would be irrelevant to the habits in question. Only when the punishment resulted in a new response to the same stimuli, incompatible with the old response, was it effective. Moreover, as the threshold method indicates, absence of punishment may be just as good a way of producing new responses as is punishment.

This attitude is characteristic of Guthrie's interpretation of punishment. Always look at what punishment makes the individual do. If punishment succeeds in changing the punished habit, it is because it elicits behavior incompatible with it. If punishment fails, it is because the behavior elicited by the punishment is not incompatible with the punished behavior. Thus, if you want to stop a dog from chasing cars, slapping its nose as it runs is likely to work, whereas slapping the dog's rear is not. The two blows may be equally painful, but the one on the nose tends to make the dog stop and jump backward, whereas the one on the rear tends to make it continue forward all the more vigorously. Hence the blow on the nose, by eliciting behavior incompatible with running after the car, makes this nonrunning more likely to occur next time. The blow on the rear has no such effect; it may even strengthen the chasing. Punishment works, when it does work, not because it hurts the individual but because it changes the response to certain stimuli.

If we wanted to use these methods of Guthrie's as cure-alls for bad habits, we would immediately encounter a problem. In order to obtain different behavior from an individual, we have to change the stimuli in some way. For the little girl, coming in the door and taking off her wraps was not the same when she had just been sent out the door by her mother as when she had just come in after a long time outside. For the army horse, not bucking to a blanket was different from not bucking to a rider. There was a considerable difference between the stimulus situation when lighting a fiftieth match under a mother's prodding and when lighting a first match for fun. Now, when the original stimulus situation is restored, how do we know whether the two situations are enough alike so that the last response in one will occur in the other? For example, will the dog that jumped back when presented with the stimulus of moving-car-plus-blow-on-the-nose also jump back when presented with moving-car-alone? The answer in all these cases seems to be: Try it and see. This difficulty weakens the general usefulness of Guthrie's advice, not to mention the problem of relating the advice clearly to the theory. However, we can scarcely expect to get advice that will work infallibly in every situation without any ingenuity on the part of the person taking it. Guthrie's interpretation of punishment and his methods for changing habits are valuable tools for interpreting situations as well as useful suggestions for dealing with them. A theorist who can give us this much need not be ashamed of his practical contributions.

Some Special Topics

Guthrie's emphasis on responses to stimuli and the ways of changing them shows up in other contexts, too. What of extinction? Since Guthrie does not talk about reinforcement, he cannot talk about extinction as resulting from the removal of reinforcement. Instead, he says that extinction is simply learning to do something else. The response was learned because it changed the stimulus situation into a different one, thus becoming the last thing that was done in the original situation. If, now, the learned response no longer produces this change, the individual will go on doing various things in the situation until some other response does change the situation. That new response will then be the one that tends to occur next time. If this new response consistently terminates the situation, it will replace the old response. If, however, there is no longer any consistency in what response will terminate the situation, behavior will be variable from time to time. No particular new response will be learned, but the old response will still be replaced by new responses—in this case, many new ones. If a dog has learned to get out of the yard by crawling through a hole in the fence, and if this hole is now mended, the dog may or may not discover some other mode of escape. In any case, however, the response of going to the place where the hole was will be replaced by some other response or combination of responses.

Guthrie's interpretation of forgetting is similar. Habits do not weaken with disuse; they are replaced by other habits. If we forget the German vocabulary we have learned, it is because the English words that serve as stimuli have become attached to other responses than the German words. If we lose our skill at horseback riding, it is because we have practiced other, competing responses in situations that were somewhat similar to being on horseback (such as being on a bicycle). In most cases the details of the relearning process are obscure, and it would be difficult to predict with accuracy how much of some knowledge or skill we would forget under a given set of circumstances. However, this interpretation of forgetting does provide a good starting point for studying the factors that influence forgetting. Even this start is more than many theorists have provided for the topic.

Forgetting, like acquisition, is usually gradual because of the many specific stimulus-response connections that make up a complex habit. If the correct responses have been attached to many different stimuli, it will take longer for new responses to get attached to all these stimuli. Hence it is possible to make one definite prediction from Guthrie's interpretation of forgetting. We can predict that a habit will be better retained if it has been practiced in a number of different situations (i.e., in the presence of a number of different stimulus combinations). In the course of forgetting, new responses may replace the old, correct one quickly in any of these situations, but the old response will still be conditioned to many other stimulus combinations. On another occasion when the stimulus combination is different, the old response is likely to reappear. Forgetting, like learning, is specific to the situation, and what is forgotten in one situation may well be remembered in another. The "forgotten" response to the changed stimulus will occur only, however, if the response in question was originally learned to a variety of different stimulus combinations. Hence we can increase the resistance of a habit to forgetting (including those verbal habits that we call knowledge) not only by practicing it more but by practicing it in a variety of situations.

The impression conveyed by most of Guthrie's writing is that human behavior is a very mechanistic matter. Behavior is rigidly controlled by stimuli, and changes in the stimulus-response connections follow simple mechanical laws. However, Guthrie has been more receptive than Watson to such concepts as desire and purpose. He recognizes that much behavior has a goal-directed character. Rather than ignoring this, as Watson was inclined to do, he attempts to interpret it in rigorously physical terms.

What does it mean to say that someone has a desire, a purpose, or an intention to do something? Guthrie recognizes four components: (1) a complex of maintaining stimuli that keeps the organism active; (2) something that blocks any simple, direct action that would remove the maintaining stimuli at once; (3) muscular readiness to make certain responses; and (4) muscular readiness for the consequences of this action. Consider a person in a burning building who has the intention of jumping to safety. In this case the four components are as follows: (1) heat from the fire, choking sensations from the smoke, and fear; (2) the fire and the height that block the person from simply running away; (3) the tensing of muscles for the jump; and (4) the preparation of the body for the shock of the fall. These four components, says Guthrie, are all that we need to describe an intention.

If someone had suggested to Guthrie that intention is something mental, over and above these four physical components, he might have replied with his story about a strange murder case. A man resolved to shoot his neighbor, and he hid outside the neighbor's house with a rifle pointed at the door and his finger on the trigger. While sitting there, he began to think better of his plan. He was about to get up and go away when the neighbor came out the door. The man pulled the trigger and the neighbor fell. At his trial, the question arose as to whether or not he fired intentionally. According to Guthrie, this is a meaningless question. That part of the man's intention which took the form of words to himself had changed, but the part that involved a ready trigger finger had not changed. There was no one intention, only a variety of bodily adjustments which did or did not prepare him to shoot.

What is attention? It encompasses a variety of responses that orient the sense receptors toward certain stimuli, as in looking or listening. There may even be scanning, involving searching movements that end when a certain stimulus is perceived. This formulation of attention makes it possible for Guthrie to reword his basic principle of learning as follows: "What is being noticed becomes a signal for what is being done" (1959, p. 186).

In all these interpretations, Guthrie is insisting that the processes involved, though they may be called by subjective terms, refer to objective physical movements. They may be hard to observe, but they are there just as surely as any other movements. Guthrie particularly emphasizes the role of *movement-produced stimuli,* the sensations produced by our own movements. These play an important part in thought, purpose, the coordination of sequences of behavior, and responses to stimuli that are no longer present. Though they often function like intervening variables in his system (since they are often impractical to observe directly), he hesitates to call them intervening variables, since for him they are just as objectively present as the independent and the dependent variables.

Guthrie's final theoretical statement (1959), written shortly before his death, is both more technical and more tentative than most of his earlier work. He seems to be trying to clarify both his own ideas and his relationships to other theorists. In this statement he is concerned both with the concept of attention and with the formal structure of his theory. However, it is likely that Guthrie will be remembered not so much for his attempts, successful or not, at formal theory building as for his informal contributions to our thinking about the learning process.

In trying to understand or to control any learning situation, Guthrie reminds us to look at the particular response that is being made and the particular stimuli that are eliciting it. He warns us not to rely on vague exhortations, not to look for magic in the administration of rewards and punishments, but to concentrate on eliciting particular patterns of behavior in particular situations. Though he tends to draw his examples largely from child rearing and animal training, Guthrie has much that is useful to offer adult human learners as well.

College students often complain that they know the material they have studied but that they somehow cannot present it on examinations. A familiarity with Guthrie's thinking would lead one to say, "If the behavior you want to produce is the behavior of writing essays about certain topics, practice writing essays, and practice in a situation as close as possible to that of an exam." In a similar example in military training, studies of combat effectiveness resulted in training situations being made more and more like combat. As a result, infantry trainees spend less time practicing exact marksmanship with bull's-eye targets on the known-distance range and more time practicing rough-and-ready marksmanship with silhouette targets that pop up to confront the trainees as they advance. Though we cannot say that these examples represent Guthrie's direct influence on the applied psychology of learning, we can say that Guthrie, perhaps more than any other major theorist, has emphasized the importance of such precise analysis of stimuli and responses. Guthrie's approach can stand one in good stead in many learning situations.

A FINAL WORD ON CONTIGUITY THEORY

Watson and Guthrie of course have in common all the characteristics of behaviorism in the general sense of that term. In addition, there is one respect in which the two of them differ from the majority of other behavioristic theorists—namely, they do not regard learning as depending on reinforcement. Watson ridiculed the idea that reward could determine what was learned, regarding it as a magical notion unfit for a scientific explanation. Guthrie similarly avoided making any reference to the reinforcing effects of rewards. In their systems, learning is assumed to depend only on the contiguity of stimulus and response, in other words, on the fact that they occur together. Hence Watson and Guthrie are called *contiguity theorists.*

In taking this position, Watson and Guthrie stand in contrast to another group of connectionist behavioristic theorists known as *reinforcement theorists.* The latter group is just as dedicated to objectivity and just as much attached to the stimulus-response language in describing learning. Its proponents do not, however, see any objection to recognizing the reinforcing effect of reward in their theories; in fact, they consider this effect essential to the analysis of learning. We have already seen that Thorndike was a great early exponent of this view. For some decades it was the dominant approach in American learning theory, and it will occupy us for the next three chapters.

Chapter 5

Hull's Formal Theory Building

*T*he most ambitious of all the connectionist learning theories is that of Clark L. Hull (1884–1952). Long a professor at Yale, Hull was the most influential learning theorist of his time. He was a behaviorist, but far more sophisticated than Watson in the philosophy of science. His early training, before he became a psychologist, was in engineering, and something of the engineer's outlook is evident in his desire to construct an elaborate, formal, precise structure of psychological theory. In him we see the full logical flowering of the connectionist reinforcement tradition.

THE POSTULATIONAL METHOD OF THEORY CONSTRUCTION

Hull's concept of the ideal theory was a logical structure of postulates and theorems, similar to Euclid's geometry. The postulates would be statements about various aspects of behavior. They would not be laws taken directly from experiments, but more general statements about the basic processes involved. Like the postulates of geometry, they would not themselves be proved but would be taken as the starting points for proofs. From these postulates, a great variety of other statements, called theorems, could be logically derived. Each theorem could be proved by arguing logically from some combination of postulates. These theorems would be in the form of laws of behavior.

So far, such a theory is simply a logical creation. No mention has been made about whether its statements are true or false, only about how they hang together logically. When a theorem is proved, all this means is that if the postulates are true, the theorem must also be true. In order for the theory to have any value as a description of the real world, it is necessary to compare the theorems with actual laws of behavior as determined by experiments. In other words, after the theorist has determined by logic that the theorems follow from the postulates, he must then determine by experiment whether they are true. If they are, the whole theory is supported; if not, the theory is weakened and requires revision.

To anyone not acquainted with the philosophy of science, this approach may seem backward. The theorists start with postulates that may or may not be true. They then prove logically that if the postulates are true, certain theorems must also be true. Next, they determine by experiments whether each theorem is in fact true. Finally, they use the truth or falsity of the theorems to argue indirectly about the truth or falsity of the postulates. If a theorem turns out to be false, they know that at least one of the postulates from which the theorem was proved must also be false, since it led logically to a false conclusion. In consequence, some postulate (the theorists may not yet know which one) must be changed so that the theorems which follow from it will be true. If, instead, all the theorems turn out to be true, this verification increases their confidence that all the postulates are true. However, they can never be absolutely sure that the postulates are true, since false postulates can sometimes lead to true theorems. As more and more theorems turn out to be true, they become more confident that the postulates are true, but there is still the possibility that eventually a theorem derived from the postulates will turn out to be false.

Although this theoretical approach may sound both complicated and strange, it is actually rather similar to what we do in many familiar situations. Consider a teacher who is concerned about the poor performance of a certain student, one who has a high IQ. She suspects that the student's difficulty may reflect two factors: (1) a fear of competition, and (2) a tendency to react to fear by "freezing up" and being unable to act effectively. These guesses are the equivalent of postulates. Either or both of them may be either true or false. They cannot be tested directly, since fear is not directly observable. They can, however, be tested indirectly. To test them, the teacher must first figure out how a student who has this fear and this reaction to fear would behave in certain situations. This is the process of deducing theorems from postulates. Thus, if the teacher's "postulates" about the student are true, it should also be true that (1) the student will do better on test items if they are presented to him casually in conversation rather than as part of a test; (2) if given an opportunity to compete for a prize, he will refuse; and (3) if offered a chance to give a talk to the class on some topic that interests him, he will accept. The teacher may try each of these approaches and see what happens. These, then, are three experiments, each designed to test one of the teacher's "theorems." If in each case the student does what the teacher predicted, her confidence in her interpretation (i.e., in her "postulates") will increase. She cannot, however, rule out the possibility that all of his behavior is really due to some other combination of factors, and that eventually he will do something that does not fit at all with her interpretation. She can become more and more confident that her interpretation is correct, but she can never be absolutely sure of it.

If it turned out that her first two predictions were confirmed, but the third was not, she would know that her "postulates" were not entirely correct. She might decide, since he refused to address the class even when no competition was involved, that his fear was not merely of competition but of any situation in which he was threatened with failure or disapproval. She could then look for new situations in which to test this revised "postulate." In this way her interpretation of his behavior would be a self-correcting process of making and testing assumptions.

The teacher's thinking in this example and Hull's thinking in constructing a scientific theory are, of course, markedly different in scope and in logical formality. These are differences of degree, however, rather than of kind. The teacher was concerned with very narrow interpretations, involving the behavior of a single student, whereas Hull was concerned with very broad ones, involving the whole range of human and animal behavior. In addition, Hull wrote down his postulates in detailed form and tested the theorems in controlled experiments, whereas the teacher merely developed hunches and tested them in a rough-and-ready fashion. Nevertheless, the two cases are basically similar enough to show the kind of reasoning that Hull followed in building his theory.

It should be clear from the above that Hull did not regard his theory as a final statement about the nature of learning. Rather, it was intended as a tentative formulation, always subject to revision to bring it in line with new data or new ideas. This tentativeness was a necessary characteristic of the kind of system he wanted to build. A set of postulates from which many laws of behavior are supposed to follow by strictly logical deduction has more chances of being wrong than does an informal system that makes fewer or less exact predictions. Watson's and Guthrie's theories, for example, are informal enough to leave considerable doubt as to just what they would predict in a particular situation. Hull, in contrast, intended to create a theory specific enough so that it would be easy to see when it was contrary to the evidence. A theory of this sort is practically certain to be wrong in some respects when it is first formulated; hence it must be open to change as errors are discovered.

It was Hull's plan to write three books expounding his theory. The first was to present and explain the postulate system. This appeared in 1943 as *Principles of Behavior.* Though various revisions of the postulate system were subsequently published, this book remains the cornerstone of Hull's theoretical writing. The second book was to contain detailed derivations of individual behavior in a variety of situations. This was published in 1952 as *A Behavior System.* It contains 133 theorems with their derivations from the postulates and the evidence bearing on their correctness as laws of behavior. The topics with which these theorems deal are as diverse as discrimination learning, locomotion in space, and the acquisition of values. As might be expected, this system of postulates and theorems is much more complicated and technical than any of the other systems we have examined so far.

An invalid during the last few years of his life, Hull was barely able to finish this second major book. In the preface, he expressed his regret that the third book in the series, which was to present derivations of behavior in social interactions, would never be written. Four months later he died. Although his trilogy thus remains incomplete, it gives us a good picture both of the grandness of Hull's conception and of the many respects in which the actual system fell short of his aspirations. It is possible that if Hull had lived longer and had been in better health during his last years, many of the shortcomings of his theory would have been corrected. As it is, we must judge both his successes and his failures by his works as they stand.

The Four-Stage Analysis

Like most theorists, Hull wanted to develop a system for predicting the dependent variables of behavior from various independent variables. Recognizing the variety of independent and dependent variables with which he had to deal, he tried to simplify the task of prediction by introducing intervening variables. We saw in Chapter 2 how the use of such intervening variables makes it possible to summarize a great many details with a small number of concepts. Hull organized his intervening variables into a four-stage predictive scheme. The first stage consisted of the independent variables from which he was predicting, the fourth stage consisted of the dependent variables to which he was predicting, and the second and third stages were made up of intervening variables connecting them. Knowing the values (amounts or degrees) of the independent variables, he could compute the values of the intervening variables at stage 2. From these he could in turn compute the value of the intervening variable at stage 3, and from that finally predict the values of the dependent variables. The general outline of this elaborate scheme is given in Figure 5.1, which may serve as a guide to the explanation below.

The independent variables include all those that can be directly manipulated by an experimenter. These may be summarized briefly, since they are discussed in more detail in connection with the intervening variables. Some of the independent variables refer to the stimulation the learner is receiving at the moment, such as the brightness of a signal light or the intensity of an electric shock. Others refer to immediately preceding events, such as the number of hours since the learner's last meal or the amount of muscular effort recently put forth. Still others refer to previous experience in the same learning situation, such as the number of times the

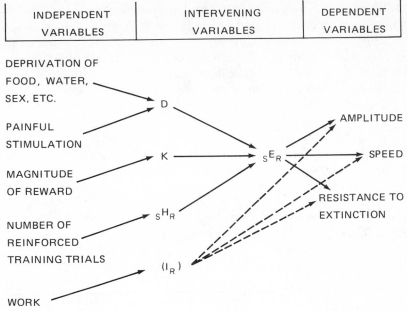

INDEPENDENT VARIABLES	INTERVENING VARIABLES	DEPENDENT VARIABLES

Figure 5.1 *A schematic representation of Hull's system.* The independent variables influence the intervening variables, which in turn influence the dependent variables. Solid arrows indicate that increases in the first variable tend to produce increases in the second; broken arrows indicate that increases in the first tend to produce decreases in the second. Note that $_sE_R$ is not an exact quantity but rather the mean of a range of oscillation. (D = drive; K = incentive motivation; $_sH_R$ = habit strength; I_R = reactive inhibition; $_sE_R$ = excitatory potential.)

subject has previously made the response to be learned or the magnitude of the reward received the last time the response was made. The number of such independent variables that could be mentioned is endless; the important thing for our understanding of Hull is the way that he has organized them in his system.

The second stage of the analysis introduces intervening variables. These are hypothetical states of the organism that cannot be observed but that are assumed to be directly controlled by the independent variables. The two most prominent ones are *habit strength* and *drive*. Habit strength refers to the strength of the learned connection between a cue or cues and a response, a connection built up through reinforced practice. Drive is an activating state of the organism, and a reduction in drive serves as a reward.

Since Hull was a connectionist theorist, habit strength is a key concept in his system. It is the strength of the bond connecting a stimulus with a response. To indicate the nature of this connection, habit strength is abbreviated $_sH_R$ (pronounced S H R), with the H standing for habit and the S and R subscripts standing for the stimulus and the response that the habit connects. This habit is a permanent connection, which can increase but cannot decrease in strength. All long-term learning involves the formation and strengthening of habits. Each time a response occurs in the presence of a stimulus and is quickly followed by reinforcement, the habit strength of this stimulus-response connection increases. In this postulate, Hull resembles all other reinforcement theorists. His system goes on to say that all reinforcement involves a reduction in the strength of a drive. The rate at which habit strength builds up with successive reinforced responses (given by an equation in another postulate) follows the well-known "law of diminishing returns," so that each successive reinforced response contributes less to $_sH_R$ than the previous one. Eventually a point is reached at which additional reinforced responses contribute very little more to habit strength.

Drive is a temporary state of the organism, produced by deprivation of something the body needs or by painful stimulation. There are many different specific drive conditions, of which hunger, thirst, and pain are typical examples. Drives have two different functions. For one thing, each drive condition, such as hunger or thirst, produces a characteristic strong drive stimulus. This stimulus indicates the particular need from which the body is suffering. A rapid reduction in this drive stimulus is reinforcing. As a result, any response that occurs just before a reduction in a drive stimulus tends to be learned as a response to whatever stimuli are present. (We have already seen this relationship in connection with the postulate about the building up of habit strength.) The other function of drives is an activating or energizing one. All drive conditions combine to make up the total drive level of the organism. This total drive (abbreviated D) serves to raise the individual's activity level. This activating effect of D can be seen both in an increased level of general body activity and in the increased vigor with which all learned habits are performed. In all these respects, Hull's D shows resemblances to Guthrie's maintaining stimuli.

Hull was also concerned with the size of the reward used as a reinforcer. We are all familiar with the law that people tend to work harder for a larger reward than for a smaller one. In other words, the level of performance is commonly higher when a larger reward is given after the response occurs. How should this law be handled by the theory? In his earlier book, Hull (1943) treated the magnitude of the reward as one aspect of reinforcement. The larger the reward, the greater the reduction in drive, and hence the greater the increase in habit strength. However, this treatment proved not to be satisfactory. Experiments showed that changes in the magnitude of the reward produced very rapid changes in the level of performance, much faster than the slow growth of habit strength could explain. This difference was particularly difficult for Hull to explain when the change was from a larger to a smaller reward. If the reward was made smaller and performance became poorer, this result seemed to mean that the habit strength had become less. Yet habit strength involved a permanent bond, one that became stronger with reinforced practice but never became weaker. Here was a striking example of a discrepancy between theory and experiment. How would Hull deal with it?

Hull's answer, in the later versions of his theory, was to introduce a third intervening variable at the second stage of the analysis. Along with habit strength and drive he added *incentive motivation* (abbreviated K). The magnitude of the reward, in the new version, affects only K, not habit strength. The level of K depends on the size of the reward (for example, the amount of food) in the few immediately preceding trials. When the size of the reward is increased, at whatever stage of practice, K increases, and when the reward is decreased, K decreases. Incentive motivation thus refers, as the name implies, to the motivating effect of the incentive that is provided for making the response. The distinction between incentive motivation and reinforcement is subtle, since both depend on the reward, but the difference is nonetheless important. In order for a habit to increase in strength, the response must be followed by a reward that reduces a drive stimulus. The size of the reward makes no difference to the rate at which habit strength is built up; any reinforcement is as good as any other. The size of the reward does, however, affect the level of incentive motivation. Large rewards make for higher values of K, smaller rewards for lower values. When a rat learns to run down an alley for food, we see a gradual increase in its speed, an increase resulting from reinforced practice. However, over and above this slow increase in speed, we can increase or decrease the speed rapidly by changing the size of the food pellet we give at the end of each run. In the same way, it may be possible to increase a worker's output immediately by offering more pay for each item produced (thus increasing K), whereas it would take much longer to increase output by training the person in better work methods (increasing habit strength).

These three intervening variables—$_sH_R$, D, and K—work together to produce another intervening variable, which constitutes the third stage of the analysis. This is called *excitatory potential* and refers to the total tendency to make a given response to a given stimulus. It is abbreviated $_sE_R$, according to the same principle as $_sH_R$. It is equal to the product of the three other intervening variables; in other words, $_sE_R = {_sH_R} \times D \times K$. This equation means that the tendency to make a given response to a given stimulus depends on a habit built up through reinforced practice ($_sH_R$) and on two motivational factors, one depending on an internal state (D) and the other on an external incentive (K). For everyday purposes, we might refer to the $_sH_R$ for a given response as "having the skill to do it," to the K as "expecting a gain from doing it," and to D as "wanting the thing that is to be gained." Hull, however, would not use this terminology, as he would consider it too vague for the precise and objective science of behavior that he wanted to promote. For Hull, $_sH_R$, D, and K are defined by the operations that produce them (reinforced practice for $_sH_R$, deprivation or painful stimulation for D, nutritive substance for K), not by any vague, everyday names that we might choose to give them.

The fourth and final stage of Hull's analysis is made up of the dependent variables, the aspects of behavior that can actually be observed and measured. Hull relates three of these to excitatory potential ($_sE_R$): (1) the amplitude or size of the response, (2) the speed of the response, and (3) the total number of responses that will occur, after reinforcement is removed, before extinction is complete. As $_sE_R$ increases, amplitude, speed, and number of responses to complete extinction all increase.

In principle, it should be possible to use this system to predict how fast, for example, a rat would run down an alley to a food reward. To make this prediction, we would need to go through a number of steps. We would use the number of times the rat had already run down that alley and been reinforced to calculate the value of $_sH_R$. We would use the number of hours since the rat last ate to calculate the value of D. We would use the size of food reward that the rat had received on the last few trials to calculate the value of K. Then we would multiply those three values together to obtain the value of $_sE_R$. Finally, we would use $_sE_R$ to calculate the rat's speed on that trial. Each of these calculations requires using one of Hull's postulates, which would give us the necessary formula. To what extent it is possible to make such calculations in practice is difficult to say; we will get some idea of why it is difficult as we go along.

What Figure 5.1 shows, and what we have considered so far, is only the barest outline of Hull's system (1952). The final version of his theory had 17 postulates and 15 corollaries (theorems that follow immediately from a single postulate), which he hoped would cover the whole range of known behavioral phenomena. For example, he postulated the existence of unlearned stimulus-response connections, but did not elaborate the topic and rarely referred to such innate connections in his theorems. He discussed the effect of a delay between the response and the reinforcement in weakening the response tendency. He went into considerable detail about generalization and about the way generalized habit strengths combine (i.e., what happens when the same response is learned to two different but related stimuli). These details are beyond the scope of this book.

Elaborations of the Theory

Other postulates and corollaries, however, are necessary in order to understand Hull's derivations. One of these is *oscillation.* This refers to Hull's assumption that any given amount of excitatory potential is not an exact value but the average of a random distribution of values. When $_sH_R$ and D and K have been multiplied together to give the value of $_sE_R$, we still cannot predict with certainty what the amplitude or speed of the response will be, since the $_sE_R$ produced by any combination of $_sH_R$, D, and K is constantly oscillating. At any given moment, the oscillation of $_sE_R$ has usually carried the excitatory potential momentarily above or below the value computed. The oscillation in the value of $_sE_R$ is rapid and random, following approximately a normal distribution. The fact that Hull found it necessary to introduce this concept shows that his system, for all its complexity, could not hope to achieve perfect prediction of behavior. An element of random, unpredictable variation had to be introduced to make the system at all realistic.

When two incompatible responses have been learned to the same stimulus, so that two $_sE_R$'s are competing for expression, the principle of oscillation may be used to predict which will occur on any given trial. The oscillations of the two $_sE_R$'s are not synchronized, so that when one $_sE_R$ is momentarily high, the other may be high, medium, or low. If the ranges of oscillation of the two $_sE_R$'s overlap, each response will occur on some trials. If the $_sE_R$ for one response is considerably stronger than that for the other, so that their ranges of oscillation overlap only slightly, the stronger will occur most of the time and the weaker only rarely. If the two are equally strong, so that their ranges of oscillation coincide, each will occur half of the time. All such situations involve the conflict between two response tendencies, and the degree of overlap of the two ranges of oscillation makes it possible to predict how often each of the two competing responses will occur.

Second, there is the concept of *reactive inhibition*. This is a tendency not to repeat a response that has just been made. The amount of reactive inhibition resulting from a response depends on the amount of effort required to make the response, so that reactive inhibition is roughly analogous to fatigue. Since this tendency not to respond works against and tends to cancel the effects of excitatory potential ($_sE_R$), it is subtracted from $_sE_R$ to give the net excitatory potential used in predicting the amplitude and latency of responses. The abbreviation for reactive inhibition is I_R. The fact that there is no subscript S indicates that the inhibition is against *any* making of that response, regardless of the stimulus that produces it. The net value of $_sE_R$ is $_sH_R \times D \times K - I_R$.

The total amount of I_R against a given response increases each time the response occurs but decreases with the passage of time. It is for this reason that subjects usually perform better on a learning task involving a lot of effort if their practice is *distributed,* with short periods of practice separated by short periods of rest. These rest periods provide an opportunity for I_R to dissipate. Hull's analysis also uses reactive inhibition to explain why extinction occurs. Once reinforcement is removed, successive responses no longer build up $_sH_R$ but continue to build up I_R. As a result, inhibition gradually overcomes $_sE_R$ until no further responding occurs. However, after a period of time, the I_R dissipates and the response again occurs, giving spontaneous recovery.

We have seen that Hull's goal was to derive the laws of behavior logically from a simple system of postulates. After considering the number of concepts and assumptions that Hull packed into his 17 postulates, we may begin to wonder if there is anything simple about the system. However, its relative simplicity is more evident if we remember that *A Behavior System* contains 133 theorems, some with several parts, all following from the 17 postulates. Moreover, these 133 represent the limitations of Hull's time and energy rather than the limitations of the theory—there could have been many more. There is no question that the system represents an accomplishment of major proportions.

STRENGTHS AND WEAKNESSES OF THE SYSTEM

Hull saw the value of his theory not so much in the particular intervening variables it included as in its rigorous quantification. The postulates do not merely state that certain variables are related; they give equations by which one variable can be computed precisely from the other. For example, the postulate regarding habit formation contains the equation $_sH_R = 1 - 10^{-.0305N}$, where N is the total number of reinforcements. Using this equation, we can state the exact level of habit strength for any given number of reinforcements. Similar equations are presented connecting the other second-stage intervening variables to the independent variables and also connecting excitatory potential to the dependent variables. The equation connecting the second-stage intervening variables to $_sE_R$, which involves simple multiplication, has already been given.

Hull dedicated much of his effort in the last years of his life to the problems of quantification. He wanted to develop a scale of measurement for excitatory potential that would be applicable to any response. How can $_sE_R$ for pressing a lever be made comparable to $_sE_R$ for running down an alley? Hull's answer (which will be meaningful only to those readers who have studied statistics) was to use the standard deviation of the oscillations of $_sE_R$ as an absolute measuring unit. This use of the standard deviation as a scaling unit is an idea Hull took over from specialists in mental testing. He could then say that $_sE_R$ for a given response was two standard deviation units above zero, and this statement would have the same meaning regardless of what response he was discussing. This unit is also convenient for analyzing competition among responses, since knowing the $_sE_R$ for each response in standard deviation units also automatically tells how much their ranges of oscillation overlap and hence how often each will occur. Hull regarded the development of this scaling unit as one of the leading achievements of his life.

The evaluation of Hull's work by others has, however, been rather different from his own evaluation. It is just on the matter of quantitative rigor that he is most vulnerable to criticism. To some extent, the reason is that his attempts at quantification were premature. The exact values in his equations, such as the $-.0305$ in the equation for habit strength, were typically based on the results of a single experiment. He made the suggestion, but never developed it, that the values in the equations might vary from individual to individual. Thus different people might have different equations for the development of habit strength, with the specific absolute value being greater than .0305 for fast learners and smaller for slow learners. Moreover, when Hull came to derive theorems from his postulates, he sometimes used different values in his equations from the ones given in the postulates. For all these reasons, it seems clear that these values were intended to be illustrative rather than literally correct. What Hull attempted to present in his books was the general outline of a rigorous theory together with some suggestions as to how the outline could be developed into a full-scale, quantitatively exact system. He was still a long way from actually having such a system when he died.

Even if we leave aside the matter of precise, quantitative values, the system does not live up to the ideals that Hull set for it. In a system such as Hull's, it should be possible, given the values of the independent variables, to compute the values of the intervening variables and from these the dependent variables. Even if the precise numbers needed to make the computations are not available, it should be possible to explain how the computations would be made. In many of Hull's cases, however, it is not possible, because a given topic is either covered by two or more contradictory postulates or not covered at all. An example of the latter kind of problem is the definition of incentive motivation (K) when the drive is a painful stimulus, such as electric shock. Presumably in that case K would be determined by the amount of pain reduction that a response produced, perhaps specified by the difference in volts between the shock received before the response and the smaller shock received afterward. However, since K is defined by the weight of food or other nutriment consumed, it is impossible to apply Hull's equations to the situation where painful stimulation is the drive.

As an example of the former type of problem, in which the same question can logically be answered in different and conflicting ways, let us consider the question of how to predict resistance to extinction. Suppose we want to know how many successive nonreinforced trials it would take to produce complete extinction. One approach would be to use Postulate 16, which translates excitatory potential directly into trials to extinction. A second approach would be to use Postulate 9 to calculate the amounts of reactive inhibition and subtract it from excitatory potential. A third would be to note (Postulate 7) that when the amount of reward is zero, the value of K is also zero, which makes excitatory potential zero regardless of the values of the other intervening variables. It turns out that these three approaches, to the extent that they give precise answers at all, give conflicting ones. We could thus obtain three different answers to the question, depending on which postulates we decided to use in deriving our theorem about extinction.

The fact that different approaches can give different quantitative answers is not necessarily a crucial problem, since we have seen that the particular numerical values Hull used were mainly illustrative. However, the lack of internal consistency which this illustration points up is a serious weakness in the system, probably more so than any other flaw. When a theory makes incorrect predictions, it can be modified, as Hull intended that his theory should be. When a theory does not deal with a given issue at all, we can accept this limitation in its scope and hope that someday it may be expanded to include the neglected topic. However, when a theory is internally inconsistent, so that it makes conflicting predictions about a given issue, its worth as a rigorous theory is seriously compromised. To some extent we can blame Hull's failure in this regard on the revisions in his theory. For example, when the intervening variable K was added to the system in a later revision, the change called for a number of adjustments in other postulates, but some of these were never made. Racing against time in the last years of his life, Hull considered it more important to show what could be done with parts of his system than to make the system as a whole complete and consistent. Nevertheless, we must recognize that the theoretical system Hull actually created falls far short of the standards he himself set for theories.

By the irony of history, it appears that Hull failed where he most wished to succeed and succeeded in the respect that interested him least. He wanted both to build a deductive theory, at once broad in scope and rigorous in detail, and to encourage others to carry on the same sort of theoretical work. We have seen how far he fell short of his first aspiration. Moreover, his failure may have discouraged others from attempting such a task. Many observers have noted a trend in learning theory away from the sort of all-encompassing theories that we have been examining so far, toward theories of smaller scope designed to explain only certain kinds of learning. This trend may well reflect in part Hull's failure. For many years, psychologists have dreamed of doing for their field what Newton did for physics—developing a theory that would be at once vast in its scope, precise in its applications, and elegant in its simplicity, a theory that would pull together the loose ends of psychology into one master system. In pushing so far toward this goal and yet falling so far short of it, Hull convinced many psychologists that the day of such a master theory in psychology is still far off.

Yet in his failure, Hull also achieved striking success. His terms, his interests, and his ways of formulating psychological questions became more widespread than those of any other theorist of his time. A large number of experiments were inspired by his work. His interpretations of drive, reinforcement, extinction, and generalization became standard starting points for discussion of these topics. He was attacked, defended, and elaborated until to many people "learning theory" and "Hullian theory" became synonymous. In the next section of this chapter we will see some aspects of Hull's dominant position through the 1940s and 1950s and into the 1960s.

HULL'S FOLLOWERS

Both during Hull's life and after his death, colleagues of his at Yale and elsewhere expanded, modified, and applied his theory in various ways. When Hull's death left the theory in an unfinished state, marred by various inconsistencies, much of the job of clarifying and simplifying it fell to Kenneth W. Spence (1907–1967) at the University of Iowa. This was a natural transition, since for years Spence had been contributing so much to the development of the theory that it was sometimes hard to decide which ideas were whose. Nevertheless, Hull and Spence differed somewhat in their approach to theory. Though Spence was a great exponent of theory construction, he was more cautious about it than Hull. His theorizing was less elaborate, less formally stated, and more obviously tentative than Hull's. Even though Hull expected to keep modifying his theory in the light of new evidence, he stated it in the form of a formal, finished structure. Spence preferred to state ideas more casually, leaving more details to be settled by experiments.

In particular, Spence was more concerned than was Hull about the *boundary conditions* of a theory. These are the limits within which a theory is expected to operate. For example, a theory of education that worked well for explaining and predicting what happens in middle-class American schoolrooms might fail completely if applied to education among African Bushmen, or even to education in American urban ghettos, because education in these other situations is a topic outside the boundary conditions of the theory. Similarly, a theory intended to deal with learning by animals or human babies, where language does not enter in, might not be appropriate for learning by schoolchildren or adults. Therefore a theory should specify the conditions to which it is and is not intended to apply. Thus in various respects Spence did not set his aspirations for theory quite as high as Hull, but he is nonetheless a major advocate of theory construction as vital to the development of science.

Four years after Hull died, Spence (1956) came out with a major revision of the theory. In addition to being simpler, less pretentious, and more internally consistent, this new version incorporated elements from a number of other theorists, some of whom we have not yet considered. Rather than explore these detailed changes, we will look at applications to personality and social behavior that were developed by various others in the Hullian tradition.

Personality and Psychotherapy

While updating Hull's theory fell largely to Spence, other researchers set out to apply it to a variety of situations. In the later years of his life, Hull gathered around him a group of people in a number of academic disciplines, including clinical and social psychology, anthropology, sociology, and psychiatry. Though working independently, they all tried to apply

Hull's ideas to their own areas of study. Many lines of work emerged from this cross-fertilization of ideas; topics included the relationship of frustration to aggression, the reinterpretation of Freudian ideas in terms of learning principles, the psychological bases of social influence, and the explanation of worldwide cultural differences on the basis of different forms of child rearing. Of these many ideas, we will look at only one: an attempt to explain abnormal personality development and the ways that psychotherapy works to cure it. The analysis was developed by John Dollard (1900–1980), a clinical psychologist and social scientist, and Neal Miller (b. 1909), an experimental psychologist, working together at Yale (Dollard & Miller 1950).

Dollard and Miller begin the analysis by pointing out three characteristics of neurotic people: that they are miserable because of their conflicts, that they are stupid about certain aspects of their lives, and that they have symptoms. The researchers then proceed to explain these three characteristics according to the neurotic's previous learning. The crucial element here is the learned drive of fear. This drive is the basis of the conflict, the source of the misery, the cause of the stupidity, and the reason for the symptoms.

What is a learned drive? Dollard and Miller begin their discussion of the topic with an experimental demonstration involving rats. A rat is placed in a box with two compartments, one of which has white walls and a grid floor, the other black walls and a wooden floor. The rat explores both parts and shows little preference between them. Then it is placed in the white compartment and given strong electric shock through the grid floor. Most rats soon escape the shock by running into the black compartment. This sequence of shock in white and escape to black is repeated several times. Then the rat is placed in the white compartment without shock. It runs rapidly to the black compartment. Since there is no longer a pain drive to motivate this escape behavior, Dollard and Miller explain it on the ground that a learned drive of fear has been conditioned to the stimuli of the white compartment.

What is the nature of this learned drive? Like all drives, say Dollard and Miller, it involves strong stimulation. These strong stimuli are produced by the rat's own responses. When the rat was first shocked in the white compartment, it made a variety of responses to the shock, such as tensing the muscles, increasing the heart rate, and other involuntary indicators of emotion. These in turn produced strong stimulation which was added to the drive produced by the pain of the shock. These strong stimuli produced by the emotional responses make up the drive of fear. These emotional responses became conditioned to the stimuli of the white compartment, owing to the fact that they occurred in the presence of those stimuli and were followed by drive reduction when the rat escaped the shock. Now when the stimuli of the white compartment are presented without shock, they produce the emotional responses which in turn produce stimuli of the fear drive.

The fact that fear is a drive can be demonstrated by using it as the basis of new learning. This demonstration was done by closing the door from the white to the black section and making it possible for the rat to open the door only by turning a wheel on the wall near the door. The animals learned to turn the wheel and then run into the black compartment, even though there was no shock in the white compartment. In this case fear was the drive, sight of the wheel the stimulus, turning the wheel the response, and escape from fear (by escaping from the white compartment) the reinforcer. Then the situation was changed so that turning the wheel would not open the door but pressing a lever would. As a result, the wheel-turning response was extinguished and the lever-pressing response was acquired. Thus the learned drive of fear operated like a primary drive to motivate learning.

How does this kind of learning occur when we go from experimental rats to neurotic humans? Let us consider a child who is severely punished for any kind of self-assertive behavior. Whenever she tries to get her own way, she is subjected to pain, which produces emotional responses, which produce the learned drive of fear. These fear-producing responses become conditioned to the stimuli which are present at the time, including the cues that come from her own self-assertion. As a result, any self-assertive behavior comes to produce fear, while submissiveness reduces the fear. Moreover, the fear is not merely of overt self-assertive behavior, but even of those self-assertive thoughts and feelings that go with it. The child is then afraid of self-assertion in the same way that the rat is afraid of the white compartment, and the child's submissiveness (in thoughts as well as deeds) is an escape from fear-provoking cues, just as the rat's running to the black compartment is an escape from the fear-provoking white compartment.

However, the child's problem is worse than the rat's. As long as the rat is able to run to the black compartment, its fear is brief and does not disrupt its life. The child, however, is often placed in positions where self-assertive behavior might get her things that she wants. These positions occur even more often after she becomes an adult. The fact that she is afraid to be self-assertive is a great handicap in such situations. She is placed in a conflict between her desire for something and her fear of the self-assertive behavior that would get it for her. This conflict, in which she loses no matter what she does, is a source of misery. If she recognized the great difference between her present situation and that in which she was punished for self-assertion, she might be able to relieve the fear and resolve the conflict. However, this course requires that she recognize her problem and think about it. But she cannot do either, since she has become afraid not only of behaving self-assertively but even of saying (to others or to herself) that she would like to be self-assertive. It is this fear of saying or even thinking that she would like to be self-assertive that makes her behavior stupid. She cannot make the thinking responses that would help her to understand and to solve her problems. She can, however, obtain

some relief in a variety of ways. She may, for example, become so dependent, perhaps through symptoms of apparent physical illness, that others
will feel obliged to take care of her and provide her with some of the things
she wants. This would not be a deliberately adopted policy but a response
learned through its drive-reducing effects. The "illness" would be called
a symptom. It is, however, only a partial solution to the problem posed by
fear and conflict, and it interferes with finding a more effective solution.
This individual has all the characteristics of the neurotic; she is miserable,
in conflict, stupid about her troubles—and she has symptoms.

How can the neurosis be eliminated through psychotherapy? Since
fear is the crucial cause, extinguishing fear is the crucial element of the
cure. If the rat is given enough experience in the white compartment
without shock, its tendency to make the fear-producing responses will
eventually extinguish. Similarly, if the neurotic can be persuaded to make
self-assertive responses (or do whatever else it is that she is afraid of) under
conditions in which she will not be punished, her fear will extinguish.
Since the cues for fear come from the individual's own responses, she must
gradually be induced to make these responses, first in very weak and
indirect form, later more directly and strongly. Thus in the early stages of
therapy the neurotic may timidly say that she sometimes thinks that if she
were permitted to she could make helpful suggestions to her boss, while
in the later stages she may express a violent desire to tell the boss off with
assorted insults. As the patient extinguishes her fear of making self-assertive statements, she becomes more able to think sensibly about her conflict. Since talking about an act and doing it are somewhat similar, she also
becomes by stimulus generalization less afraid of overt self-assertive behavior. Thus Dollard and Miller, through a considerably different theoretical system, came to a practical conclusion somewhat like Guthrie's threshold method for the elimination of undesirable emotional habits.

Some people regard Dollard and Miller's interpretation as mainly a
translation of Freudian ideas into simplified Hullian language. Others
regard their work as a direct application of learning theory, inspired in
some ways by Freud but very different from Freud's own thinking. Either
way, it represents an interesting and potentially useful combining of two
approaches from quite different sources. A third possibility is to see their
work as a historical bridge between the older Freudian ideas and newer
behavioristic approaches to personality and psychopathology. These
newer approaches begin with the work of B. F. Skinner, to whom we next
turn.

Chapter
6

Skinner's Form
of Behaviorism

During the period of Hull's greatest influence, and beginning several years before Hull published his *Principles of Behavior,* B. F. Skinner had been studying learning in his own distinctive way. He did not consider himself a theorist and had little use for the theories of others. Both the data he gathered and the pungent opinions he expressed soon brought him to general attention, but his distinctive research methods and his lack of interest in theories kept him outside the mainstream of learning theory for a long time. Yet by the same sort of irony that made Hull a great success even as he was failing in his dearest ambitions, Skinner has come to be the best-known learning theorist of the 1980s. Like Hull in a slightly earlier period, he is widely praised, condemned, and imitated, but rarely ignored, and many of his terms have become part of the standard vocabulary of learning.

Skinner was born in 1904 and received a Ph.D. in psychology from Harvard in 1931. After teaching at the Universities of Minnesota and Indiana, he returned to Harvard and has remained there ever since. Though retired, he is still a very active writer. His first book, *The Behavior of Organisms,* was published in 1938, three years after the first edition of Guthrie's *Psychology of Learning* and five years before Hull's *Principles of Behavior.* Thereafter his influence increased gradually, until somewhere around 1970 he replaced Hull as the most talked-about figure in the behaviorist tradition.

THE BASIC ELEMENTS OF SKINNER'S SYSTEM

Of the theorists we have considered so far, the one whom Skinner most resembles is Thorndike. The two are alike in being connectionist theorists of a sort who emphasize reinforcement as a basic factor in learning, who take a keen interest in problems of education, and who deemphasize theory. This lack of interest in high-level theorizing was only implicit in Thorndike's writings, but Skinner has made it quite explicit in his system. However, the fact that Skinner does not elaborate theorems, postulates, and intervening variables in the same formal way as Hull does not mean that Skinner is not a theorist at all. It does mean that his contributions as a theorist and as an experimenter are more closely intertwined than is the case with most of the system builders we have considered.

Two Kinds of Learning

In contrast to the other theorists we have discussed so far, Skinner recognizes two different kinds of learning. They are different because each involves a separate kind of behavior. *Respondent* behavior is elicited by specific stimuli. Given the stimulus, the response occurs automatically. The learning of respondent behavior follows the pattern referred to earlier as classical conditioning. A new stimulus is paired with the one that already elicits the response, and after a number of such pairings the new stimulus comes to elicit the response. The presentation of the old (unconditioned) stimulus during training may be considered the reinforcer, since without it learning will not occur. Thus the learning of respondent behavior in Skinner's system is similar to the kind of learning that Watson assumed made up all learning.

Skinner maintains, however, that most behavior is of a different sort. This kind he refers to as *operant* behavior. Whereas the distinctive characteristic of respondent behavior is that it is in response to stimuli, the characteristic of operant behavior is that it operates on the environment to secure particular consequences. There is no specific stimulus that can be identified which will consistently elicit an operant response. Skinner speaks of operant behavior as being emitted by the organism rather than elicited by stimuli. Most behavior is of this sort; walking, talking, working, and playing are all made up of operant responses.

Skinner does not mean to say that operant behavior is not influenced by stimuli. Much of his analysis of behavior is concerned with ways in which operant behavior is brought under the control of stimuli. However, such control is only partial and conditional. The operant behavior of reaching for food is not simply elicited by the sight of food; it also depends on hunger, social circumstances, and a variety of other stimulus conditions. In these respects it is in contrast to the respondent jerking back of one's hand from a hot stove, which is regularly elicited almost without regard to other conditions. Because of this distinction, Skinner does not consider it useful to think of operant behavior as made up of specific stimulus-response connections in the sense that respondent behavior is. Whereas Guthrie analyzes every bit of behavior in terms of the stimuli that produce it, and Hull includes the S in $_sH_R$, Skinner prefers to think of most behavior (the operant kind) as emitted by the organism, without bothering to consider the multitude of stimuli that have something to do with its occurrence. The difference on this point is mainly one of emphasis and convenience rather than of direct disagreement. All three theorists agree that behavior depends on the total pattern of stimuli, external and internal, that are present when it occurs, but Guthrie and Hull prefer to emphasize this point for all responses, whereas Skinner prefers to ignore it in those cases where no one particular stimulus is crucial to the occurrence of the response.

The learning of operant behavior is also known as conditioning, but it is different from the conditioning of reflexes. Operant conditioning is the same sort of learning that Thorndike described. Because for Skinner this is by far the more important kind of learning, this topic is one on which he and Thorndike are close together. If an operant occurs and is followed by reinforcement, its probability of occurring again increases. Whereas for reflexes the reinforcer is an unconditioned stimulus, for operants it is a reward (or, as Thorndike would say, a satisfier). Thus we may say that reward following an operant makes that response more likely to occur again. (Even though the stimulus for an operant is unknown, Skinner still often refers to the operant behavior as a response.) This is the pattern of operant learning, which is to say, of most of the learning discussed by Skinner.

Whereas a respondent is usually a single bit of behavior, easy to identify separately, it is sometimes less clear where one operant stops and another starts. If a series of operants must occur in a particular sequence in order to obtain reinforcement, they become organized in a *chain*. The whole chain then comes to have some of the characteristics of a single operant, since the whole chain is the response unit that gets reinforced. In order to get a drink of water, for example, a person may have to get up from a chair, walk into the kitchen, open a cupboard, take down a glass, turn on the faucet, fill the glass, raise it to the mouth, and drink. Clearly this chain is made up of many operant responses, yet in another sense it functions as a single operant. If at any point the chain is broken—if there is no glass or if the faucet is broken or if there is some other obstruction— the whole chain up to that point will tend to undergo extinction. A large part of human behavior consists of such operant chains, which function in some degree as units but can nevertheless be analyzed into their component parts.

Positive and Negative Reinforcers

Although Skinner is largely concerned with *positive reinforcers,* he also recognizes the existence of *negative reinforcers.* Negative reinforcers are aversive stimuli, ones that the individual commonly seeks to avoid. The *removal* of a negative reinforcer increases the probability of the preceding response, just as does the *presentation* of a positive reinforcer. Electric shock, for example, is a negative reinforcer because the termination of the shock is reinforcing. Thus a response can be reinforced either by presenting a positive reinforcer or by removing a negative one.

An important point about reinforcers, both positive and negative, is that they can be conditioned. If a stimulus occurs repeatedly with a positive reinforcer, it tends itself to acquire the capacity to reinforce behavior. It then is called a conditioned positive reinforcer. A sign reading "Restaurant" will serve as a conditioned positive reinforcer for a hungry person in a strange city, because such signs have been associated with food in the past. Similarly, a stimulus that occurs with a negative reinforcer tends to become a conditioned negative reinforcer, as in the familiar case of the burned child who learns to avoid the stove even when it is cold.

The topic of negative reinforcement is obviously related to punishment, but the exact relation is not obvious. Negative reinforcement results from the *removal* of a negative reinforcer, whereas punishment involves the *presentation* of a negative reinforcer. Like Thorndike in the latter part of his career, Skinner regards the effect of reinforcement as simple and direct, but the effects of punishment as indirect and less predictable. Though reinforcement, by definition, increases the reinforced behavior, punishment does not always reduce the punished behavior. The reason is that negative reinforcers, and hence also punishers, are typically also stimuli for respondent behavior. Punishment may therefore elicit both general emotional arousal and such specific respondents as crying, cowering, or biting. Because of these respondents, punishment can sometimes "backfire," as when punishing a child for crying produces more crying rather than less.

In general, Skinner regards punishment as a poor method of controlling behavior. One reason is precisely the possibility that it may backfire, producing the opposite effect from the one desired. Another is the fact that its effects in suppressing undesirable behavior are often temporary, making punishment sometimes appear dramatically successful when in the long run it is actually quite unsuccessful in changing behavior. Also, the emotional behavior it commonly produces is often undesirable. Replacing misbehavior with crying or anger is seldom a good solution. Moreover, the emotional responses may become conditioned to stimuli other than the ones the punisher wishes, including the stimuli of the punisher. For example, a child punished for some misbehavior in school may learn to respond with anger to the stimulus of the teacher or with avoidance to the whole school situation. For all these reasons, punishment is both a rather unreliable technique for controlling behavior and one that is likely to have unfortunate side effects. Finally, punishment is unpleasant, and that alone is reason enough to avoid it if an effective and more pleasant alternative (such as reinforcement of desirable behavior) is available.

Nevertheless, Skinner would not claim that punishment is worthless as a device for changing behavior. When it is possible to arrange a situation so that punishment immediately follows the undesirable behavior, but does not occur at other times, it may be effective in suppressing undesirable behavior without producing harmful side effects. Under such conditions of very specific punishment, the individual learns emotional respondents and operant avoidance responses only to stimuli closely associated with the punished behavior. Since the person is exposed to all the other stimuli in the situation at other times when behavior is not being punished, whatever responses the individual learns to these other stimuli soon extinguish. However, such carefully arranged punishment situations are hard to maintain, and are a far cry from the haphazard and sometimes vengeful way that punishment is commonly used in everyday life. So in spite of some noteworthy exceptions, in general Skinner maintains that punishment is a poor method for modifying behavior.

The Role of Stimuli

Although stimuli do not elicit operants in the sense that they elicit respondents, they may determine whether or not any given operant will occur. A stimulus acquires this influence through the process of discrimination. If an operant is reinforced in the presence of one stimulus but not reinforced when it occurs in the presence of a different stimulus, the tendency to respond when the second stimulus is present gradually becomes extinguished, and a discrimination is formed. The operant will then occur in the presence of the first stimulus but not of the second. Since the individual has learned to discriminate between the stimuli, they are referred to as discriminative stimuli. A positive discriminative stimulus is one which indicates that responding will be reinforced; a negative discriminative stimulus indicates that responding will not be reinforced. In some cases the main focus of interest is on the positive discriminative stimulus, as when the ringing of a phone indicates that someone is calling, and the negative stimulus is simply the absence of the ringing. In such cases the (positive) discriminative stimulus often is abbreviated S^D. In other cases the positive and negative stimuli are more symmetrical, as when the sign "Open" indicates that trying the restaurant door is likely to be reinforced and the sign "Closed" indicates that it is likely not to be reinforced. In such cases the positive and negative stimuli are usually labeled, respectively, as $S+$ and $S-$.

When one has learned a discrimination thoroughly, one may respond so rapidly to the onset of S^D that it looks almost as though the response were a respondent, elicited by S^D. It is not, however, since occurrence of the operant depends on factors other than the S^D. For example, a pigeon can be taught to peck a key when it is green $(S+)$ but not when it is red $(S-)$ by reinforcing with food the pecks of the green key but not those of the red key. However, the pigeon will show little tendency to peck the green key for food when completely satiated. The S^D is a major determinant of the operant pecking response, but it does not produce it in the automatic way in which a stimulus elicits a reflex. It sets the occasion for the occurrence of reinforcement. Under these conditions the operant is said to be under *stimulus control.*

Is Skinner a Connectionist?

Skinner's rejection of theorizing is largely an objection to intervening variables, which he regards as useless at best, and often actually harmful, since they focus our attention on imaginary constructs instead of on reality. As a result, he is sometimes said to study the "empty organism"—not empty in fact, of course, but empty so far as Skinner's interpretations are concerned. As a result, though Skinner will talk about the tendency for a given operant to be emitted in the presence of a given discriminative stimulus, he will not talk about any habit or stimulus-response bond as being responsible for the tendency. Even in the cases of respondents, he will say only that the stimulus reliably elicits the response, not that there is a stimulus-response connection in the nervous system. Here he diverges not only from the archtheorist, Hull, but even from Thorndike.

Skinner certainly gives a good deal of emphasis to stimuli, both as elicitors of respondents and as discriminative stimuli for operants. At the same time, he points out that stimuli are only one set of variables that influence the emission of operants; such factors as food deprivation must also be considered. Although he sometimes speaks of the strength of a given operant, he completely rejects any reference to the strength of a stimulus-response bond. Moreover, he insists that the proper measure of the strength of an operant is the rate at which it occurs, not how often or how quickly it occurs to a given stimulus. Skinner is not, therefore, a connectionist in the same sense as the other theorists we have looked at so far. The only stimulus-response connections he will discuss are relationships in behavior, not bonds in the nervous system, and at least as far as operant behavior is concerned, they are relationships that depend heavily on other factors as well. In a narrow sense of the term, therefore, we might say that Skinner is not really a connectionist at all.

Nevertheless, in a broader sense Skinner is still a connectionist. In contrast to the cognitive theorists, whom we will consider in Chapters 8–10, but like the other connectionist theorists, he analyzes behavior in terms of responses and the stimuli that influence them. His concept of causation runs rather directly from independent to dependent variables, without discussing any system of beliefs or any pattern of mental activity that might occur between. Though the connections he studies between stimuli and responses are not interpreted as habits or bonds within the nervous system, they are connections nonetheless, and as direct connections as in any other theory. So, although he relates responses to stimuli somewhat differently from other connectionist theorists, it makes sense to include him as a connectionist. Indeed, at this point in the history of learning theory, Skinner is in a broad sense the best-known exemplar of the connectionist tradition.

THE EFFECTS OF REINFORCERS

Skinner's antitheoretical bias makes it difficult to discuss his system apart from his research and its applications (a fact of which Skinner would be proud). His research has been conducted almost entirely in one version or another of an apparatus that has become known as the *Skinner box* (so named by Hull, not by Skinner). This varies in size and form according to the organism being studied, but basically it is simply a box (or, from the subject's point of view, a room) containing a simple *manipulandum* (i.e., something the subject can manipulate) and a device for delivering reinforcers. The manipulandum may be a lever for rats to press, a key for pigeons to peck, a vending-machine plunger for humans to pull, or anything else appropriate for the kind of subject using it. The mechanism for providing reinforcers is typically some sort of feeder, delivering food pellets to rats, grain to pigeons, or candy bars to humans. Other sorts of reinforcers may be used, however, from drops of water for thirsty rats to peep shows for monkeys and humans. In some cases escape from electric shock to the feet is used as the reinforcer, in which case no separate reinforcement dispenser is required.

The basic principle on which the box operates is that responses to the manipulandum produce reinforcers. These responses are called *free operants*, since the subject is free to emit them at his or her own speed. The rate at which the free operant is emitted is the response measure. Whereas other experimenters may study speed of running, number of correct choices, or other aspects of operant behavior, Skinner and his followers study only the rate of emission of free operants. Whatever variable they manipulate, they study its effects in terms of this measure. However, as we have seen, there are many different free operants that can be studied. The important thing, says Skinner, is to find an appropriate operant for the kind of individual one wants to study—that is, an operant that the subject can emit conveniently and fairly rapidly. If this condition is met, the particular operant chosen makes little difference to the laws that will be found. Levers are used for rats and keys for pigeons rather than vice versa because these manipulanda suit the response capacities of these animals, but similar laws are found for rats and for pigeons when each learns an operant appropriate for its own capacities.

Schedules of Reinforcement

The rate at which the free operant is emitted (the dependent variable) can be related to a great variety of independent variables. In practice, however, Skinner and his followers have concentrated most on one independent variable, the *schedule of reinforcement*. This term refers to the particular pattern according to which reinforcers follow responses. The simplest schedule is *continuous reinforcement*, in which a reinforcer is given for every response to the manipulandum. This schedule generally is followed when the subject is first being trained to use the manipu-landum. After the response is learned, the schedule usually is shifted to some form of *intermittent reinforcement,* in which only some of the responses are followed by reinforcement. Skinner has collaborated with Charles Ferster on a book, *Schedules of Reinforcement* (Ferster & Skinner 1957), describing a great many different schedules of intermittent reinforcement and their effects, but fortunately for the student they tend to represent variations on two basic patterns. If the frequency with which reinforcers are presented depends on the rate at which responses are emitted, this is called a ratio schedule; if it depends simply on the passage of time, it is called an interval schedule. In addition, each of these two kinds of schedules may be either fixed or variable. Combining these two bases of classification gives four main kinds of schedules.

In a *fixed-ratio* schedule, the subject is reinforced after every so many responses. Thus a reinforcer may be delivered after every fourth or every tenth or every twentieth response. A *variable-ratio* schedule differs from a fixed-ratio schedule in that the reinforcer, instead of being presented consistently after every so many responses, is presented after a different number of responses on different occasions. In this case the ratio is the average number of responses per reinforcer. Thus on a variable-ratio five schedule, reinforcers are delivered on the average after every five responses, but on one occasion two successive responses might be reinforced, while on another occasion the individual might have to make as many as ten responses after getting one reinforcer before getting another.

On a *fixed-interval* schedule, a fixed interval of time has to elapse after one reinforcer is delivered before another can be obtained. Once this interval has elapsed, the first response will be reinforced. Thus on a fixed-interval one-minute schedule, the subject cannot obtain reinforcers more often than one a minute regardless of how fast he or she responds. The subject can obtain one each minute equally well by responding rapidly all the time or by responding only once a minute. If the subject waits for a while after the minute has elapsed before making the response, the reinforcement will be correspondingly delayed. A *variable-interval* schedule makes it possible to obtain a reinforcer sometimes sooner and sometimes longer after the previous one. Thus on a variable-interval two-minute schedule, the average time after presentation of one reinforcer when another would become available would be two minutes, but on any particular occasion the interval might be considerably shorter or longer. Hence the only way to be sure of getting all available reinforcers as soon as possible would be to respond continuously.

How do these schedules differ in the patterns of responding that they produce? First, ratio schedules typically give higher rates of responding than interval schedules. This difference is not surprising, since fast responding on a ratio schedule increases the number of reinforcements in a given period of time, whereas fast responding on an interval schedule serves only to obtain each reinforcement a little sooner. Second, on both kinds of fixed schedule there is a tendency for responding to be slowest immediately after reinforcement (more so than can be explained simply by the time required to consume the reinforcer). The reason is that responses immediately after reinforcement are never reinforced. Intuitively this effect is easier to appreciate in the fixed-interval schedule, since the individual has nothing to gain from responses during the interval. On a fixed-interval schedule, the resulting pattern is a gradual increase in rate of responding from just after one reinforcement to just before the next. Because it looks on a graph like the edge of the familiar sea shell, this effect is known as *scalloping*. The fact that there is a gradual increase in rate during the interval rather than a sudden burst of responding just when the next reinforcer is due reflects the subject's inability to discriminate time perfectly.

On a fixed-ratio schedule we might expect the individual to respond just as rapidly after a reinforcement as at any other time, since a certain number of responses must be made before the next reinforcement regardless of when the subject makes them. This expectation, however, reflects a view of the organism as figuring out the most profitable strategy and acting accordingly. According to Skinner, we must simply look at the reinforcement contingencies. On a fixed-ratio schedule, the first responses after a reinforcement are never reinforced as quickly as the later ones; hence they occur at a slower rate. However, this makes a difference only when the ratio is high enough so that the subject cannot make all the necessary responses quickly and get almost immediate reinforcement. Consequently, low fixed-ratio schedules (i.e., those requiring only a few responses per reinforcer) show very little drop in responding after reinforcement, whereas high fixed ratios show a sometimes lengthy pause after reinforcement. This pause tends to be a total cessation of responding for some period of time, after which responses are emitted at a fairly constant rate until the next reinforcement. This pattern is therefore slightly different from the scalloping on a fixed-interval schedule, in which responding gradually increases during the interval, from a very low rate immediately after one reinforcement to a fairly high rate just before the next.

Finally, these variations in response rate during the interval between successive reinforcements are found only in fixed schedules, not in variable ones. Since all responses, early or late, have a chance of being reinforced on a variable schedule, responding is at a constant rate except for the brief period that may be required for actually consuming the reinforcer. Typical patterns of responding on these four kinds of schedules are shown in Figure 6.1.

Organisms will make more responses per reinforcer on most kinds of intermittent schedules than on continuous reinforcement. If reinforcement finally is terminated altogether, resistance to extinction is also greater after intermittent than after continuous reinforcement. The variable-ratio schedule is most effective for obtaining rapid steady re-

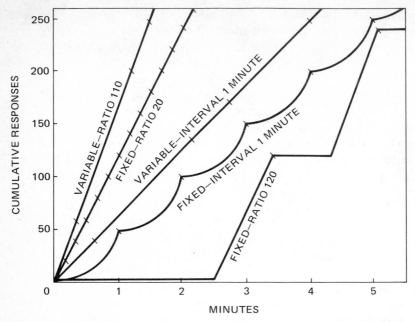

Figure 6.1 *Performance on several schedules of reinforcement.* Each curve represents the behavior of a single pigeon pecking a key on the designated schedule, plotted in the usual Skinnerian style. The vertical axis gives the number of responses emitted since the beginning of the time interval, so steeper curves indicate faster responding and a horizontal line indicates a period of no responding. The delivery of each reinforcer is indicated by a short diagonal mark intersecting the cumulative response curve.

sponding and high resistance to extinction. It is possible, in fact, to get animals to work for food reinforcement on ratios so high that they are actually operating at a biological loss: the energy expended in operating the manipulandum is greater than that obtained from the occasional food reward, so that an animal can literally work itself to death.

These schedules differ in their sensitivity to various disrupting factors. This fact has been of particular interest in connection with the effects of various drugs, and pharmaceutical companies have found it useful to test new drugs on animals responding to different schedules of reinforcement. One generalization which emerges from many studies is that interval schedules are more easily disrupted by a variety of drugs than are ratio schedules. Doses that will make responding on an interval schedule quite erratic will leave a ratio schedule largely unaffected. Apparently the rat's counting mechanism is more stable or less vulnerable than its timing mechanism. Though Skinner is pleased that his experimental techniques have been found useful for studying drugs, it is characteristic of his approach that he makes no attempt to draw inferences about what these drugs are doing to the animal's body. There is a lawful relationship between what drug goes into the body and what behavior comes out; what goes on between the two is no concern of Skinner's.

It should also be noted that studies of different schedules of reinforcement are not concerned with how the response is originally learned. Ordinarily the subject is well trained to use the manipulandum before any form of intermittent reinforcement is introduced. Thereafter a given individual can adapt fairly readily to one schedule after another, changing behavior to suit each new schedule. Thus Skinner's formal research has been largely concerned with a short-run aspect of learning, the rapid shifts in performance level to match shifts in reinforcement conditions. (Some writers, in fact, consider such shifts too short-run to be called learning at all, and refer to them simply as changes in performance.) These studies are concerned not with an individual's learning how to respond, but rather with learning how rapidly to respond under a new set of reward conditions.

Shaping

We should not conclude from this emphasis, however, that Skinner has been uninterested in the process of learning how to perform complex tasks. Much of his less formal work has been concerned with this problem, and he has given striking demonstrations of training techniques. Though many experimental psychologists study animal learning, Skinner and his followers are almost unique in their concern with animal training. The technique by which they train animals to perform complex acts that are outside their normal range of behavior is known as *shaping.* The behavior is shaped through a series of successive approximations to the desired behavior, each made possible by selectively reinforcing certain responses and not others. Thus behavior gradually is brought closer and closer to the desired pattern.

Suppose you want to train a pigeon to bowl in a miniature alley with a wooden ball and toy pins (as Skinner has done). If left to its own devices, the pigeon might occasionally move the ball around, but would quite possibly never do so in a way that would get the ball down the alley and knock over any pins. If you waited to reinforce a full bowling response, therefore, you would have a quite impractically long wait, and even if the response finally did occur spontaneously, and you reinforced it, you would probably face another long wait before it occurred again. Yet this is not a particularly hard game for a pigeon to learn to play, given proper training.

To teach the pigeon to bowl, Skinner began, of course, by depriving it of food. Next, he trained it to eat from the food magazine. The operation of the food magazine made a distinctive sound, which, since it always signaled the availability of food, became a conditioned positive reinforcer. This conditioned reinforcer was a critical feature of the shaping process. If the food magazine had been silent, some of Skinner's attempts to provide immediate reinforcement would probably have failed, since it would have taken the pigeon some time to notice that the magazine was open. With the sound, however, Skinner could be sure that the opening of the food magazine would have an immediate reinforcing effect on the pigeon.

Given this means of reliably producing immediate reinforcement whenever he wished, Skinner proceeded to reinforce behavior that approximated the desired final performance: the pigeon's striking the ball in such a way that it would go down the alley and knock over some pins. First he reinforced merely being near and facing toward the ball. When that behavior had been reinforced often enough so that it was occurring much of the time, Skinner changed to giving reinforcers only when the pigeon pecked close to the ball. When that response had become common, he moved on to reinforcing only pecks that moved the ball. From there he narrowed the range of reinforced responses even further until the pigeon was sending the ball down the alley against the pins as reliably as a (novice) human bowler (Skinner 1958).

Though shaping is an application of the scientific principle of reinforcement, it involves a good deal of art. If the trainer proceeds too fast in narrowing down the range of responses that will be reinforced, the behavior already shaped will begin to extinguish. If the trainer proceeds too slowly, the training will take excessively long to complete. The trainer must therefore be constantly alert to the effect of her or his behavior on the learner's behavior and must be constantly ready to change it as needed in order to achieve the most effective shaping.

Given skillful application of the basic principle of shaping, striking results can be obtained. Skinner has not only trained one pigeon to bowl; he has also trained two pigeons to cooperate (as well as compete) in a modified version of Ping-Pong. Rats have been trained to go through whole sequences of unratlike operations, such as pulling a string to obtain a marble, carrying the marble in their paws to a tube projecting above the floor, and dropping the marble into the tube. Pigs have learned to dance and play the piano (not well enough for the concert stage, but well enough for county fairs!). Some of Skinner's followers have found a considerable market for their talents in training animals for fairs and movies, as well as for more "serious" purposes.

Even though rapid and effective shaping requires a good deal of skill, the most striking significance of shaping is the impressive effects that can be obtained by applying the simple principle of reinforcement. Not all the demonstrations have been with animals. A technique for showing the automatic effects of reinforcement on human behavior is called *verbal conditioning*. In the first experiment of this sort (Greenspoon 1955), the subject was instructed simply to say words. The experimenter gave the subject no clue in the instructions as to what sorts of words were desired. However, whenever the subject said a noun in the plural form, the experimenter said "mmhm." There was an increase during the session in the frequency with which the subject said plural nouns. This increase occurred in spite of the fact that many subjects were quite unaware, so far as could be determined by questioning, either of the fact that they were saying more plural nouns or of any relation between the experimenter's behavior and their own. When the "mmhm" was discontinued, frequency of plural nouns declined (extinction).

In another, less formal experiment (Verplanck 1955) subjects were simply engaged in conversation without even being told that this was an experiment. The experimenter (who in this case might better be called the interviewer) expressed interest in and agreement with any of the subject's remarks that were presented as expressions of opinion (i.e., "I think . . ." or "It seems to me . . ."). Other kinds of remarks produced no reaction from the interviewer. Expressions of opinion became more and more frequent during the conversation. In both of these verbal-conditioning studies, verbal behavior was modified by reinforcing a given kind of verbal response and no other. Like any technique of operant training, this one depends on finding a reinforcer that will be effective for the particular kind of individual being studied, but once one is found the principle of reinforcement seems to apply as well here as elsewhere.

However, the "automatic" nature of these effects has been subjected to a good deal of question. In studies of animals, no problem arises: the experimenter need only note the systematic ways that behavior is influenced by reinforcement, and whether or not the effects are called automatic is pretty much irrelevant. With humans, however, the experimenter can ask subjects what they thought about the whole procedure and thus try to determine whether they reacted automatically and largely unconsciously to the reinforcement or whether they noticed what kinds of responses were being reinforced and then decided whether or not to work for reinforcers. From Skinner's point of view, the person's awareness is not a particularly important issue—the important question is whether the reinforcement influences the behavior, not whether the person can accurately describe what is going on or whether the subject feels that she or he is making a free choice. However, the issue of awareness in verbal conditioning has aroused considerable interest among other psychologists. Although the issue is far from settled, the weight of current evidence suggests that humans who are influenced by verbal reinforcement are usually at least partly aware of what is going on and have some sense of choosing how they will react to it (e.g., Spielberger & DeNike 1966). On the other hand, when a person is busy concentrating on one aspect of his or her own behavior, it may be possible to condition some other aspect of that behavior without the subject's being aware of it (Rosenfeld & Baer 1969). Probably the best conclusion is that reinforcement sometimes works automatically, without the learner being aware of what is going on, but that such events are the exception rather than the rule.

An interesting sidelight on the shaping of behavior is the way in which reinforcement can produce not only behavior that the experimenters intend but also behavior of which they have no advance idea. Suppose a timer is arranged to deliver a reinforcer every 30 seconds regardless of what the subject does. This is called a *fixed-time* schedule. (It differs from a fixed-interval schedule, in which the subject has to make a particular response after the interval is up in order to be reinforced.) Whatever the individual is doing when the reinforcement comes is more likely to occur again the next time. Purely on the basis of chance, the subject is more likely to be doing something at that moment that he or she commonly does than something that is done more rarely. Given the fact that this behavior occurs commonly to start with, plus the fact that the behavior has now just been reinforced, it is all the more likely to be occurring when the next reinforcer is delivered. This reinforcement will strengthen the behavior more and make it even more likely to occur at the right time to receive the third reinforcement. Thus this particular behavior becomes more and more likely to occur because it is reinforced, even though the experimenter did not deliberately reinforce that response rather than others. Rather, the learning was the result of a vicious circle: because the response occurred frequently, it was reinforced, and because it was reinforced, it occurred more frequently. The experimenter did not know in advance which of the various responses that the individual made frequently would be learned in this way; that selection depended on chance. There might be a period during which several different responses were reinforced before any one gained enough of a lead to start the vicious circle going. Behavior might be too variable for any one response ever to get the necessary head start. However, when it occurs, this unplanned reinforcing effect is an impressive demonstration of the automatic operation of reinforcement.

Skinner refers to this kind of unplanned learning through "accidental" reinforcement as *superstitious* behavior. The justification for this term is that the subject acts as though a certain behavior produced reinforcement, when in fact there is no necessary connection between the behavior and the reinforcement. The response is commonly followed by reinforcement only because both behavior and reinforcement occur frequently and hence often occur at the same time. The most successful experimental demonstrations of superstitious behavior have been with pigeons (though we will see a different interpretation of such demonstrations in Chapter 17). However, applications to human learning are not difficult to see. If a student carries a rabbit's foot into an examination for good luck, and does well, this experience will make the student more likely to carry it into the next examination. Repeated successes while carrying the rabbit's foot will make adherence to the foot as a source of luck stronger and stronger, even though it contributed nothing to success and the student would have done just as well without it. (We overlook the possibility that the confidence the talisman gave the student may have increased his or her effectiveness in taking the examination.) Many of our beliefs, not only in charms and magic, but also in medicine, mechanical skills, and administrative techniques, probably depend on such superstitious learning. A public speaker who thinks she is successful because she knocks three times on the podium before starting to speak is generally recognized as superstitious. But a speaker who thinks he is successful because he starts each lecture with a funny story may be equally superstitious by Skinner's definition. In humans, such superstitions are probably more often learned in the first place from other people than from chance occurrences. However, when people claim that their faith has been validated by experience, this experience probably often follows the learning pattern that Skinner has described and illustrated.

Chapter
7

Applications and Implications of Skinner's System

*A*s you have probably already guessed, Skinner has shown much interest in the application of learning principles to complex practical situations. Many of these applications are at the level either of philosophical principles or of speculation about what might work. Two, however, have been extensively tested. In the treatment of behavior disorders, and in education, Skinner's ideas have not only demonstrated their validity outside the laboratory but have also had major practical effects on psychotherapy and at least some effects on schooling. Collectively, they are referred to as *applied behavior analysis.*

BEHAVIOR MODIFICATION

The rubric "behavior disorder" covers a wide range of problems, from those mildly irritating behaviors that we all notice in one another (and sometimes even in ourselves!) through delinquency and neurosis to severe psychosis. Whether the problem is minor misbehavior on the part of a relatively normal child or a psychosis that has kept a patient hospitalized for many years, Skinner's approach to treatment is quite straightforward. Rather than focusing on early childhood, current psychodynamics, or possible organic abnormality, Skinner simply asks what this person is doing that we do not like and what we would like to have the person do instead. Once we have decided this, we can proceed to extinguish the undesirable behaviors and reinforce desirable ones. In other words, we can change the *contingencies of reinforcement,* the specific relationships according to which reinforcement is contingent on one or another behavior. This approach, basically similar to Guthrie's but with the additional element of reinforcement, forms the basis of various *behavior modification* techniques of psychotherapy.

The behavior modification approach may be illustrated by a case in which two nursery-school children were cured of excessive crying (Hart et al. 1964). The therapists (experimenters? educators?), like true Skinnerians, began by differentiating the crying into respondent (usually produced by physical pain and not influenced by the social situation) and operant (less directly influenced by specific stimulation, but occurring when an adult was nearby and involving frequent glances at the adult, apparently to see the adult's reaction). No attempt was made to modify the respondent crying, but all the nursery-school teachers were trained to recognize and to ignore the operant crying. However, when the children played constructively, the teachers often praised them and showed them affection. The attention from teachers that had previously reinforced the operant crying was thus removed, and a combination of extinction and retraining began. That the reduction in operant crying was really the result of this procedure is indicated by what happened when the teachers were instructed to resume paying attention to the children when they cried—there was rapid relearning of the crying. A second retraining was then begun, and the operant crying was virtually eliminated.

Similar techniques have been used in mental hospitals and in a variety of other settings to deal with such diverse behaviors as overeating and undereating, hoarding of towels (by a mental patient), inattention in school, and the extreme social withdrawal of autistic children and of many psychotics. In many cases where the awarding of reinforcers for certain behaviors is central to the retraining, it has been organized and formalized in the form of *token economies.* In a token economy, the people in an institution (students, patients, prisoners, or whatever) can earn tokens by engaging in certain behaviors or by not engaging in others, and can then exchange these tokens (which become conditioned reinforcers) for primary reinforcers of their choice. It is easy to belittle token economies by saying that what they show is that modern behavioral science has finally invented money! However, when a token economy changes disruptive behavior to constructive and cooperative behavior, and does so without the use of aversive stimulation, the fact that the basic idea is nothing new should not detract from the ingenuity of those who figured out when and how to apply it.

Its stronger supporters regard behavior modification as the most significant innovation ever made in psychotherapy. In support of this view, they point out its many dramatic successes—beneficial changes in behavior which, though sometimes slow in absolute terms, are still typically faster than traditional psychotherapies. Moreover, the same techniques can be used in a wide variety of settings to produce many different kinds of behavior change. Further details about the many uses of behavior modification (commonly abbreviated to behavior mod or to B-mod) can be found in Schwartz (1982) and Kazdin (1984), and evidence of its effectiveness relative to other psychotherapies is described in Smith, Glass & Miller (1980).

Critics of behavior mod have not hesitated to point out its difficulties. Interestingly, it has been attacked from two opposite directions. On the one hand, it has been criticized as producing only temporary and superficial changes. That the changes are often temporary is to be expected, since Skinner would not expect changes in behavior to last unless the changes in the contingencies of reinforcement also last. In some cases, behavior modifiers are satisfied if, by arranging proper contingencies of reinforcement, they can get students to study harder or mental patients to behave in more "normal" ways in the hospital, without worrying about anything further. In other cases they hope to produce more lasting changes, but they expect success only if they can bring about lasting changes in the contingencies of reinforcement. If a schoolchild who has acquired good studying behavior as a result of a token economy in the classroom continues to show that changed behavior after the token economy is gone, it will be because other reinforcers have taken over, whether they are the fun of learning, the usefulness of the knowledge, or the satisfaction of pleasing the teacher. If none of these reinforcers is strong enough to keep the child studying, perhaps the problem is neither in the child nor in the token economy but in the curriculum!

However, the question remains: What is the most efficient way to change from a situation in which behavior is controlled by reinforcers delivered as part of a behavior modification program to one in which behavior is controlled by the "natural" reinforcers of everyday life? The general answer given by behavior modifiers is to make the transition gradually, reducing the frequency of the programmed reinforcers bit by bit, a process known as *fading.* In addition, behavior modifiers have various ways of enhancing the natural reinforcers—for example, by enlisting the help of relatives and friends to provide such reinforcers to an extra degree. These procedures are discussed in detail in Kazdin (1984).

The opposite criticism of behavior mod is that, far from being too weak and trivial, it is too dangerously powerful. The worry these critics have is that someone exposed to planned contingencies of reinforcement loses freedom and comes under the control of the person who controls the reinforcers. Skinner's reply to this challenge is that we are all controlled by many contingencies, some deliberate, some accidental. If the contingencies of positive reinforcement used by behavior modifiers are more effective than others, and at the same time more pleasant for the learner and more beneficial in their effects, why is that a criticism? Isn't it better, says Skinner, to be controlled pleasantly by a beneficent controller than to be subjected to all the conflicting, selfish, and often aversive attempts at control that so often occur? Not necessarily, say his critics: the worst enemy of freedom may be a gentle, beneficent dictator. To pursue the argument further would take us too far afield, but at least these latter critics do behavior mod the honor, however dubious, of being afraid of it.

EDUCATION

As the above discussion indicates, behavior modification is as much an educational as a psychotherapeutic technique. It is therefore not surprising that one of Skinner's applications has had important practical effects in the field of education. This is the study of programmed learning, first popularized through its use in teaching machines. Though Skinner was not the first to suggest this approach to teaching (Sidney L. Pressey of Ohio State University is generally credited with making the first teaching machine, in 1927), he gave the idea much of its early impetus. His object was to treat classroom learning like any other situation in which certain behavior—in this case, largely verbal behavior—is to be shaped. The student must progress gradually from familiar to unfamiliar material, must be given an opportunity to learn the necessary discriminations, and must be reinforced. The classroom situation has many disadvantages from this point of view. A rate of progress appropriate for one student is too fast or too slow for another. Opportunities for each individual to make the required responses are limited, and reinforcement is often greatly delayed. Individual tutoring could solve all these problems, but in most cases it is out of the question except perhaps for occasional supplementary work. What, then, can be done to give students in school the same advantages that pigeons in boxes have? Skinner's answer to this question was the teaching machine.

The basic component of the machine is the program. This is a series of combined teaching and test items that carries the student gradually through the material to be learned. An item may or may not convey new information, but in any case it calls for the student to fill in a blank in a statement and then to look at the correct answer. If it agrees with the student's answer, this agreement constitutes the reinforcement. If not, the student can study the correct answer so as to increase the chance of being reinforced next time. However, Skinner prefers to make the learning requirements so gradual that the learner rarely if ever does make mistakes. If this effort is successful, then on every item the student makes a correct response and is reinforced, which in Skinner's view is the best possible arrangement for learning. Individual differences then are reflected in the rate at which the student proceeds through the program. (For a discussion of the logic and the advantages of this approach to teaching, see Skinner 1962.)

At this point you may be wondering, "Where does the machine come in? This is just the old, familiar workbook method." To some extent this is a valid point. Much programmed instruction has been in workbook rather than machine form. The student fills in a blank, then turns to another page to check the answer. However, these programmed workbooks differ from the more familiar types of workbooks in that they do all teaching through the items in the program, rather than serving to supplement lectures and textbooks. The same series of items that calls forth the student's responses also provides the information necessary for making the responses. This arrangement, in turn, forces the author of the program to plan the sequence of items very carefully in terms of just what the student needs to learn and just how it can best be presented. Whether the program is in a workbook or in a machine is of secondary importance. Machines have some advantages in speeding up the reinforcement and reducing the likelihood of cheating by the student. It is probable, however, that much of Skinner's preference for machine presentation results from two factors: (1) the novelty effect of the machine, which very likely makes its use more reinforcing to the student, and (2) Skinner's personal liking for mechanized procedures. Although the machine itself has sometimes been a bone of contention between those who favor increased classroom efficiency and those who fear the loss of more personal values in education, this is a misplaced emphasis. The pertinent question is about the value of programmed methods of instruction in whatever form, not about teaching machines as such.

Even now it is hard to judge how valuable programmed teaching, by machine or otherwise, will prove in the whole context of education. Many factors besides efficiency as a specific teaching device are involved. Moreover, the increasing availability of computers provides for more varied forms of presentation than either workbook programs or the original form of teaching machine. Although Skinner favors *linear programs,* in which every learner goes through the same sequence of steps, which are easy enough so that mistakes are rare, computers have increased the use of *branching programs,* in which the learner's answers determine what material will be received next. In some computer teaching programs, the learner and the computer carry on quite a spirited dialogue, including both praise and sharp admonishments from the computer as it responds to a great variety of possible behaviors by the learner. The computer can decide how lavishly to praise or how strongly to reprove the learner, as well as what material to present next, not just on the basis of the learner's last response, but on the basis of the learner's whole record of performance. Though the computer usually communicates in writing on a cathode-ray tube, it can also be designed to speak. Both of these capabilities are illustrated in a program teaching children to read (Atkinson 1974).

As a result of the computer's great flexibility, computer-assisted instruction (CAI) has largely replaced programmed instruction as an active topic of research and an expanding area of education (e.g., Chambers & Sprecher 1983). The technology of programmed instruction has now gone far beyond Skinner's initial contribution, but it continues to provide striking evidence that Skinner's applications are not restricted to tricks of animal training and to speculations about the organization of society.

OTHER APPLICATIONS

In addition to behavior mod and programmed instruction, both of which have given rise to much research and development, Skinner has presented a number of other logical applications that are still largely at the level of talk. One (appropriately enough) is the analysis of language. In his book *Verbal Behavior,* Skinner (1957*b*) analyzes language as a system of operants. He notes that each of us lives in a *verbal community,* a group of people who share a common language and who shape the language each of us uses by reinforcing correct usage and extinguishing incorrect usage. This shaping process is most noticeable with children, who must learn the language from scratch, but it continues to operate in adults as they learn new words and as they are either reinforced or not for the various spicy elements they include in their speech. Some utterances, such as requests and demands, are reinforced by another person's compliance; these utterances are called *mands.* Other utterances, which include most conversations, are reinforced in subtler ways by signs of understanding, such as smiling and answering appropriately. Utterances of that sort are called *tacts.* It is easiest to learn correct speech when the events that the speech refers to are external ones that everyone in the linguistic community can observe. When the events are unobservable, as in discussing one's own or someone else's feelings, it is much harder to decide whether a tact is correct or not. A child learns to describe his or her own feelings correctly only to the extent that others can infer those feelings from other evidence and reinforce the child's descriptions when they are accurate. No wonder our vocabularies for describing feelings lack the precision of science!

A second area of interest is the application of Skinnerian principles to complex social behaviors. Any social interaction is a situation in which two or more people are providing one another with stimuli and with reinforcers, and perhaps also failing to reinforce one another in some critical ways. Whether the interaction is formal or casual, friendly or hostile, dominant or egalitarian, it can be analyzed in these basic terms. For example, a factory worker who is paid on piecework (pay proportional to the amount produced) is being reinforced by her employer on a form of fixed-ratio schedule. For a quite different example, a mental patient diagnosed as depressive may be on a schedule where almost nothing he can do is reinforced, so that he complains of feeling helpless, hopeless, and worthless. Once you are familiar with Skinner's thinking, you can probably predict some of Skinner's comments on the mutually reinforcing or nonreinforcing contingencies in politics, business, religion, and the family.

Finally, Skinner has devised a utopian community called Walden Two (in honor of Thoreau, who might or might not feel honored), in which the principles of learning are used to create a more ideal form of social organization (Skinner 1948). In contrast to such negative utopias as those described in Huxley's *Brave New World* (1932) and Orwell's *1984* (1949), Skinner's novel *Walden Two* describes what he believes would be a desirable community, one in which principles of behavioral engineering would be used to create a more fulfilling environment for all the residents. Many of the details of this imaginary community run sharply counter to what we are used to considering appropriate. The economy is socialized; government is by self-perpetuating committees instead of by elected representatives; children are reared primarily by child-rearing professionals, rather than by their parents, and the child-rearing practices include some that are deliberately designed to frustrate the children so as to build up their tolerance for frustration.

It is not at all clear that these particular ways of doing things follow from any of Skinner's data as a researcher. How did he happen to select them for his utopian community? One possibility is that the particular suggestions were intended for their shock value in showing how different a behaviorally engineered community might be from what we would at first think desirable. In the second volume of his autobiography, Skinner leaves this possibility open by saying: "I let Frazier [the founder of the fictional community] say things that I myself was not yet ready to say to anyone" [1979, p. 298]. He adds, however, "Eventually I became a devout Frazierian" [ibid.].

Another possibility, not necessarily contradicting the first, is that Skinner made Walden Two the kind of community that reflected his own felt needs at that point in his life. He remembered as the worst year of his life the one immediately after college when he was trying to become a novelist while his parents urged him to settle down to a more conventional career. Is that why he designed Walden Two as a community in which children are largely freed from family pressures, and in which it is easy to combine artistic creativity with "honest toil"? Later, when writing the book, he was faced with problems and disruptions in both family and professional life. Is that why Walden Two sometimes impresses readers as a fine community for an overburdened person to retreat to but not much of a place for the restless or the ambitious? Is such a community one that Skinner desired only at that point in his career? Elms (1981) thinks so, and further speculates that writing the book may have been the therapy Skinner needed, since he made no effort to put his ideas into practice.

Nevertheless, several attempts have been made to establish real-life communities modeled on his book. For the most part, these attempts have had no better success than the many other secular utopian communities that have been tried over the years. One, however, known as Twin Oaks, has lasted for over 20 years and has achieved at least a modest degree of success (including one special modern criterion of success: appearing on television). Though its membership of less than 100 appears small beside the 1000 in Skinner's fictional community, it still represents a fairly stable, functioning community. The first five years of Twin Oaks were described by one of its founders (Kinkade 1973), and a more recent period has been portrayed by Komar (1983). The problems that the community has struggled with seem much like those that any commune would face, irrespective of any special behavioral principles. Judging by Komar's book, Twin Oaks has been most successful in dealing with the emotional and social needs of its members, and least successful in solving the problems of government organization and economic incentives.

Regarding this real community's relation to Skinner's utopian novel, Kinkade (1973) wrote: "The debt we owe Dr. Skinner is enormous, but there is nothing sacred about the institutions we derived from his book. All of our systems are subject to change, and most of them have changed even over the few years that we have been a community" [p. 57]. This comment Skinner presumably would approve. Later, however, Kinkade wrote (as quoted in Komar 1983): "Behaviorism at Twin Oaks was important to us in 1969 and 1970, still got lip service for a year longer, and then was overrun and sacked by a more primitive and vigorous idea which is now called the 'human potential movement'" [p. 92]. The description concludes: "I think the accepted theory now is that behaviorism was one of several early religions that Twin Oaks went through, and now that the group has matured, behaviorism is thought of as a discarded ideology" [p. 113]. The Walden Two idea, like other ideas that Skinner started, has clearly gone far from its origins in directions that its creator would not necessarily approve.

SKINNER'S RELATION TO OTHER PSYCHOLOGISTS

For many years, Skinner and his followers formed a small in-group within the psychology of learning. Whereas the followers of other theorists argued with each other and tried to best each other in experimental tests of their respective theories, the Skinnerians remained aloof and went their own way. They published their own journal, held separate meetings at psychological conventions, and eventually established a separate Division of the Experimental Analysis of Behavior within the American Psychological Association. (Many non-Skinnerians may feel that what they are doing is also "experimental analysis of behavior," but the expression has become a label for Skinner's approach.) As Skinner's research techniques and his ideas have become increasingly prominent, much of this separatism has disappeared, but some remains. What are the differences between Skinner and other psychologists of learning that account for it, and what factors have made him, in spite of it, such an important spokesperson for the field?

It is hard at first to see what differences could account for the historical schism between Skinner and other learning theorists. We have already noted his similarity to Thorndike. Though he differs from both Watson and

placing heavy emphasis on reinforcement, he resembles both
ın his practical emphasis. In analyzing a response, Guthrie's first
.on was "What stimuli evoke it?" while Skinner's is "What reinforcer
.ains it?" Both of these, however, focus on a specific, manipulable detail
ɟf the situation. Guthrie went further in relating specific situations to a
general statement of what learning is, while Skinner has gone further in
actually experimenting with the situations he analyzes. Their differences
are substantial, but their similarities are nonetheless noteworthy.

As for Watson, he and Skinner have in common a missionary zeal
about what psychology should be and what it should contribute to human
affairs. Both react vigorously against what they regard as vague, over-
theoretical interpretations of human nature and in favor of strictly scientific study of behavior. Both present systems that their supporters regard
as highly useful and their foes regard as highly oversimplified. (Both judg-
ments may, of course, be valid, for oversimplifications can be useful for
many purposes.) Both theorists appear as prophets, seeking to purge the
errors from psychology as it is and to proclaim the glories of psychology
as it should be. Both have a vision of what humankind can become if
guided by proper application of the principles of learning.

On the issue of reinforcement, Skinner is closer to Hull than either is
to Watson or Guthrie. Moreover Skinner's views of social influence and of
behavior disorders are rather similar to those already described for Dollard and Miller. Nevertheless, Skinner's difference from Hull is sharp,
since Hull was a theorist par excellence, while Skinner scorned theory
building. Even so, the difference is not as fundamental as it might at first
appear. There are two aspects to Hull's theorizing: postulating intervening variables, and deducing theorems from postulates. Certainly Skinner
does not do either of these in anything like the formal way that Hull did,
but then neither do the majority of other learning theorists. Skinner,
however, does do things that bear a certain resemblance to both of these
activities of Hull's. As regards intervening variables, Skinner has no such
concept as excitatory potential, but he does speak of the strength of a
response, even though the strength may be measured in different situations by size, or rate, or probability, or resistance to extinction. Is the
"strength of a response," then, so different from "excitatory potential"?
Also, though he scorns completely unobservable entities, Skinner does not
mind talking about ones that are merely hard to observe, like the many
different emotional respondents that can interfere with making a punished response.

As for deducing theorems from postulates, Skinner often does something one step removed from that: expressing one law of behavior in terms
of another. For example, why do subjects on a fixed-interval schedule
respond relatively late in the interval rather than early? Skinner replies
that they have formed a discrimination, since responding in the early part
is never reinforced while responding in the later part sometimes is reinforced. In other words, he starts with the law that subjects can learn to

discriminate between two specific stimuli, S+ and S−, and then applies that law to a new and somewhat different case, in which the discrimination is not between two observable stimuli but rather between whatever stimuli there may be to distinguish the first part of an interval from the last part. To Skinner, this line of reasoning is simply a matter of showing that a scientific law applies in a new situation, but it does not seem so terribly far removed from Hull's more formal deductions.

Given that Skinner's differences from the other theorists we have considered are not much greater than their differences from one another, why has there been such a schism between him and them? Part of the impetus for the separation has come from Skinner's conviction that he has a whole new approach, one that makes nearly all previous theorizing and a large part of previous research obsolete. Whether or not it is correct, his expression of this opinion in his publications has naturally tended to keep him and his followers aloof from other psychologists of learning. The rest of the impetus has come from objections by other psychologists to the research methods Skinner uses. Though he puts great emphasis on the scientific character of his work, many others have felt that his methods were untrustworthy as sources of scientific data.

The main objection to Skinner's research methods is that his experiments have typically been conducted on one or a very few subjects. Skinner believes that only by looking at the behavior of a single individual can one find the lawfulness in behavior. Many psychologists, however, take the contrary view: that stable, general laws can be obtained only by averaging the behavior of many individuals. Only thus, they say, can individual differences and accidental fluctuations be ruled out so that the widely applicable, general laws remain. The arguments on both sides of this question are too complex to consider here. Whatever the rights and wrongs of the argument, for a number of years journal editors and convention program committees often rejected Skinnerian research on these bases, thus forcing Skinnerians to find their own publication outlets and further isolating them from other researchers in learning.

Given this division, how is it possible that Skinner has come to be such a dominant figure in the psychology of learning? To some extent his dominance is due to the very methodological factors that so long isolated him. The Skinner box has proved a very valuable research tool, and Skinnerians have had enough success in demonstrating lawfulness with single individuals to impress other researchers. This success in dealing with individual cases has made Skinnerians strikingly successful in their applications of psychology, which we have already discussed, and thus given them extra credibility with practical-minded observers. Finally, Skinner has been a tireless popularizer of the ideas about psychology that many non-Skinnerians share. He has preached the gospel of objective research on learning and its practical applications, presented in a relatively simple, no-nonsense way, more vigorously and persistently than anyone else since Watson. As a result, more outsiders have heard of him and more insiders have had reason to be proud of him. As the psychology of learning has moved into more complex channels of research and theory (some of which we will see in later chapters), Skinner has stood as the most conspicuous spokesperson for those simple, traditional ideas that Thorndike, Watson, Guthrie, Hull, and Skinner himself, whatever their differences, have all shared.

In this role as spokesperson for a point of view about human behavior, Skinner has again been the focus both of enthusiastic support and of angry criticism. Supporters see his views as marking the way to a new era of scientifically based human improvement; critics see them as the mechanization and enslavement of the human spirit. He threw additional fuel on these fires of controversy in *Beyond Freedom and Dignity* (Skinner 1971). Answering those critics who claim that his system deprives people of freedom and of dignity, he argues that freedom and dignity are merely the terms we apply to behavior when we cannot detect the reinforcers that control it. All behavior, he insists, is under the control of contingencies of reinforcement, planned or unplanned. The fact that in some cases we have trouble determining what the contingencies are does not make the behavior any more desirable. We should give up pursuing these shadowy goals of freedom and dignity and instead work on building a society in which well-planned contingencies of reinforcement give rise to desirable behavior.

In spite of the sometimes sharp differences between Skinner and the other theorists we have considered, he is now the outstanding exponent of the connectionist tradition. Watson, Guthrie, Thorndike, Hull, and Spence are dead; Miller's interests have changed; Skinner remains as the current spokesperson for those approaches to psychology which they all held in common. A look at Skinner is both a look backward at this tradition and a look forward to the direction in which Skinner thinks psychology is and should be headed. Others disagree about this direction, and it is to this considerably different set of viewpoints that we next turn.

Chapter
8

Gestalt Theory

One year before Watson published his first challenge to American psychology, Max Wertheimer (1880–1943) published a challenge to the established psychology of Germany. The orthodoxies against which these two revolts were directed were, as noted in Chapter 3, much alike. Both the American and the German versions were largely concerned with the structure of the mind. They tried to analyze conscious thought into its fundamental units, such as sensations, images, and ideas. Particularly in America, there was some trend to studying behavior for its own sake, but psychology was still regarded as primarily the study of conscious experience. Experimentation was directed toward a more complete analysis of the contents of consciousness.

The forms which these two revolts took, however, were strikingly different. Watson's objection was that psychology should be concerned not with consciousness, but with behavior. He wanted to abolish the discussion of images and ideas in favor of a discussion of stimuli and responses. He still agreed with the earlier position, however, in being interested in analysis. He still wanted to work with fundamental units, though they were now to be units of behavior instead of units of consciousness.

Wertheimer, on the other hand, objected to the concern with analysis. It seemed to him that breaking consciousness into its parts destroyed what was most meaningful about it. He had none of Watson's objection to the study of consciousness; indeed consciousness was his main concern. What he wanted to do was to study consciousness as it appears, rather than break it down into parts. The traditional psychology regarded anything we look at as a mosaic of tiny patches of color.

Only as all these tiny patches are put together do they make up the scene we observe. Wertheimer challenged this view. We actually see the scene, he insisted, as a meaningful whole. Only by a very artificial process of analysis can we break down this whole into patches of different colors and shades. The same applies to thinking. The traditional psychology regarded all our thoughts as made up of images connected by a process of association. This analysis, too, Wertheimer rejected. Our thoughts are whole meaningful perceptions, not associated collections of images.

Wertheimer's first publication in this revolt against analysis was concerned with the phenomenon of apparent movement. It is well known that when a light in one place is turned off and a light in another place is immediately turned on, we experience the phenomenon as a single light moving from one place to another. This illusion is the basis of the apparent movement in lighted advertising signs. Prior to Wertheimer, the phenomenon had been regarded as a minor curiosity of no theoretical importance. To Wertheimer, however, it was striking evidence of the futility of analyzing a whole into its parts. The components were two separate lights going on and off, but the resulting whole was an impression of movement. The observer does not see the two lights flashing and infer that something is moving; the impression of movement is immediate and direct. This phenomenon of apparent movement so impressed Wertheimer that he named it the *phi phenomenon* and began a series of studies on it.

WHAT IS A GESTALT?

The phi phenomenon was only the starting point of an intellectual movement within German psychology. This movement was primarily concerned with perception, but came to include learning and other topics as well, treated according to the same principles as were used to study perception. Its emphasis was on whole systems in which the parts are dynamically interrelated in such a way that the whole cannot be inferred from the parts taken separately. Wertheimer applied the German word *Gestalt*, which may be roughly translated as "form" or "pattern" or "configuration," to these dynamic wholes. Such gestalts (treating *gestalt* now as an English rather than a German word) are of many sorts, and they occur in physics as well as in psychology. We have already considered the phi phenomenon as one example. A melody is another, since it depends on the relation between the notes rather than the notes themselves. "Die Lorelei" (to take an appropriately German example) is still the same tune when transposed into another key so that every note is different. A whirlpool is a third example, since it is a whirlpool not because of the particular drops of water it contains but because of the way the motion of the water is patterned. Because of this concern with gestalts, the movement that Wertheimer started came to be known as *gestalt psychology*.

The emphasis of the gestalt psychologists on unified wholes does not mean that they never recognized separateness. Indeed, a gestalt may be referred to as a segregated whole. Of particular interest is the way that gestalts come to stand out as distinct entities separate from the background against which they appear. This interest was expressed in the concepts of figure and ground. The *figure* in any perception is the gestalt, the entity that stands out, the "thing" we perceive. The *ground* is the largely undifferentiated background against which the figure appears. A melody, for example, is a figure against a ground that includes many other sounds. What appears as figure at one moment may not at another. If the listener stops paying attention to the melody in order to hear what a friend is saying, the friend's speech becomes figure and the melody becomes part of the ground. Such changes in figure-ground relationships play a part not only in perception but in learning and thinking as well.

It is of course possible to analyze a gestalt figure into component parts. The fact that three black dots on a white page appear as a triangle does not keep them from still being three dots. However, the important thing to a gestalt psychologist is that what we see immediately is a triangle. Afterward we can analyze the triangle into three dots and study what it is that makes these three dots appear as a triangle when another three, differently placed, do not. We cannot say, however, that the triangle is nothing but three dots. The triangularity, which depends on the pattern of the dots rather than on the dots themselves, is the most essential aspect of what we see. The gestalt figure is more than just the sum of three dots. This relationship is the basis of an expression often applied to gestalt psychology: "The whole is more than the sum of its parts."

It is evident that Wertheimer and Watson, though rebels against similar traditions at the same time, were moving in opposite directions. Each may be considered both a pioneer and an extreme prototype of a certain approach to psychology. Watson's was the mechanistic approach, concerned with the components of behavior and the connections between them. Wertheimer's was the dynamic approach, concerned with unified patterns in consciousness. Without judging their importance relative to that of other theorists, we can say that in terms of conspicuous intellectual movements, Watson was the outstanding pioneer of connectionist theory and Wertheimer the outstanding pioneer of cognitive theory.

From the first, however, Wertheimer shared the spotlight with two of his colleagues, Wolfgang Köhler (1887–1967) and Kurt Koffka (1886–1941), both of whom eventually surpassed Wertheimer as publicists for the new movement. These two men wrote a number of books on different aspects of gestalt theory. Together with Wertheimer, they formed the nucleus of a group that became known as the Berlin school. All three, however, eventually moved to the United States. Perception remained their primary interest, but learning was by no means neglected. Through-out, the emphasis was on organized wholes, separated from other wholes but united within themselves by their dynamic patterning.

The interpretations of learning presented by Wertheimer, Köhler, and Koffka tend to be presented in the terminology of perception. Instead of asking, "What has the individual learned to do?" the gestalt psychologist is likely to ask, "How has the individual learned to perceive the situation?" Gestalt interpretations thus make an interesting contrast with the connec-tionist interpretations we examined earlier. It is true that gestalt theorists speak of memory traces, which are the effects that experiences leave in the nervous system. However, these are different from the stimulus-re-sponse bonds discussed by connectionist theorists. The memory traces of the gestalt psychologists are not isolated elements, but organized wholes—in other words, gestalts. Consequently, learning is primarily a matter, not of adding new traces and subtracting old ones, but of changing one gestalt into another. This change may occur through new experience, but it may also occur through thinking or through the mere passage of time. The way in which these restructurings occur is the concern of gestalt learning theory.

GESTALTS IN LEARNING

The most important contribution of gestalt theory to our understanding of learning is in the study of *insight*. Often learning occurs suddenly with a feeling that now one really understands. Such learning is likely to be especially resistant to forgetting and especially easy to transfer to new situations. We speak of such learning as involving insight. In such cases the gestalt language of perceptual reorganization is particularly applicable. The learner who has insight sees the whole situation in a new way, a way which includes understanding of logical relationships or perception of the connections between means and ends.

Such insight is by no means restricted to humans. During World War I Köhler, interned in the Canary Islands, did extensive studies of insightful problem solving in apes. These are described in his book *The Mentality of Apes* (1925). He presented chimpanzees with problems in which bananas were displayed out of reach and could be obtained only by using techniques new in the apes' experience. For example, a banana might be hung from the top of the animal's cage, with boxes elsewhere in the cage which could be piled under the banana so that the ape could climb up and get it. Or a banana might be outside the cage, far enough away so that it could be obtained only by pulling it in with a stick. Such arrangements had the advantage, from the gestalt point of view, of making all the necessary elements of the solution visible to the animal, which is not the case in a puzzle box or maze. Köhler found that these problems not only were often solved suddenly, but frequently were solved immediately after a period of time during which the ape was not actively trying to reach the banana. Sometimes it appeared that the animal, having failed to obtain the banana by familiar methods, sat and thought about the problem and then suddenly saw the solution. Such incidents are well suited to a description in terms of perceptual restructuring. Köhler could say that an ape suddenly saw the boxes, for example, not as playthings to be tossed around but as supports to be climbed on. It saw the relationship between the boxes and the bananas. During the time that it was not actively doing anything about the problem, the ape was undergoing a process of restructuring which, when complete, made an immediate solution possible.

It should not be supposed, however, that only such dramatic examples of sudden and complete insight can be explained in gestalt terms. Gradual learning by trial and error can be interpreted as a series of small, partial insights. Köhler's problems were so arranged that the ape could see all the necessary elements of the solution at once. All that was necessary was for these parts to become organized into an appropriate gestalt. A rat in a maze, on the other hand, cannot see any relation between the pattern of turns and the food at the end until this relation has been discovered by experience. The rat's restructuring must therefore be gradual and piecemeal, since the situation permits no other kind. Nevertheless, the discovery that a certain pattern of turns is the way to food is no less a cognitive restructuring than the discovery that boxes piled on one another are the way to food. The suddenness of the restructuring depends on the problem and the way it is presented to the subject, but the principle is the same.

Gestalt Laws of Learning and Forgetting

Insight requires that certain aspects of a situation be seen in relation to one another, that they appear as a single gestalt. What factors determine whether this event will occur? In one book, *Principles of Gestalt Psychology,* Koffka (1935) pointed out that the same principles could be used to answer this question both in complex problem-solving situations and in very simple perceptual situations. He suggested, therefore, that certain laws of perception proposed by Wertheimer should also be taken as laws of learning. We will consider two of these: the law of proximity and the law of closure.

The *law of proximity,* as applied to perception, refers to the way in which items tend to form groups according to how they are spaced, with the nearer ones being grouped together. For example, if a number of parallel lines are drawn on a sheet of paper, with alternate wide and narrow spaces between them, the pairs with narrow spaces between will be seen as groups of two (see Figure 8.1, part A). It is these that are seen together, rather than the pairs with wide spaces between, because of their closer proximity to one another. This law also applies to spacing in time.

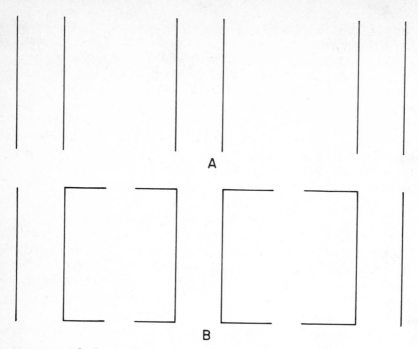

Figure 8.1 *The laws of proximity and closure.* First cover part B. The parallel lines in part A form three sets of two because of their proximity. Then look at part B, in which the same lines form two sets of two with an extra one on each end because of the closed figures formed by the middle pairs of lines.

Sounds close together tend to be heard as units. International Morse Code takes advantage of this principle by using intervals of silence of different lengths in the sequence of dots and dashes to separate letters and words, thus making these groups of sounds stand out as units. As applied to learning, the law of proximity may again refer to closeness either in space or in time. In reference to space, the law would explain why it is easier for an ape to discover that it can reach a banana with a stick if the stick and the banana are on the same side of the cage. (You may think that this is really an example from perception rather than learning, since the ape sees stick and banana together. If so, you have grasped part of the spirit of gestalt theory, in which perception and learning are inextricably tied up together.) In reference to time, it would explain why it is easier to remember recent events, which are closer to the present and hence more easily joined with the interests of the present in a common gestalt.

The *law of closure* states that closed areas more readily form units. Applied to perception, this fact can be seen by referring to the previous example of parallel lines. It is possible to change the grouping and make the more widely separated pairs of lines appear as groups. This change may be accomplished by connecting the ends of these lines so that they form two sides of a box. The connecting lines need not be complete; so long as the more widely separated pairs of lines appear to be parts of a figure that enclose space, they tend to be seen together (Figure 8.1, part B). Applied to learning, the law of closure plays the same role in a cognitive theory of learning that reinforcement plays in a connectionist theory.

As long as an individual is struggling with a problem, his or her perception of the situation is incomplete. A reward brings the hitherto separate parts of the situation together into a closed perceptual figure, consisting of the problem, the goal, and the means of obtaining the goal (Koffka 1925). The emphasis is not on obtaining a reward but on completing an activity and bringing a number of parts into relation with one another. Thus this explanation is most convincing when applied to adult humans consciously working toward certain goals. The term "closure" has indeed been adopted informally by many nongestalt psychologists to refer to the sense of completion when a task is finished or a mystery solved. However, the relation between closure in this sense and closure of a geometric figure may seem a bit forced. There is some question as to whether we should say that Koffka discovered the law of closure in perception and applied it to the study of learning, or that he called two somewhat related principles, one in perception and one in learning, by the same name.

It is interesting to note that, for all the enormous difference between Guthrie's interpretation of learning and that of the gestalt psychologists, there is a certain similarity between Guthrie's primary law of conditioning and the gestalt psychologists' law of closure. Both regard reward as producing its effect by the way that it changes the situation for the learner. For Guthrie, the reward changes the situation so that the last response which occurred remains conditioned to the stimuli of the situation. For the gestalt theorists, reward changes the individual's perception of the situation so that the stimuli, the response, and the reward form a gestalt. From the point of view of a reinforcement theorist, this feature would justify classifying Guthrie's theory and gestalt theory together as contiguity (as opposed to reinforcement) theories.

The gestalt interpretation of forgetting, like that of learning, is concerned with perceptual changes. The memory trace tends to change spontaneously with time into a "better gestalt." The concept of a good gestalt is a rather difficult one to explain. It is the pattern of organization which a system tends to adopt, whether the system is a soap bubble or a perception. Thus, a soap bubble tends to adopt the form of a sphere; if forced into a different form without breaking, it will tend to become a sphere as soon as the force is removed. Similarly, perceptions tend to adopt certain forms as closely as the conditions of stimulation permit. Good gestalts tend to be simple and regular. In the case of physical gestalts, it is often possible to describe the characteristics of a good gestalt quite precisely with mathematical equations (for example, the formula for a sphere as applied to the soap bubble). As we move into the realm of perception, previous experience begins to play a part in determining what a good gestalt is. Familiar, meaningful forms tend to be better gestalts than unfamiliar, meaningless ones. Innate factors are still of major importance, however, in determining what constitutes a good perceptual gestalt. When we consider the topic of learning, we find experience still more important, but innate perceptual criteria still apply.

Insight in Education

Wertheimer's most noted contribution to the development of gestalt psychology, once the enterprise that he started was under way, was in applications to education. He was concerned with insightful learning in schoolchildren. Whereas Köhler studied insight in apes for theoretical reasons, Wertheimer had a very practical interest in the topic in schoolchildren. It seemed to him that teachers put far too much emphasis on rote memorizing at the expense of understanding. He therefore directed his studies toward finding ways in which learning could take place with greater insight on the part of the learner.

In his book *Productive Thinking*, Wertheimer (1945) makes a distinction between two types of attempted solutions to problems. Solutions of type A are those in which there is originality and insight; solutions of type B are those in which old rules are inappropriately applied, and hence are not really solutions at all. This distinction does not imply that B solutions depend on previous experience and A solutions do not. Both depend on previous experience; the difference lies in the original organization that characterizes A solutions.

Wertheimer found geometry an especially useful area in which to study different approaches to problems. One of his problems, which he presented to adults as well as children, required the subject to find the area of a parallelogram. Wertheimer would begin by showing the subject how to find the area of a rectangle, not simply the formula of length times height, but the reason the formula works. He did so by dividing the rectangle up into small squares (Figure 8.2, part A) and showing that the area was the number of squares in a row times the number of rows. He then presented the subjects with a parallelogram cut out of paper (Figure 8.2, part B) and the instruction to find its area. Some people replied that this was a new problem and that they could not be expected to solve it without being told how. Some blindly repeated the now incorrect formula of multiplying one side times the other: a B type of "solution." Other people attempted to find an original solution, but were unable to see the essential relationships. A few, however, came up with genuine A solutions. One child, noting that the two projecting ends were what made the problem difficult, asked for scissors, cut off one end, and fitted it against the other end, thus converting the parallelogram into a rectangle (Figure 8.2, part C). Another subject achieved the same goal by bending the parallelogram into a ring, so that the two ends fitted together, and then cutting the ring vertically to convert it into a rectangle. These two in-

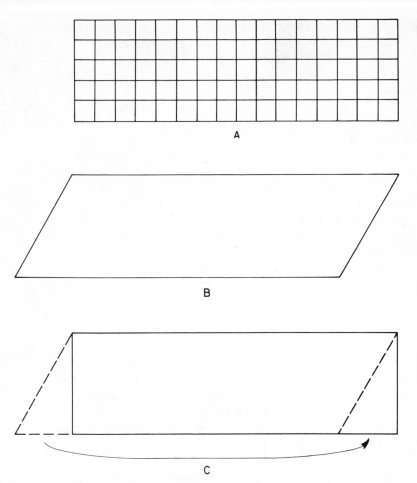

Figure 8.2 *Wertheimer's parallelogram problem.* Part A shows Wertheimer's way of explaining why the area of a rectangle equals the product of length times width—in this case, 16 by 5. Part B shows the parallelogram for which he asked subjects to find the area. Part C shows how one person solved the problem by cutting off one end and moving it to the other end, thus converting the parallelogram into a rectangle.

dividuals showed a genuine understanding of the situation that made possible correct, original solutions.

If these individuals had applied the rule "base times height," which for rectangles is equivalent to the rule "one side times the other," the computation would have been correct, but nevertheless would have demonstrated no understanding. Thus it would have been much like a B solution, even though it would have happened to be correct. What they did, however, was to find an original way of converting this new problem into a familiar one, one that they knew how to solve. The final solution depended very much on previous experience, but it was previous experience organized in a novel way. The important thing about the solutions was the insight by which the new problem situation was restructured. From the solvers' point of view, they converted the parallelogram into a better gestalt, a rectangle.

Even when a solution is correct, it is important to distinguish whether or not real understanding is involved. Understanding is not the same as logic. Both the inductive and the deductive methods of logic may be applied blindly. The inductive method, in which a person reasons from particular instances to a general conclusion, is really just trial and error. Another person might have tried various possible formulas for the area of a parallelogram, found that base times altitude gave the same answer as the book in several cases, and concluded that this was the correct formula, but without having any idea why. Though adequate for practical purposes, this would be a solution without understanding. Wertheimer enjoys giving examples of cases where such blind induction leads to absurdly wrong conclusions. The deductive method, in which a person reasons logically from one principle to another, can also be applied blindly. A student may fumble around algebraically until he or she finds a valid proof that a certain equation is correct, but the student may still not understand the equation in the sense that Wertheimer means. Understanding implies not merely logical correctness but a perception of the problem as an integrated whole, of the ways in which the means lead to the end. In going through an algebraic proof, for example, the student should ask at each step not only "How does this follow logically from the previous step?" but also "How does this lead toward the solution I am looking for?" In Wertheimer's opinion, education should make such understanding, or perception of whole gestalts, its primary goal.

The value of creative problem solving is not restricted to such "purely intellectual" situations as the above. Wertheimer illustrates its value in social situations with an anecdote about two boys playing badminton. The older boy was so much better at the game than the younger that he won nearly every point, and the frustrated younger boy finally refused to play any longer. Since this spoiled the fun for the older boy, it posed a problem for him. How could he get the younger boy to go on playing with him? He might have exhorted him to be a sport (probably in vain), or he might have offered a handicap (a better approach, but still not an answer to the fundamental problem posed by the one-sided competition). Seeing the competition as the crux of the problem, the older boy was able to propose a constructive solution. The competitive game of winning points was replaced by a cooperative game of seeing how long the two together could keep the bird going back and forth, and both were then able to enjoy playing. Again, understanding of the situation led to an insightful solution.

This book of Wertheimer's, set beside Guthrie's *Psychology of Learning,* points up the contrast between cognitive and connectionist views of learning in their extreme forms. Both books show a keen interest in the applied psychology of learning, especially as applied to children. Guthrie's emphasis is on training the child to make the right responses to the right stimuli. His question is always "What does the child do?" Wertheimer, on the other hand, is concerned with educating the child to have insights into the material. His question is "What does the child understand?" The difference is not irreconcilable, since Wertheimer is concerned with the ability to solve problems effectively and since Guthrie can talk about understanding in terms of movement-produced stimuli. Nevertheless, the difference in emphasis is tremendous. This emphasis on understanding, on the perception of relationships within an organized whole, is the great contribution of gestalt psychology to the interpretation of learning.

Chapter
9

Other European Cognitive Theories

Gestalt theory originated in Europe, and it remained largely a European viewpoint. It never became very popular in America, where various forms of behaviorism long dominated the scene, but it had much more influence within Europe. A number of theoretical approaches in Europe show this influence in various ways. Not all are directly derived from the original gestalt theory of Wertheimer, Köhler, and Koffka, but they show the same concern with how people perceive and understand the world and with the importance of organization. We will look at two of them, one particularly concerned with motivation, the other with development.

LEWIN'S SYSTEM

Among the gestalt psychologists who worked with Wertheimer, Köhler, and Koffka in Berlin was Kurt Lewin (1890–1947). Like the other leading gestalt psychologists, he eventually settled in the United States. His interests were different from theirs in a number of respects. Whereas they were mainly concerned with rather technical problems in perception, learning, and thinking, he was interested in motivation, personality, and social psychology. Gestalt psychology, in dealing with learning, tended to take the desire for certain goals for granted and to concentrate on the way the goals are obtained through cognitive restructuring. Lewin wanted to concentrate on the desires and the goals themselves, studying them in relation to the personality. The system he developed for conducting this study

(Lewin 1936) is not primarily a theory of learning; rather, it is a system of description within which learning, motivation, personality, and social behavior can all be discussed.

The Life Space

What Lewin wanted was a theoretical system for predicting the motivated behavior of a single individual. He found the answer in the concept of *life space*. This may be defined as the totality of facts which determine the behavior of a given individual at a given time. It is represented conceptually as a two-dimensional space in which the individual moves. This space contains the person himself, the goals he is seeking, the negative "goals" he is trying to avoid, the barriers that restrict his movements, and the paths he must follow to get what he wants.

This concept of life space is more complicated than is at first apparent. For one thing, it must not be confused with physical or geographical space. This is not the world of physical objects and real other people, but the world as it affects the individual. Hence an object of which the person is unaware and which does not influence him would not appear in his life space, even though physically it may be close to him. Similarly, something he thinks is there and reacts to as if it were there is present in his life space even though physically absent. If a child thinks there is a tiger under the bed, the tiger is part of the child's life space, even if everyone else insists that the tiger is purely imaginary.

Can we say, then, that the life space is the person's environment as he himself perceives it? This is a hard question to answer, since it depends on just what we mean by "perceive." We cannot say that the life space is made up only of the things of which the person is consciously aware. An individual may be influenced by factors of which he is unconscious. For example, a certain high school teacher would like to take an administrative position, and feels quite able to do so. Nevertheless, whenever an opportunity to apply for such a position comes along, she finds some excuse not to apply. After this has happened several times, her friends suspect that something is holding her back from seeking an administrative position, perhaps some deep-seated lack of confidence in her own ability. In Lewin's terms, there is a barrier in her life space between her and the goal of an administrative job. Yet she insists that she wants such a job and is going to apply as soon as just the right opportunity comes along. If we go by what she says, we would conclude that she does not perceive any important barrier between herself and the goal of an administrative job. If we go by what she does, we would conclude that she does perceive such a barrier, since she acts as if one is there. Which does she *really* perceive? This is a question we cannot answer, but fortunately we do not need to answer it. If she acts as if the barrier is there, then it is in her life space. It is from the way she behaves that we know what is present in her life space. It is often convenient to speak of the life space as "the environment as the person views it," but we must keep in mind that what we really mean is "the environment as it affects the person's behavior."

The life space includes the person himself and his behavioral environment, which consists of everything that influences his behavior. Of particular importance in the life space are the goals the person is seeking, the things or situations he is trying to avoid, and the barriers that restrict his movement toward or away from them. Lewin represents the life space by two-dimensional diagrams (see Figure 9.1). Any place, object, or situation that the individual wants to approach (strictly speaking, *acts as if* he wants to approach) is said to have *positive valence* and is represented in the diagram by a plus sign. Any that the individual wants to avoid is said to have *negative valence* and is represented in the diagram by a minus sign. Barriers are represented by heavy lines separating one part of the life space from another.

These diagrams are, of course, highly schematic. They usually do not correspond to physical space. For example, a politician's life space might include the state governorship as a positive valence and the election as a barrier. The distances in the diagram between the politician, the election, and the governorship have no particular meaning in the life space that the diagram represents. What is important in the life space is the regions through which the politician must pass to reach the goal and the difficulties of getting from one region to another (i.e., the barriers). These considerations led Lewin to decide that the ordinary geometry of distances was not appropriate for picturing the life space. He therefore turned to the special kind of geometry known as *topology.* Topology sometimes is called "rubber-sheet geometry," since topological space can be stretched in any di-

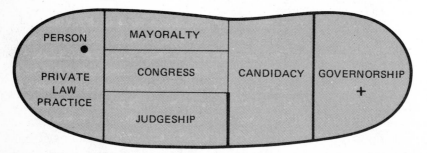

Figure 9.1 *A topological diagram of a politician's life space.* At present the individual is practicing law. He sees three other regions available to him. From the mayoralty or from Congress he could become a candidate for governor, but the boundary between the judgeship and candidacy appears to be impenetrable. The boundary between the region of candidacy and the positively valenced region of the governorship also forms a barrier, indicating serious doubts as to whether he could win the election. Note that the sizes and shapes of the regions could be greatly changed without changing the meaning of the diagram, as long as the boundary relationships remained the same.

rection without making any difference. Topology is concerned only with the boundaries between regions, not with the sizes or shapes of the regions or the distances from one place to another. When an area is divided up topologically, all that matters is what regions separate one point from another. Such topological space was much more convenient for Lewin's purposes than the space of ordinary geometry.

Whereas it is meaningless to ask the distance, in inches or miles, between a politician and the goal of being governor, it is meaningful to ask what regions one must pass through to get to the goal. Certainly the final region before the region of being governor is that of being a candidate. Before that there may be alternative paths—perhaps one by way of the mayoralty of a large city and another by way of Congress. These regions are not, of course, particular places in physical space, but they are meaningful parts of the life space. They are positions that the individual can occupy. Positive and negative valences are attributes of certain regions, as with the positive valence of the governorship. Barriers are boundaries between regions that are especially hard to penetrate. The barrier formed by the gubernatorial election, for example, is the boundary between the region of candidacy and the region of governorship. If a barrier is impenetrable for the person in question, that person cannot enter the next region, and any path going to or through that region is blocked.

These topological diagrams can be used to represent all the significant elements in any life situation. Positive valences may be attached to regions as specific as "eating candy" or as vague as "maintaining social status." Negative valences may apply to situations as diverse as a spanking for a child and guilt feelings for a criminal. Barriers may be physical (e.g., a locked door), intellectual (e.g., a difficult examination), or social (e.g., the exclusiveness of a positively valenced club). The regions through which a person must pass may be places (e.g., city blocks), social statuses (e.g., child, adolescent, adult), activities (e.g., practicing tennis before becoming a star), or any other situations that necessarily occur to the individual as sequences. In all these cases we must remember that it is the situation as it influences the person, not the "objective" situation, with which we are concerned. If the politician felt sure to lose the election and thus declined to become a candidate, then the election would be an impenetrable barrier in the person's life space, even though this pessimism might actually be quite unjustified. (For a politician, such unjustified pessimism probably makes the example quite unrealistic!) In any case, it is subjective rather than objective reality that makes up the life space.

Predicting Behavior

The topological regions in a person's life space and the barriers between them indicate what paths it is (subjectively) possible to follow. The positive and negative valences of various regions suggest which of the possible paths one is actually likely to follow. However, Lewin also wanted to be able to indicate the relative strengths of tendencies to approach or to avoid different points in the life space. There are often a number of positive valences in the life space at a given time—which one will be approached? To answer this question, Lewin added *vectors* to his system. A vector is a force operating in a certain direction. It is represented by an arrow, with the direction of the arrow indicating the direction of the force and the length of the arrow indicating the strength of the force. Vector analysis has been most prominent in physics, where forces of different magnitudes operating in different directions play an important part. Lewin adopted only the idea of vectors, not the mathematical analysis that usually goes with them. In his diagrams, he indicated the tendency to approach a positive valence by a vector pointing from the person toward the valence, and the tendency to avoid a negative valence by a vector pointing from the person away from the valence. The length of the arrow indicates the strength of the tendency. This makes it possible to show which of the forces acting on an individual is the strongest.

Although the description of the life space provides a considerable basis for predicting an individual's behavior, a number of questions remain unanswered. When two or more paths toward a goal are available, which will be followed? When two or more vectors operate on an individual, will only the stronger be effective or will some compromise occur? If a barrier proves insurmountable, will some other goal be substituted for the inaccessible one? Lewin's reply is that topological psychology determines what behaviors are possible and what ones are impossible. It does not tell us which one definitely will occur. However, the more we know about the details of a person's life space, the more we can narrow down the range of possibilities that are open to him. Thus more and more information will make our predictions better and better, until perhaps eventually they will become almost perfect.

Let us consider, as an example, a student who has a strong vector toward the region of being a teacher, and also a moderately strong vector toward the region of being well-to-do. We may suspect that this situation will lead to problems. However, if we know nothing about the topology of his life space, we cannot predict his behavior. If we know that in his life space these two positively valenced regions overlap (i.e., he perceives teachers as well-to-do), then there is no problem (regardless of what the objective situation may be). He will simply approach this goal of being a well-to-do teacher. If, instead, we know that in his life space the two regions are separate (i.e., teachers are not well-to-do), we are again unable to predict. He may simply react to the stronger vector, or he may find some compromise, or he may investigate the matter further and perhaps as a result restructure his life space (as by finding out that some teachers actually are well paid), which would make the two regions move together and overlap. However, if we can find out more about his life space, our chance of predicting successfully which of these things he will do will increase. If the region of being well-to-do includes a subregion similar to teaching (such as industrial training or school administration), this fact makes him more likely to approach that subregion as a compromise. If he has a vector toward further investigation of the possibilities, this increases the chance that he will get new information leading to a restructuring of the life space. As our knowledge of his life space increases, our ability to predict his behavior also increases.

Lewin's theoretical analyses of the person and the life space, along with the many experimental studies that he based on these analyses, made him famous as a psychologist of personality and of social behavior. He was always interested in the application of psychology to these areas. The organization of groups, the causes and cures of prejudice, and the effects of frustration are among the topics to which he made important contributions.

Lewin's Weakness in Predicting Learning

From the point of view of the psychology of learning, however, Lewin's contributions are quite limited. He provided us with a system for describing and to some degree predicting behavior, but he did not give us a theory of learning. Much of the value of studying his system in this book lies in understanding why he did not. A knowledge of the life space as described by Lewin enables us to predict reasonably well what the individual will do. But how do we determine the structure of the life space? We do so by observing the individual's behavior and inferring from it what the structure must be. Having observed someone's behavior, we figure out the structure of his life space. From this structure we predict what his behavior in the future will be. In order for this method to work, his life space must remain the same except for his own position in it. Learning, however, involves a change in the life space. How can we predict when and how such changes will occur? In some cases a knowledge of the life space (and the person in it) is enough, as for example when we predict that long exposure to a region of positive valence will produce satiation and make the valence less strongly positive. In most cases, however, we must take into account external, physical reality. If an individual comes to a door that he thought was unlocked, tries to open it, and finds it locked, the door changes in his life space from a permeable boundary to a barrier. How could we have predicted this change in the life space? We could have only by knowing that the door was, in fact, locked. But such questions of physical reality do not really enter into Lewin's system.

Lewin was, of course, aware of this problem, and he discussed the ways in which external events can produce changes in the life space. However, this part of his theory is very minor, and he never developed it in detail. In his research he showed a lively interest in finding out how best to change attitudes, but little of this practical interest found its way into his formal theorizing. In his theoretical work, for the most part, he was too busy examining the structure of the life space, the organization of the person, and the way these influence behavior to be concerned with the ways in which they are themselves changed by external events. As a result, his theoretical system is useful for stating the results of certain kinds of learning, but of little value in predicting what learning will occur under what conditions.

This lack of concern with learning as such reflects Lewin's philosophical view of science. He sees most psychologists as looking for statistical laws that apply more or less to people (or animals) in general, but not specifically to any given individual. To apply these laws accurately to a given person, you need to know a lot about that individual. In principle you might be able to find out enough about the individual by a detailed study of his ancestry and previous history of learning, but in practice such an approach would be enormously cumbersome, since each experience in the person's life may have affected how each future experience would be perceived. Consequently Lewin rejects that approach and seeks instead to find out about each individual's life space at the present time, without regard to how it got that way. With this bias, it is understandable that Lewin did not want to concentrate on problems of learning. However, in not doing so, he left a serious gap in his theory. Without more information on how the life space can change, we are hard put to make long-term predictions and even more hard put to make recommendations about teaching, psychotherapy, or other problems in learning. In spite of this problem, Lewin's approach is regarded by many psychologists as of great practical value, as we will see at the end of this chapter.

PIAGET AND COGNITIVE DEVELOPMENT

The cognitive theorists we have considered so far were interested in describing perception, motivation, and problem solving as they operate in individuals at a given time. As we have noted, they were not much interested in how these activities change for a given individual over time. However, the European cognitive tradition has not neglected such changes. Children reason and solve problems in ways that are often different from the ways of adults, and the process by which juvenile thinking develops into adult thinking has been of interest to a number of psychologists, European and otherwise. Of all the psychologists who have been concerned with this process of cognitive development, the most famous is Jean Piaget (1896–1980). He was a French-speaking Swiss (so his name is pronounced somewhat like "John Peeah*jay*") who spent about the last half century of his life in Geneva studying processes of thinking in children. His early scientific interest was in biology, and at the age of 15 he had already achieved renown for his publications about mollusks. However, his interest in logic and the sources of knowledge led him into cognitive psychology. He first became widely known among psychologists through his book *The Language and Thought of the Child*, which was published in French in 1923 and translated into English in 1926. This has been followed by so many other books, articles, and lectures, continuing up to his death, that even a sampling of the titles would be excessively long. Since his writings are not only voluminous but also theoretically rather complex, we can get a better overview of his system from such secondary sources as Flavell (1963) and Phillips (1969). The increasing interest in cognitive theories in recent years has raised Piaget's status in the English-speaking world from that of a somewhat strange outsider who could not be completely ignored to that of a major theorist.

Basic Concepts of Piaget's System

One way of identifying a theorist is by the key intervening variable(s) that he postulates. Piaget used as his favorite intervening variable the *schema* (plural, *schemata*). Schemata are a little more general than most of the cognitions we have considered so far. They are ways of perceiving, understanding, and thinking about the world. One might speak of them as frameworks or organizing structures for mental activity. They are broad types of expectancies, dealing with general ways in which events occur. The formation and change of schemata are the essence of cognitive development.

A child, of course, has schemata relevant to a great many topics, and the number becomes even greater as the child approaches adulthood. Piaget was particularly interested in those schemata pertaining to the physical world. In what ways does a given child understand relationships of size and weight and causality? How does the child reason about physical changes, about constants and variables, about the sources of actions and the nature of living and nonliving things? Though the exploration of these schemata was Piaget's greatest contribution, he has not been unaware of children's social worlds as well. How does a child understand social relationships? How does the child reason about moral issues? What justification can be provided for the rules of games or the rules of decent behavior? Piaget has studied these schemata, too, as well as influencing the research of others interested in those aspects of development.

Schemata can change, and such change is important in cognitive development. The process by which they change is known as *accommodation.* When a child (or any person, for that matter) has an experience which is inconsistent with a schema, there will be some tendency for the schema to change so as to accommodate this new input. For example, it is common for children around the age of 6 to operate on the schema that objects which are light to lift will float and those which are heavy to lift will sink. When asked to make predictions, they indicate that a large (and therefore heavy) block of wood will sink, while a small piece of metal will float. However, as they repeatedly see disconfirmations of these predictions, the schema becomes increasingly difficult to maintain. Gradually they fumble their way toward a new, more adequate schema. For a while they may manage with a group of more specific schemata such as that wood floats, while metal and stone sink. Eventually they achieve a new schema that is as simple and general as the old, but more accurate: that objects of low density float, while those of high density sink.

The process of accommodation by which children improve their schemata is similar to that by which scientists improve their more technical ones. Indeed, the question of how to differentiate consistently between objects that float and those that sink was once as much of a problem for scholars as it is now for children. All of us sometimes find our views of the world disconfirmed, try to explain why, and (perhaps) learn from the experience. Accommodation applies equally well to an infant discovering that an object which has gone out of sight has not ceased to exist and to Einstein replacing Newton's description of the world with the theory of relativity.

An emphasis on the process of accommodation might suggest that schemata are unstable, constantly being changed by new inputs. Actually, however, the opposite is true; schemata tend to be quite stable. A child is no more likely to give up an old schema in response to one or two disconfirming inputs than is a scientist to give up a pet theory because only one or two experiments failed to work out as expected. Even more common than accommodation is the opposite process, by which schemata influence the interpretation of experiences. This process is known as *assimilation.*

Everything we experience, from the simplest physical stimulus to the most complex new scientific or philosophical idea, is interpreted in the light of what we already know and believe. Lewin emphasized this most strongly, in his claim that it is not the physical environment but the life space that matters to our behavior. Most theorists have not been willing to put the matter quite that strongly, but all have agreed that our reaction to stimulation depends on something other than the physical characteristics of the stimulus. One way of expressing this relationship is to say that the stimulus (however simple or complex) is assimilated into the existing schemata. The meaning of the stimulus is determined by the schemata which the person uses to recognize and interpret it. This "modification" of the stimulus into a part of the individual's total cognitive world is what Piaget means by assimilation.

When a schema is stable and can easily assimilate whatever relevant new experiences come along, a state of equilibrium exists. As new experiences come along that cannot easily be assimilated, disequilibrium results. If eventually accommodation occurs, so that a new schema can assimilate these troublesome experiences, a new equilibrium results. This process of striving toward equilibrium of schemata and experiences—by assimilation where practical, more gradually by accommodation where necessary— sounds rather like the notions of the gestalt psychologists about the characteristics of a good gestalt. Piaget's schemata are more durable than their gestalts, but both involve an organization within the nervous system, resulting from the interaction of experience with existing structures, and always striving toward its best possible form. Though Piaget's background is not that of a gestalt psychologist, his thinking is congenial to theirs.

Piaget is not, however, open to the same criticism as Lewin—that he ignores the external world and talks only about the life space, thus providing no basis for a true theory of learning. Piaget is very much aware of the external world. Whereas the concept of assimilation emphasizes that our behavior is determined by the world as interpreted, the companion concept of accommodation emphasizes that the external world is constantly in a position to modify the way we view it—to "keep our schemata honest," so to speak. Piaget is thus in the position of combining a complex and flexible cognitive theory with an insistence that the influence of the "real world" cannot be ignored.

Stages in Cognitive Development

If we look only at the process of accommodation, we can imagine a person's schemata constantly changing throughout life. Though in a sense this is true, it would not give a very accurate picture of Piaget's writings. Much of what he has written deals not with changes in schemata but with their characteristics at any given period in life. Since schemata change slowly, it is possible to describe the way a person interprets the world at any given time during life without worrying about the changes that are slowly going on in those interpretations. One of the most conspicuous features of Piaget's theory is his list of developmental stages. At each stage, children's schemata have certain characteristic features that are different from those of earlier or later stages. Knowing at what stage a given child is now, we can predict with a fair degree of accuracy how the child will answer various questions about the way things happen and why.

Many psychologists have described development as a series of stages, and several comments are appropriate to all of them, including Piaget's. For one thing, the number of stages and the boundaries between them are somewhat arbitrary. What one scholar would call two stages, another might call two parts of a single stage. Moreover, a given person at a given time might be judged by one observer to be in an earlier stage, but starting to make the transition to the next stage, and by another observer to be in the later stage, but still showing many remnants of the earlier.

Further, some children will enter a given stage earlier than will other children, and some children will pass through the stage more rapidly than others. The order of stages is assumed to be the same for all children, but the timing is somewhat variable and the ages specified for any given stage are therefore only approximate. In addition there is typically some ambiguity as to why everyone passes through the same order of stages and whether there is any way the order could be changed. Psychologists who describe systems of stages nearly always assume that the order, at least, is fixed, regardless of the environment. It may be possible to speed up progress through the stages, or slow it down, or even stop it completely, but it is not possible to reach a "higher" stage before passing through the lower ones. Though this assumption of stage theories often is challenged, Piaget could defend it in his case by pointing to the way in which schemata build on one another. Since one cannot solve a problem without first having mastered the necessary components, Piaget would claim that one cannot enter a later stage until one's schemata have reached the necessary level of complexity and abstraction, represented by the previous stage.

With these general warnings, let us look at Piaget's system of stages. The matter of distinguishing between main headings and subheadings, mentioned above, is a bit of a problem. Probably the clearest version of his classification is in four stages: sensory-motor, preoperational, concrete operations, and formal operations. Each stage represents an increase over the previous one in the child's ability to think abstractly, predict the world correctly, explain reasons for things accurately, and generally deal intellectually with the world.

The first stage is known as the *sensory-motor.* It extends roughly from birth to age 2. As the name implies, the schemata that develop during this stage are those involving the child's perception of the world and the coordinations by which he deals with the world. It is during this period that the child forms his most basic conceptions about the nature of the material world. He learns that an object that has disappeared can reappear. He learns that it is the same object even though it looks very different when seen from different angles or in different illuminations. He relates the appearance, sound, and touch of the object to one another. He discovers ways in which his own actions affect objects, and acquires a primitive sense of causality. Thus his world becomes increasingly an orderly arrangement of more or less permanent objects, related causally to each other and to his own behavior.

The second stage is the *preoperational,* extending from about ages 2 to 7. In this stage the child begins to show the effects of having learned language. He is able to represent objects and events symbolically: not just to act toward them, but to think about them. However, Piaget does not regard this change as due entirely to language. The child has internal representations of objects before he has words to express them. These internal representations give the child greater flexibility for dealing adaptively with the world, and attaching words to them gives him much greater power of communication. However, his intellectual abilities are still very limited compared with those of an adult. His thinking is still decidedly concrete by adult standards. He tends to focus on one aspect of a situation to the exclusion of others, a process that Piaget calls *centering.* His reasoning can be a logician's nightmare, and he finds it difficult to understand how anyone else can see things from a point of view other than his own. He is thus, as the name of the stage implies, still early in the process of acquiring a logical, adult intellectual structure.

The third stage is that of *concrete operations,* extending from about ages 7 to 11. Again, this stage represents an increase in flexibility, in this case over the preoperational. The sorts of operations to which the name of the stage refers include classifying, combining, and comparing. The child in the stage of concrete operations can deal with the relationships among hierarchies of terms, such as robin, bird, and creature. He is aware, as the preoperational child is not, of the reversibility of operations: what is added can be subtracted, and a substance that has been changed in shape can be restored to its original shape. A girl in this stage will not fall into the fallacy that a preoperational girl may, of saying: "I have a sister, but she doesn't have any sister!" Just as the advances of the preoperational stage can be related to the beginning of language, so the advances of the stage of concrete operations can be seen as related to the beginning of school. Again, however, Piaget points out that this is not the whole story. One child may have learned arithmetic operations by rote but fail to apply them when appropriate, while another child may deal effectively with problems without ever having been exposed to arithmetic. Learning of symbolic manipulations may be helpful to the child in going from the preoperational to the concrete-operations stage, but experience with a wide variety of concrete situations is more important.

The fourth and final stage is that of *formal operations,* starting around age 11 and involving improvements in abstract thinking continuing to about age 16. In this stage the capacity for symbolic manipulation reaches its peak. Though children in the previous stage have been able to perform a number of logical operations, they have done so within the context of a concrete situation. Now the person (intellectually no longer a child) can view the issues abstractly. He can judge the validity of syllogisms in terms of their formal structure, independent of content. He can explore different ways of formulating a problem and see what their logical consequences are. He is at least ready to think in terms of a realm of abstract propositions that fit in varying degrees the real world that he observes. (In short, we might suggest, he is ready to study Hull's theory!) He may not demonstrate all these tendencies in every possible situation—how many of us ever do?—but he has reached the stage at which he is capable of doing so. The intellectual apparatus of formal reasoning that provides the basis for so much human achievement is at least potentially at his disposal.

As the child passes from one stage to another, as well as through substages we have not considered, his schemata are changing through accommodation to new experiences. At each stage he tries to assimilate new experiences to his existing schemata, but often finds discrepancies. (The same observations at a younger age would not have been discrepant, since his schemata were not well enough developed for him even to recognize an inconsistency.) Though a single such discrepancy is merely puzzling, a series of them will gradually produce accommodation and change the relevant schema toward the next stage. Formal schooling helps the process along, but confrontation with discrepant information is critical, and even that produces its effect only slowly.

Of the many schemata that change during development, there is one group that Piaget has studied in particular detail. They are the most studied changes that take place as the child moves from the preoperational stage into and through the stage of concrete operations. They are grouped together under the heading of conservation, to which we now turn.

Conservation

Most people, on hearing the term *conservation,* probably think of virgin redwood forests or some other natural resource in danger of depletion. Piaget's use of the word, however, is more like that in the physical expression "conservation of matter." It refers to the fact that some quantitative property of matter remains the same in spite of changes in other properties. For example, a lump of clay keeps the same weight no matter how its shape is changed, and a given number of buttons is still the same number whether the buttons are bunched close together or spread out widely over a table top. These constant properties may seem ridiculously obvious to us, but they are not at all obvious to most children in the preoperational stage. Just as an infant must learn that an object remains the same object as it moves, so a somewhat older child must learn that a substance conserves its weight through changes of shape and a group of objects conserves its number through changes of spacing. The mastery of these various forms of conservation takes place typically at somewhat different ages, extending from the beginning to the end of the stage of concrete operations.

A favorite demonstration among Piagetians is to show a preoperational child two pitchers of different-colored liquids, the same size and shape, and equally full. When the child has agreed that there is the same amount in both pitchers, the experimenter pours the contents of one of them into a tall, narrow beaker and asks the child which liquid there is now more of. Some children will say there is now more of the one that was poured ("since it's higher"), others will say there is more of the one that is still in the pitcher ("because it's fatter"), but they generally agree that there are no longer equal amounts of the two liquids. The children have failed to show conservation of volume. This failure may be attributed in part to their unawareness of the reversibility of operations. It is obvious to most adults that the liquid could be poured back into the pitcher and would then take up the same space as before; its volume never changed. To the child, however, the change was more fundamental; he was not aware of its reversibility. This characteristic of his thinking interferes with his achieving conservation.

Failure to conserve number or weight follows from the same characteristics of the preoperational child. A child lines up eight buttons next to eight pennies and agrees that there are the same number of pennies as buttons. Then the pennies are spread out to make a longer line, and in reply to the experimenter's questioning the child now indicates that there are more pennies. Again, this failure of conservation represents a non-recognition that the change in spacing is reversible. Similarly, when a child has seen two balls of clay balance on a scale and has then watched the experimenter mold one of them into a different shape, he is likely to decide that now the changed piece is either heavier or lighter, not realizing that the clay can be restored to its original shape.

Failure to show conservation seems so strange to most adults that one is tempted to think that the problem is merely a trivial misunderstanding about words. Maybe the child really knows that the number, or volume, or weight remains the same, but just gets the words for them mixed up with words for length or height, and so appears not to be showing conservation. This is a tempting interpretation, and there is evidence to suggest that confusion about words does play some part in children's failure to show conservation. However, most people who have worked with children on these problems, asking children the same question in different ways, have concluded that there is much more to it than that. If the child is confused about the words, it is largely *because* he is confused (from an adult point of view) about the whole matter of quantities—what they are and how they behave. However strongly he may defend his "wrong" interpretations, he is still, as Piaget claims, in the process of developing and refining the schemata by which he interprets the world.

THE GESTALT TRADITION AND LEARNING

Gestalt psychology was not primarily a theory of learning, and our examination of Lewin's theory shows why its attempts to incorporate the subject of learning were not always successful. As for Piaget's theories, developmental changes that result from learning are mostly slow changes, and it is often difficult to tell just what independent variables are responsible for which changes. As a result, these theories are short on answers to questions that many learning theorists consider of central importance. This does not mean, however, that these theories have no relevance to the issues considered by psychologists of learning. As Lewin notes, his theory (and related theories) can be of considerable value in predicting and understanding individual behavior.

Let us consider a psychologist working with individuals whom she wants to help—perhaps a school counselor working with mildly disturbed children. Since she knows little of the children's life histories, she may well find that the most effective way of understanding them is to reconstruct their life spaces, to "see the world as they see it." She will then have a good basis for guessing what they will do under various circumstances. She may be able to predict more accurately in this way than in any other what events will make a given child less anxious or less hostile or happier. This does not tell her how to help the child change, but it does provide a basis for trying to change the environment in a way that will help. Moreover, once she has identified the chief features in a child's life space, she at least knows where to focus her attempts at changing the way he relates to the world. Many counselors feel that this approach is more useful than any other in understanding and helping individual children and adults.

However, this is not the only approach that claims practical usefulness in dealing with individuals. Skinner, like Lewin, feels that to be useful an approach needs to apply to individuals, not just to the statistical trend of groups of people. To control the behavior of people and animals, he needs independent variables that will work for most individuals regardless of their unique characteristics. The counseling psychologist should be able to use these independent variables to modify a child's behavior in ways that will help both the child and the other people around him.

Here we have two contrasting approaches. Both are relevant to the problems of individuals, both are potentially useful to a counseling psychologist (and to many other people), but their assumptions are widely different. The first is cognitive, growing out of the gestalt tradition and focusing on the individual's life space; the second is connectionist, based on behaviorism and focusing on learning. Each has its devoted followers, and the followers of each have tended to regard the other as either ineffective or perhaps even harmful. Nevertheless, since our counseling psychologist wants to help children by whatever means will work, she might well wish to combine the best of both approaches, to have both a way of understanding the child's life space and a way of changing it.

If so, she would certainly not be alone in that desire. A number of theorists have felt that the cognitive approach, with its emphasis on people's perceptions and beliefs, has more to offer than does the connectionist's emphasis on habits. At the same time, they have not wanted to give up the behavioristic interest in how behavior relates to independent variables in the external world and in how learning can change this relationship. We will consider these cognitive theorists, influenced as much by behaviorism as by gestalt psychology, in the next chapter.

Chapter
10
Cognitive Theories in the Behaviorist Tradition

*D*uring most of the history of American learning theory, connectionist theories have been dominant and what cognitive theories there were have been in the very different gestalt tradition. Only fairly recently has it become popular to combine the basic attitudes and goals of behaviorism with intervening variables of a cognitive sort. In retrospect, it seems surprising that it took so long. There were, however, a few pioneers in this approach whose work goes back as far as many of the connectionist psychologists we have considered. Of these pioneers, the most conspicuous was E. C. Tolman.

TOLMAN'S PURPOSIVE BEHAVIORISM

Edward Chace Tolman (1886–1959) spent most of his professional life on the faculty of the University of California at Berkeley. His major work, *Purposive Behavior in Animals and Men,* was published in 1932. Though his system later underwent a number of modifications, its essential spirit remained the same. Writing in the heyday of behaviorism, Tolman was impressed with behaviorism's objectivity, its concern with the precise measurement of behavior, and its faith in the improvability of man. At the same time he felt that behaviorism showed too little appreciation of the cognitive aspects of behavior. We do not simply respond to stimuli, he argued; we act on beliefs, express attitudes, and strive toward goals. What we need, therefore, is a theory that recognizes these aspects of behavior without sacrificing objectivity. To fill this need, Tolman undertook to create what has been called a *purposive behaviorism.*

What is a purposive behaviorism like? Much of its meaning can be inferred from the name. First, since it is a form of behaviorism, it is concerned with objective behavior, not with conscious experience. Moreover, it is concerned with the effect of external stimuli on behavior, not merely with a "life space" inferred from behavior. Second, it is concerned with learning, with the way that behavior changes with changing experience of the external world. It is thus a genuine learning theory in a sense that Lewin's, for example, is not. Third, it is concerned with the purposes that impel and guide behavior. Whereas most connectionist theorists treat behavior as a matter of responses to immediately present stimuli, Tolman emphasized the relation of behavior to goals. Most of our behavior is not so much a response to stimuli as a striving toward some goal. Stimuli of course guide us toward the goal and determine at every step what means we will use to reach it, but the search for the goal is what gives unity and meaning to our behavior. We may shift from one approach to another as circumstances require, while still continuing to direct our efforts toward the same goal. As a result it would be necessary for anyone who wanted to predict our behavior to know the goal we were seeking as well as the particular stimuli we were encountering along the way. Tolman's system is called a purposive behaviorism because it studies behavior as it is organized around purposes.

The behavior that Tolman wanted to study is *molar* behavior. This term refers, not to the kind of behavior, but to the way in which it is analyzed. Molar behavior is analyzed in fairly large commonsense units, such as driving to work or cooking a meal. In practice, this is the way all theories of learning analyze behavior. However, some theories include an interest in *molecular* behavior, which is behavior analyzed in terms of single movements of particular muscles. Walking a city block, for example, is a molar act made up of an enormous number of molecular movements— expansions and contractions of the various muscles of the legs and other parts of the body. Guthrie is an example of a theorist who puts a good deal of emphasis on molecular analysis. Tolman, however, states explicitly that he is concerned only with molar behavior. The ways in which molecular movements work together to produce molar acts are of no concern to his system.

Cognitions as Intervening Variables

A given goal may be approached by a great variety of different acts, not only as sequences of responses but also as alternative possible ways of gaining the objective. Tolman's problem was to develop a theory for dealing with this complex variability of molar behavior as it operates in search of goals. To do this, he considered it necessary to take account of the individual's cognitions—one's perceptions of and beliefs about the world. These correspond to Lewin's life space. How could Tolman take them into account without sacrificing the objectivity of behaviorism? His answer was to make use of *intervening variables.* To appreciate the importance of this answer we must see it in historical context. The existing behaviorist theory (more than a decade before Hull's *Principles of Behavior*) regarded anything intervening between the stimulus and the response as itself a response, just as physical and potentially just as measurable as any other response. If the word *cognition* had any meaning at all for such behaviorists, it was as a shorthand name for tiny movements of the speech muscles; any other meaning they rejected as a figment of some mentalistic theorist's imagination. Tolman, however, considered it possible to use the term *cognition* objectively without treating it as a physical, directly measurable movement. He therefore designated cognitions as intervening variables. In doing so he both made the concept of cognition more respectable in behaviorist circles and introduced the concept of intervening variables into psychology.

As an intervening variable, a cognition is not a thing. It is an abstraction defined by the theorist. While it is possible that physiologists may some day find some particular activity in the brain that corresponds to a cognition, this possibility is no concern of Tolman's. The meaning of the word *cognition* is determined by the definition that the theorist gives it. For Tolman, this definition is in terms both of stimuli and of responses, since it intervenes between them. Experience with certain stimuli results in the formation of certain cognitions.

In addition, certain needs produce *demands* for certain goal objects. (Deprivation of food, for example, produces a demand for food.) These demands are also intervening variables. Cognitions and demands work together to produce responses.

The difference between this system and the other cognitive theories we have discussed so far is mainly one of emphasis. For Lewin, the relation of the life space to external stimuli is to some extent a side issue. For Tolman, it is of central importance. He is a theorist of learning, and learning involves changes in cognitions resulting from experience with external stimuli. In this sense Tolman could be considered a stimulus-response theorist even though he is not a connectionist. However, the notion of life space fits easily into Tolman's system. He did, in fact, adopt large parts of Lewin's system into his own. Basically, Tolman's system is a cognitive theory, but with more emphasis on external stimuli than Lewin's and more emphasis on learning and on motivation than gestalt psychology.

Predictions from Tolman's Theory

How is Tolman's theory different from a connectionist one? Both attempt to predict behavior from stimuli and other antecedent conditions. Does the fact that Tolman uses cognitions as intervening variables make any real difference? Consider an individual who makes a certain response to certain stimuli and obtains a reward. What learning does this experience tend to produce? For Guthrie, Hull, or Skinner, it produces a tendency for those stimuli to be followed by that response, provided other conditions such as drive are appropriate. For Tolman, it produces a cognition that making the response will lead to the reward. If one now has a demand for the reward, one will make the response. How are these two interpretations really different?

The answer to this question is that not all cognitions take the form "If I do this, I will get that." We form many other kinds of cognitions about the way the environment is structured, about things that go together, about what paths lead to what places. These various sorts of cognitions can then be used when needed to help the individual achieve life goals. Cognitions from several different learning experiences may be put together so that the individual can respond adaptively to new situations. Attention to such combination makes it possible for Tolman's theory to deal with more original and flexible behavior than is covered by the connectionist interpretations of learning that we have discussed so far.

One example of this greater flexibility is in cognitions about what leads to what. Once an individual has learned how to get from one place to another, this knowledge can be used to obtain rewards quite different from the one obtained while learning. A rat that has learned its way around a maze while satisfying its demand for exploration can use this knowledge later to obtain food. This changeover is illustrated in an experiment by Buxton (1940). Rats were given several experiences of spending a night in a large maze. There was never any food in the maze, and the rats were taken out of the maze at different places on different occasions. This variation was designed to ensure that no part of the maze or path through the maze would be rewarded more than any other. After this experience, the rats were fed in the goal box of the maze while they were hungry and were then put in the start box of the maze. About half the rats ran to the goal box without a single error on this first trial, a record far above that of a control group without the previous experience in the maze. Since the rats had never been reinforced with food (or, presumably, with anything else) for following this particular path, it is difficult for stimulus-response theories to deal with this experiment. For Tolman, however, it is simple enough; the rats had formed a cognition (or perhaps a group of cognitions) about how the maze was arranged. They did not make use of this knowledge until they were given a reason to do so. In other words, the learning about the layout of the maze remained latent until food was experienced in the goal box. Hence this study is said to demonstrate *latent learning*. Several different kinds of latent learning have been studied; this experiment illustrates one of them. Whenever learning goes on without its being evident in performance at the time, latent learning is taking place.

Another way in which Tolman's theory achieved greater flexibility than connectionist theories was through its emphasis on learning the location of reward. Once an individual has learned where a given kind of reward is located, that location can often be reached by means other than those originally used. If a shopper finds an intriguing store while exploring the city on foot, the person can return later by car or bus. Similarly, a rat that has learned the location of food may, if the experimental arrangements permit, take a detour to get there faster. This is illustrated by another experiment (Tolman, Ritchie, & Kalish 1946). Rats ran a roundabout route across a tabletop, through an enclosed alley, and then along a series of elevated pathways to obtain food (Figure 10.1, part A). After they had learned to use this route, the alley was blocked, but 18 new pathways were made available, leading in various directions from the tabletop (Figure 10.1, part B). The rats did not, as one might expect from the principle of generalization, choose the paths closest to the one they had previously used. Instead, they tended to choose the one that pointed approximately toward the location of the goal. Many, to be sure, chose other paths, but the goal-pointing path was the only one chosen by a large proportion of the rats. In other words, the rats tended to choose the path that appeared to be a shortcut to the goal rather than those close to the original path. They had not merely learned a route to food; they had also learned the location of the food in space.

The two above experiments are typical of many that were done by Tolman and his students or were done by others but quoted by Tolman in support of his position. Because of their importance to the controversy between cognitive and connectionist interpretations of learning, these studies often were criticized for various details of their procedures and often were repeated by both friends and foes of Tolman's ideas. In some

Figure 10.1 *Learning the direction to a goal.* This is a top view of Tolman, Ritchie, & Kalish's (1946) apparatus. In part A, rats followed the roundabout route from the round tabletop to the goal, where they found food. In part B, the original route was blocked and 18 new paths were made available. The rats tended to choose the path pointing toward the goal.

cases it turned out that animals show the insightful behavior predicted by Tolman only under quite special conditions. However, whether or not rats behave according to Tolman's theory in any given situation, there is no doubt that this kind of flexible, insightful behavior does occur in some species (particularly humans) under some conditions. The very fact that Tolman considered these experiments necessary shows how strong a hold connectionist interpretations of learning had on American psychology.

Tolman used a number of terms to refer to the cognitions that are learned in various situations. Perhaps his most popular term is *cognitive map.* It is easy to see how the two experiments discussed above can be interpreted by saying that the rats had cognitive maps of the areas they had explored. Those in the maze had a cognitive map of the various alleys, indicating which were blind and which led on to other choice points. Those in the roundabout path had a map that included not only the path but also the surrounding space with its possible shortcuts. If someone asks how it is possible to have maps in the brain when the brain is made up of nerve fibers that conduct impulses from one place to another, Tolman is not concerned. Cognitive maps are intervening variables, and if they explain learning Tolman does not care how they relate to physiology.

Clearly, Tolman's ideas are close to those of the cognitive theorists we have already discussed. In many respects he was particularly close to Lewin, and he borrowed heavily from Lewin in later formulations of his theory. Tolman's later theoretical publications are full of diagrams of vectors and valences. He also added to Lewin's system of diagrams by making a distinction between *pragmatic performance vectors* and *identification performance vectors.* Pragmatic performance vectors refer to the tendencies actually to go to various places or to make other responses of acting on the environment. Identification performance vectors refer to the tendencies merely to observe things. They are concerned with exploring the situation, with observation of the environment. Thus Tolman distinguishes tendencies to observe the environment, either out of curiosity or in order to decide what to do about it, from tendencies to take action toward some part of the environment.

At various points in his theorizing Tolman borrowed ideas not only from Lewin and the gestalt psychologists but also from Freud, from the reinforcement theorists, and even from Guthrie. His breadth is also reflected in the variety of variables that he took into account in explaining behavior. In addition to all the aspects of the situation, he listed four main kinds of individual-difference variables. Only one of these, we may note, involves learning. The four are heredity; age; training; and endocrine, drug, or vitamin conditions. Using the initial letters of these four, Tolman labeled them the HATE variables. (One wonders how Tolman, a devout Quaker, came to arrive at this particular set of initials.) The HATE variables help to illustrate the breadth of Tolman's concern with different aspects of behavior. Discussions of such diverse factors as age and vitamin conditions are rare in learning theory. They are valuable as a reminder that learning, for all its great importance, is far from being the only determinant of behavior.

Of Rats and Humans

Tolman was atypical among cognitive theorists in having given more attention to the behavior of animals than of humans. (This was also Köhler's emphasis at one stage of his career, but he did extensive work in human perception as well.) To some extent, the preference reflects the same factors that have influenced behaviorists in general toward animal work: the greater simplicity of animals and the greater opportunity to control their environments. It probably also reflects Tolman's special concern to show that a cognitive system could still be objective, that it need not depend at all on anything the individual says. Tolman himself, in the tongue-in-cheek manner so characteristic of his writing, presented a third possible explanation. He suggested that psychologists typically begin with an interest in solving the great problems of human life, then become frightened by the awesome implications of such a task and flee to safer aspects of the study of behavior, such as learning in the rat. Certainly Tolman was right in saying that many psychologists are aware of a conflict between their desire to attack the great questions of life directly and their desire to concentrate on other questions that are less exciting but that they have more chance of being able to solve. Tolman's own career reflects this conflict clearly.

On the one hand, Tolman was a man of strong social conscience. (He was one of the faculty members who left the University of California rather than sign the controversial loyalty oath in 1950). In 1942 he published a small book called *Drives Toward War,* in which he analyzed the psychological causes of war and presented some suggestions for removing them. His analysis of the biological drives, social techniques, and psychological dynamisms leading to behavior—warlike or otherwise—combined experimental, clinical, and historical sources. On the basis of this analysis he suggested several fairly radical changes in our political, economic, and educational systems, changes which he thought would reduce the impetus toward war. Among these was a plan for a world state, along with some psychological suggestions for making this admittedly visionary idea a bit more practical.

On the other hand, Tolman had as his principal ambition the development of a schematic rat world, a system from which he could predict completely the behavior of rats in a laboratory environment. This is reflected in his whimsical dedication of *Purposive Behavior* to *Mus norvegicus albinus* (actually the white mouse, but he meant the white rat). He wanted to include enough different variables and to have flexible enough constructs to achieve this goal completely. When we consider the tremendously complex human social situations that people usually want psychologists to deal with, this seems like a very modest ambition. Tolman did not, however, achieve his goal.

Evaluation of Tolman

If we consider how Tolman incorporated the best aspects of behaviorism within a cognitive theory, what a broad range of variables he took into account, and how early he anticipated future developments in the logic of theory building (e.g., the use of intervening variables), we could easily conclude that Tolman is the greatest learning theorist we have considered. In its conception, his theory may very well be the best there is. The conception, however, was never really carried into execution. Tolman discussed the kinds of laws psychology needs, but he did not develop these laws. He did experiments intended to show that cognitive formulations are better than connectionist ones, but he did not do experiments to make these cognitive formulations precise enough to be really useful for prediction. He pointed the way toward an extension of cognitive theory to include the best aspects of connectionist theory, but he did not carry the program through. He is therefore open to the same criticism as the other cognitive theorists, that he does not give us a basis for predicting from objective stimuli to objective behavior. He gave us a cognitive framework (or perhaps we should say a gestalt!) for interpreting learning, but he did not provide us either with detailed laws of learning like Skinner's, or with a detailed theory like Hull's, or with a general principle of learning like Guthrie's. Thus his system is more a road sign or a preliminary attempt than it is an accomplished fact.

This shortcoming is not really a failure on Tolman's part, however, for his attitude toward his own theorizing was always tentative and whimsical. He regarded theory construction not as a serious business of building great intellectual edifices for the future but as a half playful trying out of different approaches. As a result he was constantly revising his theory, making suggestions and then abandoning them before he had time to explore their implications. His writings are a mixture of earnestness and whimsy, of high-flown theorizing constantly being pulled up short by a chuckle. His desire to construct a schematic rat world was thus partly an aspiration but also partly a joke. He wanted not so much to build a truly adequate theory as to explore the whole activity of theory building, both playing with it himself and puncturing the excessive claims of others. As a result, he was widely respected and widely loved, but not widely followed. In fact, of all the major learning theorists in the last half century, he may well have been regarded most affectionately by his students but at the same time have had the fewest students follow in his footsteps. This apparent contradiction was analyzed 15 years after his death in a symposium (see Campbell & Krantz 1974) which concluded that to be a "tribal leader," that is, to found a school of loyal followers, one must have a strong and somewhat intolerant conviction of the rightness and importance of one's ideas. Tolman lacked that conviction. Possibly his intellectual style was influenced by his being the younger brother of a distinguished scientist in a better-developed science: physics. In any case, compared with other major theorists, he had little faith in the lasting rightness of his theories, but much interest both in exploring ideas and in encouraging students to develop in their own directions.

Tolman himself put it best. His final theoretical statement appeared in the same book as Guthrie's (and he and Guthrie died in the same year). He ended his chapter with this concluding statement, which thus became in a sense the concluding statement of his professional life.

> The system may well not stand up to any final canons of scientific procedure. But I do not much care. I have liked to think about psychology in ways that have proved congenial to me. Since all the sciences, and especially psychology, are immersed in such tremendous realms of the uncertain and the unknown, the best that any individual scientist, especially any psychologist, can do seems to be to follow his own gleam and his own bent, however inadequate they may be. In fact, I suppose that actually this is what we all do. In the end, the only sure criterion is to have fun. And I have had fun [Tolman 1959, p. 152].

BOLLES'S MORE RECENT BEHAVIORISTIC COGNITIVE THEORY

The same casual approach to theorizing that prevented Tolman from founding a school also made it easier for him to present many tentative suggestions about the interpretation of learning. We have noted his openness to other people's ideas, to aspects of learning that many other theorists neglected, and to different formulations of different kinds of learning. As a result, it has been hard for later cognitive theorists to come up with anything that Tolman had not already suggested. Much of the work of later cognitive theorists, therefore, has been to make ideas quite similar to Tolman's somewhat tighter and more formal than he did. From among the various recent formulations of cognitive theory we will look at one which illustrates more recent theory in the tradition of Tolman.

Bolles's Cognitive Interpretation

One attempt to formulate a neo-Tolmanian theory was made by Robert C. Bolles (b. 1928) of the University of Washington. Since the University of Washington was Guthrie's stronghold for many years, and Arthur Lumsdaine continues to represent Guthrie's viewpoint there, Bolles (1972) may have been particularly sensitive to a gibe that Guthrie once directed at Tolman. Tolman's theory, said Guthrie, dealt with how a rat's cognitions were formed, but then left the rat buried in thought. If the rat ever got to the food at the end of a maze, it would have to do so by itself, with no help from the theory. Whether or not Bolles found that remark amusing, he certainly did not consider it fair. Why, he asks, should we say that a habit produces behavior while an expectancy produces nothing but the thought? Both habits and expectancies are intervening variables, which produce behavior if and only if we postulate that they do. (It is clear where Bolles stands on the question of whether intervening variables are real entities that we discover or explanatory fictions that we invent.) Hull, for example, says that the right combination of habit, drive, and incentive will produce a given response. Tolman, in contrast, says that a response results from an expectancy that a given response will produce a given outcome, plus a demand for that outcome. Is one formulation any more logical than the other? asks Bolles. Either set of intervening variables, if correctly formulated, permits us to predict what response will occur under what conditions, but neither produces the response any more directly than the other.

How does Bolles formulate a cognitive theory to predict behavior? He begins with three kinds of events about which an organism can learn. The first two sound familiar enough: a stimulus that serves as a signal (S), and a response (R). The third, which refers to a biologically important stimulus, is S*. The kinds of stimulus events to which S* refers are the same kinds that other theorists have called positive and negative reinforcers. A stimulus event S permits us to predict the occurrence of a significant consequent event S*.

Two kinds of expectancies can be formed about the relationships among these three kinds of events. An *S-S* expectancy* is a cognition that when S occurs, S* will follow. If we have learned that the sight of an approaching waiter (stimulus) means we will soon get food (significant positive consequence), we have formed an S-S* expectancy connecting the approach of the waiter with the arrival of food. If a child has had the misfortune to learn that some barking dogs do bite, it has formed an S-S* expectancy connecting the sight and sound of a barking dog with the significant negative consequence of being bitten. The reader will note the relationship of S-S* expectancies to classical conditioning, with S as the conditioned stimulus and S* as the unconditioned stimulus. The S also resembles Skinner's conditioned positive or negative reinforcer, since it predicts the occurrence of a primary positive or negative reinforcer. Where S* is aversive, S also resembles what Dollard and Miller would call a stimulus for the secondary drive of fear.

The other kind of cognition is an *R-S* expectancy*. Here it is the individual's own act that predicts the biologically significant consequent. If one expects that opening the refrigerator door (R) will reveal food (S*), and that touching a lighted stove (R) will produce pain (S*), one has formed R-S* expectancies. Since Bolles is more concerned with why behavior occurs than with why it does not occur, most of the R-S* expectancies with which he deals are ones in which the S* is positive. However, it may be positive in the sense that it relieves a negative condition, as in the expectancy that if you take this aspirin (R), your headache will go away (S*). An R-S* expectancy thus relates a response to what Skinner would call either positive or negative reinforcement.

There are two questions we can ask about these expectancies. First, how are they learned? The answer to this question is easy enough: by experience. Whenever an S is followed by an S*, an S-S* expectancy is formed or strengthened, and whenever an R is followed by an S*, an R-S* expectancy is formed or strengthened. There is no need to refer to reinforcement, even though S* is the kind of event that others have referred to as positive or negative reinforcers. The acquiring of expectancies is thus a forming of cognitions by a process of learning by contiguity.

Second, how do these expectancies lead to behavior? In other words, what specific assumption does Bolles make to avoid leaving the person or the rat buried in thought? He assumes that when an event S occurs, it will give rise to behavior R if the individual has both an S-S* and an R-S* expectancy connecting that S and that R. For example, a sign "Restaurant" on a building will lead to the behavior of entering the building only if the person has both the S-S* expectancy that the sign really indicates that there is food to be obtained and the R-S* expectancy that going into the building is the way to get to it. The strength of the tendency to make the response will depend on three things: the strength of the S-S* expectancy, the strength of the R-S* expectancy, and the value of S* to the individual. In the example, how sure is the person that the sign indicates food, how sure is he that going into the building is the way to get the food, and how hungry is he? Bolles suggests that in some rough sense an S-S* expectancy corresponds to Hull's incentive motivation (K), an R-S* expectancy to habit strength ($_sH_R$), and the value of S* to drive (D).

In the above example, the S* in the S-S* expectancy is positive and the R in the R-S* is the means of getting to it, so the S* in S-S* and the S* in R-S* are the same. However, this relationship does not always hold. A mistreated child might learn the S-S* expectancy that an angry shout means she is about to be struck. That S* is negative, and an appropriate R-S* would refer to how to avoid it. The child might have the expectancy that running away would save her from the blow. In that case, the S* of the R-S* expectancy would refer to safety, while the S* of the S-S* expectancy refers to danger. Thus, for the two kinds of expectancy to work jointly to produce action, they may refer to the same positive S*, or one may refer to a negative S* and the other to its absence. These predictions fit well with common sense, and Bolles does not feel it necessary to make any special distinction between the two kinds of situations.

Although a theory of learning naturally focuses on learned expectancies, they are not the only kind. Both S-S* and R-S* expectancies can also be innate—resulting from the organism's heredity rather than from previous experience. The fear of a sudden loud noise that infants often show might be considered an innate S-S* cognition that such a noise (S) indicates danger (S*). However, Bolles is interested more in innate R-S* expectancies. The existence of such innate expectancies is indicated by various stereotyped responses which different species of animals make in the presence of food, danger, or other biologically important situations. Most species have fairly stereotyped ways of taking and eating food, and also stereotyped reactions to danger. Among the food responses, we may note not only the various ways of grasping, tearing, chewing, and so on, but also such special patterns as the raccoon's food-rubbing ritual (sometimes called "washing"). For danger, fleeing and freezing are the two most common patterns. Although a connectionist psychologist would interpret these *species-specific behaviors* as evidence of stimulus-response connections, Bolles prefers to look at them as reflecting innate R-S* expectancies. For example, "freezing in fear" results from a combination of an S-S* expectancy that this noise means danger and an innate R-S* expectancy that freezing means safety. A combination of the two kinds of expectancies can thus predict behavior equally well whether the expectancies are innate, learned, or one of each.

Bolles and collaborators have conducted research to try to determine how much of a rat's learning is of the S-S* sort and how much of the R-S* sort. Specifically, when a rat has learned to make two different responses to the same object, and then is punished for one of them, to what extent does it learn a fear of making that response (R-S*) and to what extent a fear of that object (S-S*)? The answers so far are not simple (Bolles et al. 1980), nor would we expect them to be, but this research represents a promising beginning at using these concepts to clarify just what is learned from a given experience.

Even with its various complications, Bolles's system may seem rather spare as contrasted with Tolman's spread of cognitive maps and vectors. Part of this difference is due to the fact that Tolman focused more on the arrangement of events in space, whereas Bolles focuses on the sequence of events in time. Tolman did research on rats finding their way around in mazes, whereas Bolles has worked most on what happens when a rat receives a signal that indicates a shock is soon to follow. Since mazes involve two-dimensional space (or occasionally three-dimensional, if the rat climbs out the top), while time extends in only one dimension, it is perhaps understandable that Bolles feels he can get along with simpler assumptions than Tolman did. However, as the theory is applied to more situations, further "postulates" may be needed.

Chapter
11

Connectionist Moves in Cognitive Directions

*F*or the first half of the twentieth century, connectionist interpretations of learning were dominant in American psychology, while cognitive theorists remained as critics from outside the mainstream. However, their criticisms attracted enough attention so that connectionist theorists felt a need to deal with them. If behavior is simply a matter of responses to stimuli (or of operants controlled by stimuli, in Skinner's case), how can connectionist theorists explain those phenomena that cognitive theorists attribute to beliefs, plans, and attitudes?

Connectionist theorists have answered this question by noting that responses produce stimuli which can in turn produce other responses. Some responses seem to have as their main function the producing of stimuli. We saw one striking example in Watson's view that thinking is merely subvocal speech—a series of fractional speech movements that serve the function of talking to oneself. A similiar analysis can be applied to responses of looking at something or imagining something or thinking or anticipating the possible results of a course of action. In each of these cases we make a response (looking or imagining or thinking or anticipating) that provides us with stimuli, external or internal. Responses that serve mainly to produce stimuli are known as mediating responses.

In some cases it is fairly clear that mediating responses function by changing the orientation of our sense receptors and hence of the stimuli we receive. A person staring at something and a dog pricking up its ears are obvious examples. In such cases we can speak of the mediating responses as *observing responses* (Wyckoff 1952). In other cases we cannot identify any specific observing response, but it is still plausible to say that the mediating response changes the effective sensory input in subtler ways, through a change in attention. Often it is difficult to say whether we are dealing with changes in receptor orientation or in attention at the level of the central nervous system. If a driver who is reading a sign suddenly notices an oncoming car, is the change in what she looks at (observing response) or in the part of what she looks at that she notices (attention)? Perhaps it depends on something as trivial as how far away the car and the sign are, and hence on whether it is possible for her to focus her eyes on both at once. So, although a full understanding of mediation would require knowing just what form the mediating responses take, for our present purposes we can group together all those cases where mediating responses of whatever form serve primarily a cue function.

CUE-PRODUCING RESPONSES

One phenomenon that can be explained by mediating responses is what D. H. Lawrence of Stanford University (no relation to the novelist) has called the *acquired distinctiveness of cues.* This term refers to learning about which cues in a situation are important. When a first-grader discovers that it is the shape of letters rather than their size that is important in reading, the cue of form has acquired distinctiveness. This acquisition will then affect the student's subsequent learning of letters and words. The response of paying attention to form is separate from any particular response made to any particular form. This separateness has been demonstrated in several ingenious experiments with rats (Lawrence 1949, 1950) and in an impressively thorough experiment with humans (Goss & Greenfeld 1958).

Acquired distinctiveness of cues is not an unmixed blessing. Once we learn what aspects of a situation to pay attention to and what ones to ignore, we may miss opportunities for useful learning about those we have come to ignore. Such a situation has been labeled *blocking* (Kamin 1968). For example (Haggbloom 1981), rats were trained to run down an alley and were rewarded on every other trial. As a result, they learned to run fast on trials following nonreward (since the next trial after a nonrewarded one was always rewarded) and not on trials following a reward. In other words, they learned to discriminate between the internal cues of just having eaten and of just having not eaten. Once this discrimination was learned, a new cue was introduced: on rewarded trials the alley was always black, whereas on nonrewarded trials it was always white. They were given as many trials on this new regime as other rats needed to learn to run when the alley was black and not when it was white. However, these rats did not need to learn this discrimination, since they could always respond appropriately on the basis of the internal cues they had already learned to pay attention to: run after a nonreward but not after a reward.

What happened when they were tested with the rewarded and nonre-warded trials in random order, so that the only cue was color? In fact, they showed little evidence of discrimination on the basis of color, indicating that the earlier learning about the internal cues had blocked later learning about color. Because of the blocking, they were baffled by the new dis-crimination problem. How often do people have similar experiences—learning enough so they think they "know it all" and therefore not learn-ing any more?

Another closely related example of a situation where observing re-sponses are important is in the formation of *learning sets.* These were first demonstrated by Harry F. Harlow (1905–1981) of the University of Wis-consin (Harlow 1959). To demonstrate a learning set, an individual is given a long series of discrimination problems. On each problem the learner is presented with two objects, such as a toy plane and a rubber ball. One of these has a food reward hidden under it on every trial; the other does not. The same one is correct on each trial—in this case, say, the rubber ball. This is an ordinary discrimination-learning task, in which the individual gradually learns always to choose the rubber ball because that choice is always reinforced.

After this task is learned, the learner is switched to another discrimina-tion, between two new objects, such as a cap and a shoe. Since the objects are different from those on the previous task, there is no way for the individual to transfer what was learned about the plane and the ball to this new task. There is one thing that may transfer, however: the principle that only one object has food under it and that it is the same object on each trial. This similarity in structure between the two tasks does indeed make a difference. Over a series of such discrimination tasks, each with two new objects, learning gets faster and faster.

Once the principle is understood, all the learner has to do is to choose either stimulus at random on the first trial of each new problem. If it is correct, the learner chooses the same one on all the other trials. If it is wrong, the individual chooses the other one on all the remaining trials. With this method the food will be found consistently on every trial except the first of every discrimination problem (and also, by chance, on the first trial of half the problems). This strategy may seem so obvious that we wonder why the learner does not start using it at once. Actually, however, for inexperienced learners it is not obvious at all. Why should they expect food always to be under the same object, even though they just took the food from there a moment ago? One source of confusion is that the right-left position of the stimuli is changed from trial to trial, and some learners tend to respond to the position rather than to the object. There is also a widespread tendency to choose the other one on trial 2 regardless of whether the first one was rewarded on trial 1. These and other systematic wrong ways of responding to the situation are known as *error factors.* Because of the various possible error factors, inexperienced learners are likely to do poorly on the task. Gradually, however, they do learn this principle, so that learning gets better and better from problem to problem. After having experience with enough different problems, all of which can be solved in the same way, learners commonly reach the point where their scores on new problems are nearly perfect. They are then said to have formed a learning set.

A learning set is an example of learning how to learn. It involves being set to approach the problem in a certain way. Since the approach to the problem requires paying attention to certain cues rather than others (form rather than position, for example), acquired distinctiveness of cues is one aspect of the formation of learning sets. Most of the studies of learning sets have been with animals, particularly monkeys. There are large species differences and age differences in the rate at which learning sets are formed, more so than in the learning of a single discrimination. The rate at which learning sets are formed has come to be regarded as one of the best measures of differences in intelligence among animals.

Much of education may be regarded as the formation of learning sets. We hope that in teaching students we are not merely providing them with specific stimulus-response connections, but are giving them the necessary background for continued learning after they leave school. We want them to be able not merely to parrot answers to questions but to solve problems by making use of what they have learned. Studies of learning sets show individuals going through such a process of learning how to solve problems. The solution to one problem cannot be transferred directly to another problem, but the general method of solution can. Just as the "intelligent" behavior of the experienced monkey solving a discrimination problem reflects its prior experience in forming a learning set, so the "intelligent" behavior of an adult human reflects prior experience in learning how to solve problems.

The cue function of mediating responses is particularly valuable for resolving the differences between connectionist and cognitive theory. If our own responses can provide us with cues and if these can include complex verbal cues, we are well on the way to a connectionist cognitive theory. If one can make the responses of drawing a map on paper, can one not also make responses of imagining such a map? If one can give oneself instructions in words, why not in images, in muscular sets, or in any other sort of stimulus-producing response? And if such nonverbal mediating responses are available to humans, why not to animals also? This line of reasoning can be carried to the point where nearly all of the cognitive theorists' statements about life space, expectancies, and cognitive maps are accepted, but all are reinterpreted as stimuli produced by the individual's own responses.

Clearly, not all of the suggestions about mediating responses that have been made by various connectionist psychologists have gone this far. Though Hull and Guthrie both make use of mediating responses, neither one regards the response-produced stimuli involved as having the extensive gestalt properties that cognitive theorists favor. Moreover, Wertheimer would probably have considered learning sets more like blind applications of a principle than like true insights, leading to B rather than A solutions. Nevertheless, these various elaborations of connectionist theory help to bridge the gap that separates them from cognitive theory. If they are still far from Wertheimer and only moderately close to Tolman, they are perhaps not so far from Bolles.

MOTIVATIONAL MEDIATING RESPONSES

So far we have focused on mediating responses that provide neutral information, without paying much attention to their motivational effects. However, the stimuli from our own responses can also be quite motivating, as we note whenever we speak of happy or sad or frightening thoughts. Skinner noted this effect in his discussion of emotional respondents, and Hull and his followers have made considerable use of similar interpretations. One theorist in the same tradition went still further, and in the process came close to developing a cognitive theory of motivation within a connectionist framework.

This theorist was O. Hobart Mowrer (1907–1982) of the University of Illinois, who had been an important contributor to the Hullian analysis of personality, fear, and neuroses. He agreed with Dollard and Miller that we first learn what to be afraid of and then learn what to do about it. However, he went further than Dollard and Miller in emphasizing the distinction between these two stages of learning. Learning what to be afraid of is an example of *sign learning,* in which a stimulus comes to serve as a sign of what is coming next. Whenever anything serves as a signal that something either good or bad is about to happen, the process by which it becomes such a signal is sign learning. Learning what to do about it is *solution learning.* In the case of fear, solution learning is learning what response to make to escape or avoid the feared situation.

In Miller's experiment with the two-compartment box, learning that the white section is dangerous is sign learning, and learning to turn the paddle wheel in order to escape from the white compartment into the black one is solution learning. Likewise, when a child learns to recognize her mother's frown and raised voice as danger signs of parental anger, this is sign learning, and whatever she learns to do to deal with the threatening situation is solution learning. Sign learning thus corresponds to classical conditioning, and solution learning corresponds to instrumental learning.

Some years after Mowrer (1947) originally presented his two-factor theory, he modified it by pointing out that solution learning has many of the characteristics of sign learning. Suppose an individual learns not to do something for which he has been punished. According to two-factor theory, in stage 1 of this learning the sensations produced by his own behavior became a conditioned stimulus for fear. In stage 2, the response of changing his behavior away from that which was punished was reinforced by reduction of the fear, and learned. In stage 1, sensations from his own behavior became danger signs. Why, asked the later Mowrer, should we not say the same thing about stage 2: that sensations from the individual's own behavior became signs of hope? When the fearful person felt himself making the new, never punished response, he felt safer, because the sensations from this response had previously been followed by a reduction in fear. This new interpretation of Mowrer's replaces his older two-factor theory with a new, cognitive-sounding one-factor theory. All learning, in this new version, is sign learning.

Through learning, according to this theory, stimuli become signs of fear or hope or disappointment or relief. Even the acquisition of bodily skills can be interpreted as sign learning. When we learn certain movements in riding a bicycle, for example, we are learning that some sensations from our bodies mean we are doing it right, while other sensations indicate that we are about to tip over and must act quickly to keep our balance. The important thing about these stimuli is not that they elicit certain responses but that they have certain meanings, that they are signs of success or of impending failure in our attempt to ride. The history of Mowrer's thinking, in coming to this position, is covered in his book *Learning Theory and Behavior* (1960).

This new interpretation of learning makes Mowrer more cognitive than any of the other theorists we have discussed who developed their systems within the connectionist tradition. It is therefore interesting to compare him with the two cognitive theorists whom we considered in the previous chapter. Mowrer's earlier system bore considerable resemblance to Bolles's, with sign learning corresponding to the formation of S-S* expectancies and solution learning to the acquisition of R-S* expectancies. Mowrer's later system does not entirely get rid of the distinction between S-S* and R-S* expectancies, but it reinterprets R-S* learning in a way that makes it more like S-S*. We learn an expectancy that our own responses will lead to S*, but what this really means, says Mowrer, is that the S's from our own behavior become signals for S*. At a theoretical level, therefore, Mowrer regards R-S* learning as a special kind of S-S* learning.

Mowrer's interpretation, like Bolles's, still lacks the full cognitive complexity of Tolman's. Like Bolles, Mowrer talks about sign learning but not about cognitive maps. Though his later theory is as cognitive as some that emerged from the cognitive tradition, he still shows traces of his connectionist background.

BANDURA'S SOCIAL COGNITIVE THEORY

Another respect in which theorists in the connectionist tradition have moved in a cognitive direction involves the things that people learn from other people. In the early days of connectionist theory, such learning was downplayed in favor of learning by doing. One conspicuous exception, however, was a book by Neal Miller and John Dollard (written before their book on personality and psychotherapy) called *Social Learning and Imitation* (Miller & Dollard 1941). Although this book pointed to the importance of social learning, it did so in a thoroughly behaviorist way. Many of the stimuli that influence our behavior are those from other people, and one way we can respond to these stimuli is to model our behavior after someone else's. If we are reinforced for imitating others, say Miller and Dollard, we will continue to imitate them, and if we are reinforced for imitating some people but reinforced for doing the opposite of what other people do, we will learn the discrimination and follow that pattern.

Later theorists have gone well beyond Miller and Dollard's simple behaviorist view of imitation. Of the various contributors to this resurgence of interest in imitation, probably the most influential has been Albert Bandura (b. 1925) of Stanford University. He and Richard Walters collaborated on a book in which they presented their views, not only on imitation, but on a range of related topics (1963). Their one small book, in fact, covered much of the same range of topics, including social learning processes, personality development, and psychotherapy, that Miller and Dollard covered in the two books on which they collaborated.

An Analysis of Modeling

As regards imitation, Bandura and Walters start at about the point where Miller and Dollard stopped. The form of imitation that Miller and Dollard analyzed in detail was like a simple version of follow-the-leader. They showed that rats could learn to follow (or not follow) other rats in a T-maze, and that children could learn to make (or not make) the same response that an adult or another child made. The responses the rats or the children made were ones that they would have made in that situation anyway; all the leader did was to provide a cue as to which response would be reinforced. Certainly humans, probably monkeys, and perhaps various other species can learn by imitation in considerably more complicated ways than that. A person can learn how to perform some fairly elaborate sequence of operations by observing someone else doing it and then modeling her own behavior after what she has observed. Whether or not that person can acquire completely new responses by imitation is largely a matter of definition, but she can surely learn to arrange simple responses in a complex sequence purely by observing and imitating someone else.

Consider how hard it would be to learn to drive a car if every step in the process had to be shaped by Skinnerian procedures. Reinforcing the learner for each successive approximation to the final correct use of each of the controls would not only be maddeningly slow; it would also give little assurance that the learner would survive the training course, considering how a person would be likely to drive who had achieved only a first approximation to mastery of the steering wheel and the brake. The fact that a learner can observe and imitate an experienced driver greatly increases both the speed of learning and the chance of living to the end of the course.

You may feel that this example ignores the importance of language. A person can learn a lot about how to drive a car by observation, but that person can also learn a lot by being told how to work the controls and what sorts of precautions to take. You might guess that certain aspects of driving could be better acquired by watching and others by listening, while a combination of both might be better still. Bandura and Walters do not worry much about this distinction. They are really concerned with a concept even more general than imitation: *modeling.* When behavior is modeled after someone else's, that someone else may be called the model, and the whole process referred to as modeling. Modeling thus includes not only simple imitation of one person by another, but also those more pervasive processes (often called identification) by which a person tries to be the same kind of person as another. Given this broader concept, the model need not be a particular real person whom one observes. He or she may, instead, be a character in history or fiction or a generalized ideal person whom one has only heard described. When we think in terms of modeling behavior after that of some real, imaginary, or hypothetical person, the distinction between learning by observing and learning by being told becomes less important. We may still ask which will work better in a given case, but both are examples of modeling and hence, in a sense, of imitation.

The example of learning to drive a car refers to the acquisition of at least relatively new responses. Considering all the skills and social behaviors that people acquire from one another, such acquisition of new responses is certainly a very important kind of imitation. However, it is only one of three processes of imitation that Bandura and Walters consider. The second involves the inhibition or disinhibition of already learned responses. In other words, the person has already learned to make a response, but he learns by observing other people whether or not to make a given response under a given set of conditions. In the case of *inhibition,* he learns from observing someone else not to make the response that he otherwise very likely would have made. Teachers hope that such inhibition by observation will take place when they reprimand a student for being noisy in class—that other students will thereby learn not to be noisy either. As with every other hope in education, the process often does not work that way, but it works often enough to illustrate that observational learning of inhibition is a real process. *Disinhibition* refers to the case in which a person has already both learned how to make a response and learned not to make it in a given situation, but now observes someone else making the response and proceeds to do so also. The inhibited response has been disinhibited through a process of imitation. Just as the inhibitory effects of imitation were illustrated by what teachers hope will happen, the disinhibitory effects may be illustrated by what they fear may happen after they have trained a class to be quiet. One student making a commotion may have a disinhibitory effect, inducing the rest of the class to abandon its inhibitions and join in rowdy noisemaking.

The third way in which imitation can operate is by eliciting an already learned response. Such *elicitation* is particularly noteworthy in children, though common enough in adults; as soon as one person starts to do something, several other people want to do the same thing, even though they had given the possibility no thought until that moment. This tendency can be a nuisance if the resources for that one activity are limited (only one set of crayons for a dozen children who suddenly want to color), but a benefit if the activity is one that requires a number of people for best results. It is not always easy to tell whether a given case of imitation is elicitation or disinhibition, since both involve an increased tendency to perform an already learned response when someone else is observed to be doing it. In principle, however, the two processes are distinctly different, since in elicitation the sight of the model creates a positive desire to perform the activity, whereas in disinhibition the desire is already active and all that is needed is some indication that the desire can safely be indulged.

Both the second process of imitation (inhibition and disinhibition) and the third (elicitation) depend at least in part on the consequences of the activity to the model. If the model is punished for whatever was done, the result is likely to be inhibition, and the chance of the model's being imitated goes down. If there is no obvious consequence, good or bad, the model may be imitated either through disinhibition or through elicitation, but the chance of imitation is greater if the model is conspicuously rewarded for the behavior. In effect, reward or punishment of the model acts much like reward or punishment of the observer, in that we tend to imitate those we see rewarded and refrain from imitating those we see punished. This process by which consequences to the model influence the behavior of the observer is often called *vicarious reinforcement.*

Although vicarious reinforcement is important for the second and third kinds of imitation, it seems not to be very important for the acquisition of new responses. That is, an observer learns what it was that the model did, and becomes able to imitate it irrespective of reinforcement to the model. What reinforcement to the model does is to influence whether the observer will show what she has learned about the model's behavior. Studies have shown that even when children do not spontaneously imitate a model, they can still imitate the model with a good deal of accuracy if specifically asked to do so. Studies have also shown that whether or not the children spontaneously imitate the model depends considerably (though by no means entirely) on the reinforcement or punishment that the model received.

Much of the research carried out by Bandura and Walters dealt with the imitation of aggressive behavior. Both were concerned with the problems posed by aggression, and Bandura in particular worried about the

which aggressive models on television might contribute to ag-
behavior by children who watched television. Research by Ban-
and others has amply demonstrated that children learn the aggres-
responses they observe and that in many cases their subsequent play
is influenced into more aggressive forms by what they have observed. This
change in behavior involves the learning of new responses, the disinhibition of old ones, and probably the elicitation of old ones without disinhibition. It is less clear to what extent observing aggression on television
induces viewers to engage later in real-life aggression. As with so many
practical applications of psychology, speculation goes well beyond data,
and there is plenty of room to argue both sides of the case. However, the
weight of evidence suggests that there is at least some real effect (e.g.,
Eron et al. 1972).

Observational Learning

Walters died not long after their book was published, but Bandura has
continued to work and write on modeling and its implications and applications. In doing so, he has dealt increasingly with the "how" and "why" of
modeling (Bandura 1971). As regards the "how," his interpretations are
quite cognitive. The main thing that goes on in modeling is learning by
observation. The observer sees what the model does, notes what the consequences to the model are, remembers what he has learned, makes various
inferences from it, and either then or later takes account of it in his own
behavior. What is learned is not responses in the connectionist sense, but
knowledge about responses and their consequences. On this matter,
therefore, Bandura is clearly with Tolman and Bolles rather than with
Guthrie, Hull, or Skinner. Indeed, he suggests that instrumental conditioning might best be viewed as observational learning about the consequences of our own actions, just as we may learn from observing others.

How is learning by observation achieved? Bandura points to four
necessary components: *attention, retention, production,* and *motivation.*
Attention indicates that we do not automatically learn everything to
which we are exposed. We notice events selectively, both in obvious physical ways, such as what things we look at, and in various subtler ways.
Retention indicates that what we learn doesn't have any practical effect
unless we remember it long enough to do something about it. Production
is perhaps more challenging, since anyone who has either given or received coaching in a skill knows that observing someone else's behavior
does not automatically convey the ability to imitate it accurately. How is
that ability acquired?

In some cases, says Bandura, we have already mastered all the components of a performance, so all we need to learn from observation is when
to do them. If this is not the case, so that we need to acquire the component skills themselves, the learning is harder, but there are a number of
ways it can be achieved. A coach can help by guiding us through the

performance with a mixture of talking, demonstration, and moving our bodies through the proper motions. However, polished skill also requires that we try making the responses and receive sensory feedback from our own responses. Thus Bandura admits that there is no perfect substitute for practice when it comes to the production of a new skill, even though he also insists that practice per se is only a limited part of human learning.

Whereas these three factors determine how much observational learning will occur, the fourth, motivation, determines whether observational learning of someone's behavior will lead us to imitate that someone. For Miller and Dollard, this factor meant that we imitate because we are reinforced for imitating, and can also learn not to imitate under those conditions where imitation is not reinforced. Bandura rejects this view, which is too connectionist to fit in his more cognitive theory. However, for most practical purposes, his own interpretation amounts to much the same thing as theirs. We model our behavior after that of others when we expect to be rewarded for doing so, and one factor that leads us to expect reward is having been rewarded before under similar conditions.

What makes this view different from the simple reinforcement interpretation is that it also allows for other factors to influence our expectations. We may expect that imitating someone in a particular situation will lead to reward because we have been told that it will, or because we see other people similar to ourselves being rewarded for such imitation. Each of these sources of information gives some indication of whether imitation will be rewarded on this particular occasion, but none is infallible. We make a judgment on the basis of any or all of them, and imitate or not accordingly. Depending on the outcome, our confidence in that source of information will go up or down, which in turn will affect our tendency to imitate different people under various future conditions.

We do not need to assume that people are always aware of what goes into these decisions as to whether or not to imitate. If a child in one of Bandura's experiments were asked why she imitated the model, her answer would probably be no more informative than "I felt like it" or "It looked like a fun thing to do." Nevertheless, there is evidence that the likelihood of imitation depends on reward to the model, reward to the child, the apparent power and status of the model, and other motivational variables. Such cases of what looks like automatic imitation resulting from reinforcement obscure the difference between Bandura's interpretation and Miller and Dollard's, but the difference is still real, and typical of the differences between connectionist and cognitive views.

Like many theorists, Bandura has gradually increased the scope of his theorizing, spreading out from the study of modeling to consider a wide variety of other topics. His most recent book, *Social Foundations of Thought and Action* (Bandura 1986), deals not only with general principles of learning and modeling but also with development, judgment, self-regulation, and social processes—a considerable part of the subject matter of psychology.

Some Special Topics

Two of the topics Bandura has studied have received particular attention. One, as already mentioned, is aggression (Bandura 1973). He has little use for interpretations of aggression as either an innate human drive or an automatic reaction to frustration. Instead, he emphasizes aggression as a way of obtaining rewards that might have been obtained in other ways. One way of reducing aggression, therefore, is to teach people more socially desirable ways of getting what they want. Moreover, as we might guess, Bandura considers modeling an important factor encouraging people to behave aggressively. On the controversial question of whether violence on television tends to increase violence in real life, he is strongly on the "yes, it does" side. If we want less aggression, we should show fewer aggressive models, particularly fewer successfully aggressive ones, and more models who achieve their goals effectively in nonaggressive ways.

The other topic is what Bandura refers to as *self-efficacy*—a person's sense of his or her ability to deal effectively with the environment (Bandura 1982). An application in which Bandura has been particularly interested is the treatment of phobias. Whereas many psychologists, including Dollard and Miller as well as Mowrer, focus on reducing the person's fear of the phobic object, Bandura focuses on increasing the person's self-efficacy with regard to it. In other words, the key question is not how afraid the person is but how able she feels to deal with the fear and with the object—her self-efficacy. Bandura has shown that after a phobic has gone through training designed to reduce her fear of snakes, for example, her judgment of how close she will be able to approach a different species of snake is a better predictor of how close she actually will come than is a measure of fear based on her behavior during therapy (Bandura, Adams, & Beyer 1977).

Another application of self-efficacy is to social activism. Among people who are unhappy with the status quo, which ones will take action to try to change it? Bandura cites evidence (for once not from his own research!) showing that it is the people with higher self-efficacy who are most likely to take such action. Presumably they are the ones who believe that their own actions are likely to make a difference, and who therefore are willing to make the necessary effort and sacrifice, whereas those with low self-efficacy feel that the chances of success are not enough to be worth it.

Assuming that we want to increase someone's self-efficacy, how might we go about it? As we might easily guess, an approach that Bandura particularly recommends is modeling, and he has obtained a good deal of evidence as to what kinds work best. Suppose, for example, that a coach tried to increase a snake-phobic's willingness to approach and handle a snake by showing someone else doing so. We might at first guess that this would work best if the model handled the snake fearlessly. Actually, however, it works better if the model at first shows fear of the snake but gradually overcomes that fear and begins to handle the snake (Meichenbaum 1971). This is, of course, what we would expect if we think of the modeling, not as reducing fear of the snake, but as increasing the person's sense of efficacy in dealing with it.

Bandura has been a prolific writer on a number of topics, and his approach has become quite widely known under the title of *social learning theory.* Under that name, it occupied an intermediate position between cognitive positions like those of Tolman and Bolles on the one hand and connectionist positions like those of Miller and Dollard and Skinner on the other. Recently, however, it has become more fully cognitive, as noted above, and been renamed *social cognitive theory.* Though it is still not quite as cognitive as, for example, Piaget's, it still represents a long move in a cognitive direction from its connectionist beginnings.

Mowrer's move in a cognitive direction began with the study of avoidance learning, and Bandura's with the study of imitation. A third starting point for such a move has been the psychology of education and training. We have already seen Skinner's views on that subject. In the next section we see how someone starting with similar views to Skinner's has come to develop a rather different, more cognitive view.

THE HIERARCHICAL STRUCTURE OF LEARNING

The use of programmed instruction began as an attempt to apply such Skinnerian principles as immediate reinforcement and the gradual shaping of the responses to complex verbal situations in education. However, as more programs were written and the more and less successful ones compared, it became evident that there is a lot more to programming than eliciting and reinforcing responses. Programs need to be constructed in ways that clarify the logical structure of the material. What needs to be learned are not merely particular responses, but a structure of principles from which particular responses can be derived. Programs are successful to the extent that they are organized so as to clarify this structure for the learner.

The importance of the structure of material applies not only to the writing of teaching-machine programs but also to such related topics as industrial and military training. One psychologist who has been particularly impressed by this aspect of practical training is Robert M. Gagné (b. 1916), currently of Florida State University. How, Gagné (1962*b*) asks, can we most usefully apply psychological principles to training people on such tasks as radar operation, aerial gunnery, and troubleshooting in complex electronic systems? The sorts of suggestions that a typical learning theorist might come up with, such as providing immediate reinforcement or making the crucial stimuli more distinctive from one another, turn out not to be as useful as an optimistic psychologist might hope. Some are simply not applicable to a given learning task, and those that are, all too often make relatively little difference in rate of learning. What does help is an analysis

...sk into its component parts. The psychologist needs to ask the ...ving kinds of questions: "What items of knowledge and skill must a ...rson have in order to do this job?" "How do these items of knowledge and skill depend on one another in such a way that certain ones should be learned before others?" "Into what more basic components can these items be analyzed, and how are they in turn organized?" The answers to these questions tell the psychologist what needs to be taught, in what order, and to some extent how.

When one analyzes a complex task into its components in this way, one finds a hierarchical structure. The final task can be broken down into various component items of knowledge or skill, each of which can then be broken down into subcomponents, and so forth. Gagné (1962a) provides a further analysis of this hierarchical structure in an educational setting, where the focus is on knowledge rather than on manual skills or mechanical operations. Suppose we ask what knowledge a person must already have in order to perform a certain task, given only instructions. The answer will be mastery of some other tasks that are simpler and more general. For example, one can tell an algebra student that the way to solve two simultaneous linear equations is to use one equation to get a value for one of the unknowns and then substitute that value in the other equation. To act on this instruction, the student must know both how to solve a single linear equation and how to substitute one value for another in an equation. If the learner does not have these two items of knowledge at his disposal, he will not achieve the final performance of solving the simultaneous equations, even if the instructions are clear and he attends carefully. If he does have both items of knowledge available, he will quite possibly be able to act on the instructions and carry out the task, but he may not; the instructions could be inadequate to bridge the gap between the components and the final task. Each of the two components, in turn, depends on others. Solving a single equation, for example, depends on knowing that a term can be moved from one side of the equation to another with a change of sign, that both sides can be multiplied by the same factor, and so forth. These component items of knowledge are necessary, but not always sufficient, to solve a single linear equation. Thus the final performance is at the apex of a pyramid of component items of knowledge.

Given such a hierarchical arrangement of knowledge, in which a performance can be achieved only by those who have already mastered its components, it is clear why Gagné considers task analysis the key to effective teaching. To teach any task, one must at a minimum ensure that all the necessary components are learned, which may in turn require teaching *their* components. When the components are mastered, simple instructions may be enough to obtain the final performance. Often, however, simple instructions are not enough; some more complex presentation may be needed to bridge the gap, to get the components put together in the proper way. Such a presentation should make clear what performance is required, focus attention on the necessary components, identify crucial stimuli, and otherwise point the learner in the right direction. These are what a good teaching program does, in addition to simply providing information, as it moves the learner up the hierarchy to higher and higher levels of knowledge.

Gagné's views have implications beyond either schooling or applied training: they indicate the way in which our whole structure of knowledge and skills is gradually built up throughout life. Early in life, simple items are acquired, such as the skill to grasp an object in the hand and the knowledge that objects still exist even when they are out of sight. Such items form the components for the next higher level, such as knowledge about the ways in which various objects can or cannot be changed, or skills in performing such manipulations of objects. The learning of spoken language, and afterward of written language, mathematics, and other symbolic systems, makes possible many additional levels of learning, so that the hierarchies of knowledge for an educated adult are extremely complex.

This analysis of cognitive development begins to sound quite a bit like Piaget's. Indeed, the idea that knowledge, skills, and understanding are arranged in hierarchies that gradually develop through life has come to be quite widely held. It is interesting that Piaget's research on children's cognitions, Gagné's work on education and training, and the application of ideas about computers, along with other current approaches, have all converged on this idea about cognitive organization. The idea of hierarchies is not inherently a cognitive idea, for connectionists likewise assume that simple habits get organized into complex skills, but the idea is currently more associated with cognitive thinking. Whether connectionist, cognitive, or a mixture of both, the idea of hierarchical organization is important in the study of learning, thinking, and human development.

Chapter
12

Mathematical Analysis of Learning

As theories of learning become increasingly formal and attempt to make more exact quantitative statements about behavior, they increasingly tend to adopt language and concepts from mathematics and from more precise branches of science and technology. We have seen examples of this tendency in Lewin's topological life space, in Tolman's vectors, and particularly in Hull's equations. Some theorists have gone still further in making mathematical analyses central to their theories. Such theories have become increasingly prominent in the past 40 years, reflecting the increasing use in modern society of computers, servomechanisms, and probabilistic interpretations of events.

Beginning about 1950, there was a burst of interest in a statistical approach to learning. This approach assumes that the processes in learning are not entirely predictable, but vary randomly in certain ways that can be described statistically. Just as actuaries cannot predict who will marry or die this year, but can predict within a small margin of error how many marriages or deaths there will be, so statistical learning theorists do not claim to predict what a given learner will do on a given trial, but do claim to predict the average behavior of one individual over many trials or of many individuals on a single trial. Whereas Hull worked out a system for making exact predictions and then added the factor of oscillation to show the inevitable random component in behavior, the statistical theorists make this randomness the basis of their systems. One might satirize the difference in approach by saying that Hull started with perfect order and eventually had to make a concession to chaos, while the statistical theorists start with chaos and proceed to find order in it!

ESTES' STIMULUS-SAMPLING MODEL

Since the several statistical models that appeared in the early 1950s had a lot in common, we will look only at the one developed by William K. Estes (b. 1919), who began his career as a statistical learning theorist at the University of Indiana, pursued it for some years at Stanford and at Rockefeller University, and is now at Harvard. His original system and a number of elaborations are presented in Estes (1959).

Estes studied with Skinner during the period that Skinner was at the University of Minnesota, and he received his Ph.D. in psychology there in 1943. His work with Skinner on the effects of punishment was an important contribution to Skinner's thinking on that topic. However, his interest in building mathematical models of learning is of course a departure from Skinner's antitheoretical bias. Moreover, the assumptions in Estes' theory seem to show the influence of Guthrie, with whom he did not study, more than of Skinner.

Estes' system may be spoken of as a *model* of learning because, at least at the beginning, it made no attempt to be a complete, all-encompassing theory. In this respect it is more modest than the systems of Guthrie, Skinner, and Hull, and perhaps reflects some of the same concern about boundary conditions that Spence expresses. Rather, the model is a very simplified statement of assumptions from which a few aspects of learning can be predicted with (one hopes) a good deal of accuracy. It is a model in the same sense as a three-dimensional model of an atom, with wooden balls for electrons, protons, and neutrons. No one claims that such a classroom model is a complete and accurate representation of an atom; we know very well that electrons are different from wooden balls and that their orbits are not much like pieces of wire. Nevertheless, there are certain respects in which the model and the real atom are alike. Given these similarities, the model enables us to predict certain things about the way the atom itself will behave. To the extent that a model enables us to predict some aspect of reality, it is useful. We need not argue whether or not the model is true, since at best it is never more than a partial representation. This is much the same logic of theory construction that Hull used, but Estes carried it further, beginning with a simple model and expanding it gradually at the same time that he was testing its usefulness.

One way to look at Estes' model is as an attempt to make certain ideas of Guthrie's more precise, to turn a part of Guthrie's broad, practically oriented theory into a model appropriate for laboratory study. Remember that Guthrie regarded the learning of a skill as the conditioning of a great many particular stimulus-response connections. Estes simplified this suggestion by grouping all possible responses into two categories: those that produce a given outcome and those that do not. Thus, in Guthrie's terms, he is concerned with acts rather than movements, or, in Tolman's terms, with molar behavior. Estes would record, for example, only whether a basketball player successfully shoots a basket or not, without regard to the innumerable muscle contractions that go to make up either outcome. Similarly, a circus dog either jumps through the hoop or does not, regardless of whether a jump is graceful or clumsy and regardless of whether a nonjump involves jumping and missing, sitting quietly, or running away. In this way Guthrie's concern with what the learner does is changed into a concern with what the learner accomplishes, with the successful and unsuccessful outcomes of the behavior. (Note, however, that success is defined by the observer, not necessarily by any purpose of the learner's.) Since these two classes of responses (or, strictly speaking, of response outcomes) constitute the two possible acts, Estes calls them A1 and A2.

Stimulus Elements

Having simplified the matter of responses, Estes is prepared to face the complexity of stimuli. He regards any stimulus situation as made up of many small stimulus elements. In principle, such an assumption is clearly realistic. At any given moment we are being bombarded by a great number and variety of stimuli. As we read a book, we may be stimulated by the words on the page, the pressure of the book on our hands, the furniture around us, and the sound of a passing car, to give only a very incomplete list. Together these make up the stimulus complex that influences our behavior. However, if we try to analyze this complex into specific components, we immediately find ourselves in difficulty. Is the pressure of the book on our hands a single element, or is it 10 elements for our 10 fingers? If the temperature and the texture of the book's cover enter into the sensation, are these additional elements? It is a good example of Estes' model building that he does not concern himself with this question. If it is reasonable to suppose that there are such stimulus elements, Estes does not care just what the elements are, or how many there are, or how we decide where one element ends and another begins. He wants to know whether learning acts as if it is under the influence of such elements, not whether such elements "really" exist in the sense of being separately identifiable.

Another problem about this analysis of stimulus complexes into elements is that it implies that these elements operate separately, that there are no effects of patterns, or gestalts. Since we do not know what the elements are, it is hard to judge just how unrealistic this assumption is, but it certainly seems likely that there must be patterning effects of some sort. Estes eventually dealt with this issue, but his original model used the assumption that there are no patterning effects, that each element operates independently of the others. Again the question is not whether this assumption is true but whether it is useful. To answer this question, we must wait until we see the predictions Estes has been able to make from a model that included this assumption.

So far Estes has divided all the possible responses in a given situation into two classes, and he has divided all the possible aspects of the stimulus situation into an unspecified large number of elements. He now further assumes that each element is conditioned to one or the other of the two response classes. In other words, each stimulus element tends to evoke either A1 or A2. An element cannot be conditioned at the same time to *both* A1 and A2, nor can it ever be conditioned to *neither*. (If it seems unreasonable that all elements must be conditioned to one or the other of these response classes, keep in mind that all possible responses are included in one or the other class.) Accordingly, at any given moment, all elements can be classified as either conditioned to A1 or conditioned to A2.

As used in this connection, *conditioned* does not mean that there has necessarily been prior learning. It might be clearer just to say that every element is "attached" to one or the other response class, so that that stimulus element tends to produce that response. However, these connections are subject to change, with stimulus elements which were formerly attached to A1 becoming attached to A2, or vice versa. In fact, for Estes such changes are what is meant by learning. These changes are a process of conditioning, and hence Estes speaks of an element as being conditioned to a response when it tends to elicit that response.

Stimulus Sampling and Conditioning

To understand how the conditioning process operates in Estes' model, we must first look at the process of *stimulus sampling*. Estes assumes that only a small number of the stimulus elements in a given situation actually influence the response on any given trial. Estes refers to all of the stimulus elements in a given situation, taken collectively, as S. At any particular moment, only a small fraction of the elements in S are actually effective in determining the response. Which elements will they be? Estes assumes that the individual samples elements randomly from S. We need not assume that this sampling process is conscious and deliberate, as though the individual were window shopping before an array of stimuli. The sampling may be explained by momentary changes either in the environment or in the individual's attention. Again, however, it is important to note that Estes does not try to explain just how this sampling occurs. He assumes that it does occur, and whether it is a good or a bad assumption depends on whether it leads to valid predictions.

Each element has a certain probability of being sampled on a given trial. It is mathematically simpler to assume that all elements have the same probability of being sampled. Since the whole concept of stimulus elements is hypothetical anyway, there should be no objection to assuming that these probabilities are equal. Moreover, Estes has demonstrated that, at least for certain purposes, it makes very little difference whether or not this assumption is made. He therefore assigns the Greek letter θ (theta) to represent the probability that any given element will be sampled on any given trial. Put another way, θ represents the proportion of all the elements in S that are sampled on any one trial.

On successive trials, different groups of elements are sampled. This sampling is random, so that each element has the same chance of being sampled on each trial. Whether or not an element was sampled last time has no effect on its chance of being sampled this time. Moreover, whether or not any one element is sampled this time has no effect on any other element's chances this time. Hence the degree of overlap among successive samples is determined solely by chance. This assumption, like so many others in Estes' model, may seem unrealistic if we think of stimulus elements as particular, identifiable sources of sensations. The important question, however, is whether Estes can use these simplified assumptions to make correct predictions about learning.

Let us consider two successive trials. For the sake of simplicity, let us say that in this situation θ is equal to .1. This means that one-tenth of the elements in S are sampled on each trial. Since the sampling is random, we can find the proportion of elements sampled on both trials by multiplying .1 times .1 to obtain .01. This means that one-hundredth of the elements in S are sampled on both trials. How many are not sampled on either trial? Since .9 of the elements (1 minus .1) are not sampled on the first trial, and .9 are not sampled on the second, we find the number not sampled on either trial by taking .9 times .9, which gives .81. By subtracting .81 from 1.0, we find that .19 of the elements *were* sampled on at least one of the two trials.

The stimulus elements sampled on a given trial are the ones that determine which response, A1 or A2, will occur on that trial. But if some elements are attached to A1 and others to A2, which of these two responses will occur? The answer to this question shows why this is called a statistical learning theory. Estes does not tell us definitely which response will occur; instead he gives the answer in the form of a probability statement. The probability of A1, abbreviated as p, is equal to the proportion of the elements in the sample that are attached to A1. Thus if 60 percent of the elements that are sampled on a given trial are attached to A1 and the other 40 percent to A2, there are 60 chances in 100 that A1 will occur on that trial and 40 chances that A2 will occur. Since the sample is drawn randomly from S, we could just as well say that the probability of A1 occurring on that trial is equal to the proportion of all the elements in S that are attached to A1.

Since the prediction of which response will occur is in the form of a probability, we can never say for sure which response will occur (unless the probability of A1 is either 1.00 or 0). This uncertainty of prediction may seem like a considerable weakness. However, Estes is really only saying, a bit more bluntly, what the other theorists we have considered also said. Guthrie said that the combination of stimuli would "tend" to be followed by the movement. Skinner discussed the factors controlling rate of emission of an operant, but he never tried to predict exactly what that rate would be. Hull, as we have noted, accomplished the same thing by including the concept of oscillation. Thus predictions from Estes' theory are no less definite than those from other theories. He has, however, put the whole theory in terms of probabilities: the probability that an element will be sampled and the probability that a given response will occur. (These probabilities can in principle be converted into speeds if desired.) Since probabilities are analyzed by statistical techniques, Estes' theory is called a statistical theory.

In his original formulation, Estes assumed that learning takes place by the principle of contiguity. This relation means, in his formulation, that whenever a response occurs, all the stimulus elements sampled on that trial become conditioned to that response. Nothing is said about reinforcement as such. This formulation is particularly well suited to classical conditioning. Consider a case of eyelid conditioning. We will call an eye-blink response A1 and the absence of a blink A2, so that on every trial either A1 or A2 but not both will occur. On the training trials the blink always occurs, since the unconditioned stimulus is always presented. As a result, all the stimulus elements sampled on a given trial become conditioned on that trial to A1 (the response of blinking). On successive trials, additional elements are sampled and become conditioned to A1, so that the proportion of the elements in S that are conditioned to A1 keeps increasing. Whenever an element is conditioned to A1, it is of course also unconditioned to (or "disconnected from") A2. Thus conditioning is a process of transferring elements from being conditioned to A2 to being conditioned to A1. As this process goes on, the probability of a *conditioned* eye-blink response (A1) increases. The unconditioned blink occurs on every trial, since it is elicited by the unconditioned stimulus, but the conditioned blink may or may not occur, its probability depending on the proportion of elements conditioned to A1.

Learning Curves

With all this background of assumptions, we are finally ready to look at the predictions that follow from them. First, what of the shape of the learning curve? Suppose we take the situation in which, at the beginning of learning, all the elements in S are conditioned to A2, so that the probability of a conditioned A1 response is zero. This case would be very near that in eyelid conditioning, where the chance that the subject will make a response to the conditioned stimulus before conditioning has begun is quite small. In this state all the elements sampled on the first trial will already be attached to A2 (not responding). However, on this trial they will become conditioned to A1. On the next trial another sample will be drawn. Most of the elements in this new sample will still be attached to A2, but a few will now be attached to A1 because they will have been sampled, and hence conditioned to A1, on the previous trial. Only those that are attached to A2 can become conditioned to A1, since the rest already are attached to A1. Thus fewer elements will be transferred from A2 to A1 on the second trial than on the first. (Remember that the total number of elements sampled is the same on all trials.) On the third trial still more of the elements that are sampled will already have been conditioned to A1, so that even fewer will be transferred from A2 to A1. Learning will continue in this fashion, with fewer elements being transferred from A2 to A1 on each successive trial, until all the elements in S are conditioned to A1. At that point, no further learning can take place.

If we know the value of θ, we can make predictions about the proportion of elements in S that will be conditioned to A1 at the end of each trial. Let us return to the previous discussion of sampling in which we assumed for convenience that θ was equal to .1. At the end of the first trial, .1 of the elements in S had been sampled once. As a result, .1 of the elements were then attached to A1. After two trials, .19 of the elements had been sampled at least once, so that .19 of the elements were then conditioned to A1. The increase in the proportion of elements conditioned to A1 was .1 as a result of the first trial and .09 as a result of the second. In both cases, this increase was .1 of the elements still conditioned to A2. In other words, on each trial, 10 percent of the elements still conditioned to A2 were transferred to A1. This value, .1, is the value of θ. If we continued these calculations further, we would see that this ratio fits a general principle: On each trial the proportion of elements transferred from A2 to A1 is equal to θ times the proportion still conditioned to A2. However, since

Figure 12.1 *The first part of a learning curve as analyzed by Estes.* The vertical steps represent the conditioning that takes place on each trial, as illustrated in detail for trial 2. The smooth dashed curve connecting the values of p for each trial would eventually reach 1.0.

fewer and fewer are still conditioned to A2 on each trial, the actual number of elements transferred from A2 to A1 is less than on the previous trial. This process is illustrated in Figure 12.1.

This formulation has resemblances to both Guthrie's and Hull's discussions of the learning curve. Guthrie assumed that conditioning of a movement to a stimulus occurs on one trial, but that conditioning of an act requires many trials because it is made up of many stimulus-movement connections. Similarly, Estes assumes that an element is conditioned to A1 on one trial, but that the change in probability of A1 is gradual because there are so many elements to be conditioned. Thus in this respect Estes has taken an idea very much like Guthrie's and changed it from a loose verbal interpretation to a precise mathematical one. The mathematical description of the learning curve then turns out to be identical with Hull's. The advantage of Estes' formulation over Hull's is that instead of simply postulating that the curve should have this shape, he has derived this curve as a prediction from the more basic assumption (postulate) of sampling. He has, in a sense, out-Hulled Hull.

ELABORATIONS OF THE MODEL

Once a reader has grasped the fundamental assumptions of Estes' system, he can exercise his ingenuity by trying to predict how Estes will deal with various phenomena of learning. The phenomenon of generalization poses no problem. If a response has been learned to one set of stimuli, generalization is indicated by the occurrence of that same response when another, similar set of stimuli is presented. For Estes, a "similar set of stimuli" is one which has a number of the same stimulus elements as the original training set. If all of the elements in the first set are conditioned to A1, and if half of the elements in the second set are also in the first set, then at least half of the elements in the second set are conditioned to A1. The probability of an A1 response to the second stimulus set cannot then be less than .50.

Discrimination is more of a problem. If two stimulus sets have a number of elements in common, how can an individual learn consistently to give response A1 to one of these sets and response A2 to the other? For such perfect discrimination to be established, it would be necessary for all the elements in one set to be conditioned to A1 and all those in the other set to be conditioned to A2. Such a situation is impossible, however, since some of the same elements are in both sets. To deal with discrimination, we must assume either that the individual learns not to pay attention to those stimuli that are in both sets or that she responds to patterns of stimuli rather than simply to total numbers of elements. Either of those solutions gives a more cognitive flavor to an otherwise connectionist theory. It is probably not coincidence that Estes himself, since developing this theory, has gone into other, somewhat more cognitive lines of theorizing (Estes 1976).

Drive, however, should be an easy topic to predict within the framework of stimulus-sampling theory. For Estes, as for Guthrie and for Dollard and Miller, drive is a stimulus (or, more precisely, a set of stimulus elements). Estes' principal contribution in this regard has been to argue that Hull's intervening variable D is unnecessary. Hull used D to refer to the general energizing function of all drives. In an ingenious mathematical example, Estes showed how what appears to be an overall energizing effect of drive could be explained as simply a matter of the number of drive stimulus elements conditioned to different responses. This revision does not necessarily mean that drives do not have an energizing function, since Estes' example is hypothetical, but it throws the burden of the argument on Hull's supporters.

Extinction, for Estes, is simply another example of conditioning. If in acquisition stimulus elements are conditioned to response class A1, then in extinction they are reconditioned to A2. The laws of learning are exactly the same in acquisition and extinction. This interpretation is essentially the same as Guthrie's. Guthrie says that extinction is learning to do something else, which raises the question "What else?" Estes can dodge this question because, by definition, any response that is not A1 is A2. In extinction, A1 is being replaced by something else, but Estes considers only the rate at which that replacement goes on, not the details of what the "something else" looks like.

Forgetting and Spontaneous Recovery

Spontaneous recovery is a bit more of a challenge, but again Estes deals with it in a typically Guthrian fashion. To do so, he has to consider a larger category of stimulus elements than before. He assumes that S, the set of stimulus elements from which a learner samples in a given learning situation, is only a subset of all the elements that are sometimes available for sampling in that situation. In other words, if we consider all the stimulus elements that might be available for sampling in a certain learning situation, only some of them will actually be available for sampling on any given occasion. This seems like a quite plausible assumption. There are many characteristics of learners, teachers, and other aspects of a learning situation that vary from one occasion to another. If the learner is more tired or more distracted on one occasion than on another, for example, this difference could be expected to affect what stimulus elements were available for sampling on the two occasions. We can therefore divide all the stimulus elements that might be available during this learning into two categories: S (those available on a given occasion) and S' (those not available on this particular occasion but potentially available on others). On any two occasions, some elements will be in S on both occasions, some in S the first time and in S' the second, some in S' the first time and in S the second, and some in S' on both. This assumption makes it possible to predict not only spontaneous recovery but also various other phenomena of learning.

Consider a learning situation in which originally all stimulus elements

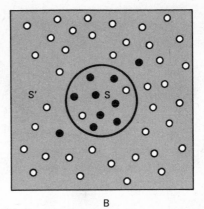

A   B

Figure 12.2 *An analysis of forgetting in Estes' system*. Black circles represent elements conditioned to A1, open circles those conditioned to A2. In part A, all the elements in S have been conditioned to A1. In part B, a day later, 20 percent of these elements have drifted out of S into S' and have been replaced by elements still conditioned to A2. As a result, only 80 percent of the elements in S are now conditioned to A1. The probability of an A1 response has therefore dropped from 1.00 to .80 during the elapsed time.

are conditioned to A1 (see Figure 12.2, part A). In the course of conditioning, all the elements in S are sampled at some time and become conditioned to A1. The next day the individual is tested for retention. By then, 20 percent of the elements in S have moved into S' (i.e., are no longer available for sampling) and have been replaced by elements that were formerly in S' (Figure 12.2, part B). Since all of these new elements in S are still conditioned to A2, 20 percent of the elements now in S are conditioned to A2. As a result, the probability of an A1 response drops from 1.00 at the end of the first day's training to .80 at the beginning of the session on the second day. This drop would ordinarily be described as 20 percent forgetting. The more different the conditions are on the second day than on the first, the more elements will leave S between the two days and the greater will be the amount of forgetting.

In this context, spontaneous recovery may be regarded simply as the forgetting of extinction. Suppose that over a series of days acquisition training is carried out until all the elements in both S and S' (i.e., all the potentially available elements) are conditioned to A1. Unless there was additional training involving some of the same elements, forgetting would thereafter be impossible. Suppose now that extinction is carried out for one day until all elements in S are conditioned to A2. If 20 percent of elements in S move into S' before the next test and are replaced, S will then consist of 80 percent elements conditioned to A2 and 20 percent conditioned to A1. This means that 20 percent of the response strength before extinction will have recovered spontaneously. A whole series of extinctions on successive days would be necessary in order to prevent any further spontaneous recovery.

This formulation of spontaneous recovery and forgetting emphasizes the importance of practice over a series of occasions. It takes not merely a lot of practice, but practice spaced in time to give maximum possible learning. Herein rests one of the difficulties with cramming and with very concentrated courses. Estes' theory, like Guthrie's, thus supports the view held by many educators that learning is most effective when there is time enough to spread out the process. Reviewing learned material every now and then, or taking a series of courses in which each begins with a review of the previous one, is a procedure that fits well with this interpretation of learning.

Reinforcement

What does Estes have to say about reinforcement? Relative to many other theorists, very little. As far as he is concerned, a reinforcer is simply any event that determines to which response class the stimulus elements that are sampled will get conditioned. What other properties a reinforcer may have, such as perhaps being a reduction in drive, do not interest him. He is, then, somewhat like Skinner in the way he interprets reinforcement, but he puts less emphasis on the importance of the topic than does Skinner, thus increasing his resemblance to Guthrie.

Estes' treatment of reinforcement also resembles Skinner's in another respect: both are greatly interested in intermittent reinforcement. What happens, asks Estes, if some of the trials in a series end with reinforcement (thus conditioning all the elements sampled on that trial to A1) and other trials end with nonreinforcement (conditioning all the sampled elements to A2)? A favorite learning situation for answering this question is the *light-guessing experiment.* Here A1 and A2 are defined not as making or not making a given response but as making one of two possible guesses. The learner is seated in front of a board with two light bulbs on it. On each trial he is instructed to guess which of the two lights will be turned on. After he guesses, one and only one of the lights does go on, and which one it is does not depend on his guess. The two possible guesses are response classes A1 and A2, and the two possible *events* (the left and the right light going on) are called E1 and E2. Thus E1 reinforces A1 and E2 reinforces A2. However, Estes assumes that E1 conditions all the sampled elements to A1 and E2 conditions all the sampled elements to A2, regardless of which response occurs on that trial. In other words, the left light going on reinforces the response of guessing "left," even if the guess the learner made was "right." This assumption that a response which does not occur on a given trial can nevertheless be reinforced on that trial is a departure from the usual assumptions of connectionist reinforcement theories.

If E1 always occurs in this situation, the individual gradually learns to make A1 consistently. (He also rapidly becomes bored with the experiment.) What if E1 occurs 75 percent of the time and E2 occurs 25 percent of the time, in a random order so that the learner can never be sure which light will go on on any given trial? What usually happens is that the learner comes to make A1 75 percent of the time and A2 25 percent of the time. Any reader who is ambitious enough to work through the mathematics can confirm that this is just what Estes' model predicts. (To do so, the reader will have to decide what percentage of the sampled elements will be conditioned to A1 by E1, or to A2 by E2, when the probability of A1 is greater than, equal to, and less than .75. It will take a little thinking, but it's a good opportunity to obtain an insight experience while studying a connectionist theory!)

This finding, so satisfying to Estes, has disconcerted many other theorists because of its apparent irrationality. If the learner wants to guess correctly as often as possible, the best strategy is to guess the more frequent event all the time. (If this isn't obvious, try calculating the percentage of correct and incorrect guesses for each strategy.) A cognitive theorist might expect an individual to follow such a rational strategy, since it would be the best possible insightful solution to the problem. Instead, however, subjects follow the "irrational" behavior that is predicted by Estes' conditioning model. Why? Many experiments have been done and many words written in an attempt to explain this behavior to other people's satisfaction. In the process, some situations have arisen in which learners do adopt the rational solution, but they are not typical. Estes, however, can take pride in having correctly predicted an unexpected finding.

How does Estes' approach compare with those of other theorists we have considered? Since he was a student of Skinner's, we might expect him most to resemble Skinner, but if so we would be mistaken. Such an abstract theory as we have described for Estes is far from Skinner's style. Skinner's comment on Estes was that he caught a bad case of "theoryitis" from which he never recovered, and as a result an excellent experimenter was lost to psychology. (Estes could fairly reply to this teasing, however, by some teasing of his own, pointing out that Skinner's book on verbal behavior had far more ideas than data, as much so as Estes' theory.)

The details of Estes' model sound most like Guthrie's; indeed, one could almost say that what Estes has done is to turn Guthrie's loose, nonmathematical theory into a more precise mathematical one. However, the whole idea of developing such an elaborate deductive theory is most like Hull's. An admirer of Estes might say that he used Hull's general method more effectively than Hull and also used Guthrie's general ideas about learning more effectively than Guthrie, while still demonstrating his individuality by *not* following in the footsteps of his own mentor, Skinner. Others might not be quite as flattering, but it would be hard to deny the impressiveness of Estes' theoretical edifice.

Though his stimulus-sampling model might seem like enough of an accomplishment for one theorist, Estes went on to develop other models with somewhat different assumptions—similar to the original one in some respects, but different in others. Such an approach is consistent with Spence's ideas about the boundary conditions of theories. A theoretical model that is appropriate for one situation may not be appropriate for another, and having different models for different situations makes possible the most accurate prediction for each.

The attitude reflected in having different models for different situations is somewhat atypical of most theorists. However willing various theorists might be to try to improve their theories to fit the data better, they have generally assumed that their particular theories were the best. They might realize that the theories worked better for some situations than for others, but they were not prepared to recognize any other theories as better. The logic of theoretical models, however, is to see what predictions follow from certain assumptions and then to see how well those predictions fit the data in a given situation. Models are judged not so much as true or false in general but as more or less useful in making accurate predictions of certain events for certain purposes.

Estes is only one among a number of theorists who have developed mathematical models, some quite broad, others very specific to a given set of data. Some are really only equations that predict what the learning curve should look like under various sets of conditions. Others, like Estes', are models in a more physical sense, like the physicist's model of an atom. Some are designed for specific situations; others try to be more general. Some are based on connectionist assumptions, others on cognitive models. However, as they generally make difficult reading, we will settle for having looked at only one of them.

The value of mathematical theories for the general student of learning is not so much in what they reveal about the process of learning as in the method they provide for studying learning. Theorists who present their ideas only in words can argue a long time about their theories, partly because it is not clear what each predicts in a given situation. When a theory is stated mathematically, it is easier to be sure what it predicts, and therefore also easier to test whether it is correct as applied to a given situation. It is for this reason that theories stated in mathematical form, however different they may be in other respects, have become increasingly important both for psychology in general and for the study of learning in particular.

Chapter
13

Cognition and
the Computer

*A*s we have noted, connectionist models were dominant during most of the history of American learning theory, and only recently have cognitive models become preferred by a large proportion of psychologists. Since most people attribute much of their own behavior and at least some of other people's behavior to knowledge, beliefs, and ideas, why did psychologists for so long avoid that type of analysis? Many factors may have contributed to this, but probably the most significant was the desire to treat human as well as animal behavior as part of the natural world of science. Connectionist intervening variables seemed appropriate to that purpose, since they were consistent with a nervous system in which physical input led fairly directly to measurable responses. Cognitive intervening variables, on the other hand, impressed many psychologists as mentalistic, as belonging to a realm of mind or spirit rather than to the physical and biological realm of natural science. Much as Tolman tried to convince the world that this was not the case, that cognitive intervening variables could be as well integrated into the physical world as could connectionist ones, most psychologists of learning were unconvinced, and connectionist theories remained dominant.

What happened to change this situation? Why were psychologists more willing to listen to Bolles in the 1970s than to Tolman in the 1930s or 1940s? Part of the reason was the development of biological theories. As biologists and psychologists became increasingly aware of the complexities of the nervous system, it became less and less clear that the central nervous system operates according to connectionist principles. As a result, cognitive principles came to seem increasingly acceptable. Even more important, however, was another development, one which made cognitive activity not only part of the scientific world but of technology as well. This development was the rise to prominence of computers in science, in business, and eventually throughout society.

WHAT COMPUTERS CAN DO

The phenomenal rise in the use of computers in the past third of a century has had several effects on psychology. Computers are used to analyze data, to generate stimuli for experimental subjects, to present instructional programs, and to perform various other tasks. For theorists, a particularly interesting application has been the attempt to draw an analogy between the operation of computers and the operation of the human intellect. Computers carry on various processes that bear marked resemblances to human learning, remembering, and thinking. Can the way that computers carry on these processes tell us anything about how humans do so?

Robots

In these days of computerized games it may be appropriate to begin with a relatively simple connectionist "toy," not even using a computer. A small machine can be built, far less complicated than a computer, that will behave like a real organism in that it moves around, seeks certain goals, avoids others, and demonstrates simple forms of learning. Walter (1953) produced such a machine a number of years ago and named it (imitating biological taxonomy) *Machina docilis* (the teachable machine). This little machine would ride around on its wheels, approaching lights of moderate intensity and moving away from very bright lights. It could be conditioned to approach a whistle that was paired with the turning on of a "reinforcing" light, and this conditioning was subject to both extinction and forgetting. It would avoid obstacles, show "fear" of a stimulus that had been paired with a kick, and behave ambivalently toward other members of its "species." In the days before computers became widespread, when the behavior of machines was widely regarded as something completely different from the behavior of living organisms, such a machine constituted quite a striking demonstration. Even after looking at its wiring diagram, one tended to feel that there was something magical about a "mere machine" behaving in so lifelike a fashion. Now, when computers have taken over many business operations and computerized robots are a stock-in-trade of movies and television, some of the magic has gone out of such a demonstration, but it has still not completely lost its power to beguile us.

As computers have become smaller, it has become increasingly practical to build robots with on-board computers, so that more recent robots have far more "intellectual power" than *M. docilis.* One example, created in the late 1960s, was named Shakey. Whereas *M. docilis* was designed to resemble an animal, Shakey was designed to resemble a human manual laborer. Its (or should we say his?) principal job was moving and stacking boxes. Though this might be considered "mindless labor" for a human, it requires quite sophisticated behavior from a machine. Shakey had to perceive the environment well enough to locate boxes, avoid obstacles, and know in which of eight rooms it (he) was located at any given time. Shakey had to be able to pick up a box, carry it into another room, and put it on another box stably enough so that the stack would not fall over. Given such a moving job to do, it had to figure out just what sequence of moves would accomplish the task. Moreover, it could remember such a plan and use it again later in another context.

Knowing what complex operations computers can perform, we might think such simple manual labor would be trivial for a computerized robot. Why didn't Shakey do something more impressive? Actually, however, computers are best at calculating and at making logical decisions (activities that many humans find difficult). Computers have difficulty, on the other hand, doing things that are simple for most humans, such as recognizing patterns in a visual display and making well-coordinated movements in a variable environment. In other words, when the input and the output are simple, computers can do impressive jobs of processing the information in between, but both getting the information and controlling the output are difficult. Shakey's abilities thus represent more of an achievement than we might at first think.

One example of such limitations of computerized robots is their form of locomotion. Like *M. docilis,* Shakey rode on wheels. Given the number of stair steps in most human environments, walking on legs would have made these robots more adaptable. However, walking is a complex operation that, however natural for humans, is a major problem for robots, even with the power of computers. The robots of fantasy, striding skillfully on insectlike legs, will probably come to pass, but for the time being robots do much better on wheels. Whereas people joke about "reinventing the wheel," robots need to reinvent legs!

Computer Problem Solving

For the most part, computer analogs have been of more complex, cognitive processes. They typically involve problem solving, game playing, language comprehension, and the like—not so much models of learning per se as of those behaviors that in humans are the results of learning. A number of them are discussed in Feigenbaum and Feldman (1963) and in Schank and Colby (1973). One impressive model is the Logic Theorist developed by Newell, Shaw, and Simon. This is a computer program whose function is, given the postulates of geometry, to prove certain theorems. The manner in which it goes about doing so is quite comparable to what a good high school geometry student does. It works forward from theorems already proved to try to find ways of turning one of them into the theorem to be proved. It works backward from the to-be-proved theorem to other statements which, if true, would permit the proof, and then treats these statements as subgoals to be proved. Clearly, it deals with cognitive structures rather than with stimulus-response connections or even with the sorts of signals that Bolles considers. Though Logic Theorist's concern with postulates and theorems would appeal to Hull, Tolman would feel more at home with its mode of operation than most of the other theorists we have discussed, and Wertheimer would be proud of its creative problem solving!

Soon after Newell, Shaw, and Simon developed Logic Theorist, it was expanded to deal with a wider variety of problems. The result was known, appropriately, as General Problem Solver, or GPS (Ernest & Newell 1969). A problem may be regarded as any discrepancy between an actual state of affairs and a corresponding desired state of affairs, and the job of a problem solver is to reduce that discrepancy. In real life, problems vary from "I am in Chicago and want to be in New York, but a snowstorm has closed O'Hare Airport; how can I get to New York?" to "I need an A in organic chemistry to get into medical school, but at this rate I'll be lucky to get even a B; how can I raise my grade?" Though a computer program to solve such problems for us would indeed be useful, illustrations of how GPS works are generally more artificial problems. They are, however, still challenging enough to keep most people occupied (and sometimes frustrated) for at least a few minutes. Here are two examples of problems that GPS can solve:

PROBLEM 1

Present state: There are three missionaries and three cannibals on one side of a river.

Desired state: To have all six of them on the other side.

Difficulties: The only way across is by a boat that can carry only two people at a time and must always have at least one person to row it (i.e., it cannot cross the river empty). If more cannibals than missionaries are ever left together on one-side while the boat is crossing, the cannibals will eat the missionaries. (Getting missionaries across in cannibals' stomachs is not considered a solution!)

Question: What sequence of crossings with the boat will accomplish the transfer?*

PROBLEM 2

Present state: DONALD
              + GERALD
              ROBERT

---

*The boat crossed five times, each time carrying one missionary and one cannibal. The first and fourth times a missionary brings the boat back; the second and third times a cannibal. (There are numerous versions of this problem, varying in difficulty.)

Desired state: An example of correct addition in which one particular numeral corresponds to each of the letters above.

Difficulty: The codebook to tell what numeral each of the above letters represents is lost, and we know only that D = 5.

Question: What code will convert the letters into numerals to give a correct example of addition? (Simon & Newell 1971)*

A computer program that can solve problems as different from one another as logic proofs and the puzzles above is clearly quite an accomplishment, and GPS is one of several that can. Nevertheless, some people feel that problems of this sort are rather trivial. Humans have been able to analyze completely the various possible approaches to these problems and to say which will work efficiently, inefficiently, or not at all, so perhaps it is not such a wonder that computers can be programmed to find a solution. However, computers have also been programmed to work on problems that no one has been able to analyze so exhaustively. Chess playing is probably the most famous example. Though no chess-playing program has yet achieved very high ranking in the chess world, one did win the Pennsylvania State Championship in 1987 in a field that included 15 chess masters—and it is not rare for a program to beat its author.

Even though a computer can search the implications of many possible moves very quickly, it cannot win by that power alone. Fast as it is, it still cannot come anywhere near to following every possible sequence of moves through to eventual victory or defeat; there are just too many possible combinations of moves in the course of a game. The program must therefore recognize, as a human player does, which situations are promising and which are threatening and then try to create or avoid those situations. In other words, it "understands" that it is typically desirable to trade a knight for a rook or to threaten the opponent's king, but undesirable to lose one's queen or to have one's own king put in check. Each sequence of possible moves is then analyzed according to whether it leads to desirable or undesirable consequences within the next few moves.

Though human players and computer programs are alike in that they examine and evaluate various possible moves, it does not follow that they do so in just the same way. Computers, because of their great speed, can examine more total moves. They are much less efficient, however, in deciding which possible moves to explore most deeply. As a result, they tend to play rather uninspired chess (as do most human players), with little ability to formulate long-range strategy. The best human players can beat the best chess programs partly because of such long-range strategy and partly because of having gradually learned the significance of a great many specific chess positions—which are favorable, which are risky, which call

---

*The solution is as follows: 526485
197485
723970

for a particular move or series of moves. Programs might obtain such detailed knowledge about chess positions either by having it included in the original program or by being programmed to learn by experience (an approach discussed, though not specifically for chess, in Chapter 14). So far, neither approach has been very successful, so it will probably be a number of years before the world's chess champion is a computer program. These similarities and differences between human players and computer programs, and their implications for understanding both people and computers, are explored in Frey (1983).

Though these examples suggest (correctly) that computers are more effective thinkers than one would have imagined, 40 years ago, that any machine could be, they are a long way from being able to do all that humans can do. One of their conspicuous failures is translating from one language into another. Fairly early in the development of computers, it looked as though they should be ideally suited for translation. To translate Russian into English, for example, you should need only to provide the computer with a Russian-English dictionary and to program it with appropriate grammatical rules. These hopes have not, however, been realized. The main reason for the failure is that the meaning of a sentence cannot be determined by vocabulary and grammar alone. Does "We don't have enough different woods" refer to a shortage of forest preserves, cabinet-making materials, or golf clubs? It depends on the context. Does "That kills me!" mean that the speaker is dying? Fortunately not in most cases. Because of such ambiguities, a passage translated into a foreign language and then translated back again by another person may be unrecognizable, as when "He shot off his mouth without thinking" comes back as "He absentmindedly fired a bullet into his jaw!" Given such difficulties, it is understandable that computerized translation has not yet achieved great success.

Efforts to make computers better problem solvers are continuing. Recently Newell and a new set of collaborators developed a program called SOAR (for "State, Operator, And Result") that goes well beyond GPS (Waldrop 1988a, b). It provides better ways of resolving indecision about what step to take at any given point, and it can store the solution to a problem efficiently for future use. SOAR is currently being tried out in a number of contexts and modified in various ways. (Presumably Hull would have approved.) How well it can solve the various difficulties we have considered remains to be seen.

Computers and Learning Theory

What do computer programs tell us about the actual processes of learning and thinking in living organisms? Nothing directly; as just noted, the fact that a computer can be programmed to learn or think by certain processes does not demonstrate that either humans or rats learn or think by the same processes. What these programs can show are the implications of certain assumptions about how organisms learn. A theorist can write a computer program to follow the laws of learning that he or she thinks organisms follow, then run the program to see what happens. If what happens is similar to the outcome of human or animal learning, this finding makes it more plausible that humans or animals do in fact follow those hypothesized processes when they learn. If what happens is quite different from the outcome of "real" learning, the theorist's assumptions are probably false. Thus the computers provide a more precise way of doing what Hull wanted to do; if he had made use of computers he might have avoided some of the contradictions in his system. The role of the computer program is much like that of mathematical analysis—not to change the logic of theory construction, but to carry out that logic more precisely and more thoroughly.

Though most psychologists working with computers have not been concerned primarily with the arguments between connectionist and cognitive theorists, their work is quite relevant to that controversy. As a piece of engineering, a computer is a connectionist "organism"; its transistors, which do or do not pass currents, are comparable to neurons in the nervous system that do or do not fire. At a molecular level, therefore, a connectionist analysis of a computer would be accurate. At the molar level, however, what we mainly note is the computer's ability to store and retrieve information, reason logically, break problems into subproblems, and otherwise behave in very cognitive ways. A computer is thus a basically connectionist "organism" that gets programmed to operate in cognitive ways. If a "mere machine," built by humans from basically connectionist parts, can operate so effectively in such cognitive ways, cognitions can scarcely be as unscientifically mentalistic as earlier psychologists feared. Perhaps, indeed, there may be a resolution of the connectionist-cognitive argument in the definition of a human being as "the only movable, general-purpose computer that can be produced by unskilled labor!"

In the case of computers, the programming is done by humans. How do humans themselves get programmed? Their programming takes place through a lifetime of experience, some of it arranged deliberately by parents and teachers, some of it happening without anyone having planned it. At first our programs are simple, but they soon get combined into more complex ones. A computer program often includes a command to call some simpler program to do a particular job needed by the larger program. Similarly, a person working on a large task can draw on previously learned ability to do smaller tasks that contribute to the larger one. For example, a carpenter's "program" for building a bookcase will be full of specifications to saw a board or pound a nail. The details of these actions do not need to be spelled out, since the carpenter is already thoroughly familiar with how to do them and can take the details for granted. When the appropriate point in his "program" for the bookcase arrives, the carpenter simply has to note that the board should be sawed, and his previously learned "subprogram" of skills will take care of it, after which the main program continues on its way.

The analysis in terms of programs and subprograms could be extended to more than two levels, with programs made up of subprograms and in turn combined into larger programs. The result would be a hierarchy of skills at different levels. This sounds much like the view we considered at the end of Chapter 11, an example of theorists moving from different starting points to similar conclusions.

ACT THEORY

One way in which computers have influenced learning theory is by providing a general pattern or analog for theorizing. Just as earlier theorists interpreted humans as animals and both humans and animals as simple stimulus-response mechanisms, more recent theorists have analyzed people, and sometimes animals, as "wet computers," doing by means of neurons what computers do by means of transistor chips. Since some of the things that computers do sound rather cognitive, such as storing information in their memories and making decisions on the basis of that information, these computer-based models are closer to traditional cognitive than to traditional connectionist theories. They also take seriously the challenge to cognitive theories to show how cognitions give rise to actual behavior. As a result, some of them are called *production theories*, theories that attempt to show how cognitions actually produce action.

Declarative and Procedural Knowledge

One such theory is appropriately called ACT, developed by John R. Anderson (b. 1947) of Carnegie-Mellon University (Anderson 1982, 1983, 1987). The name ACT stands for "Adaptive Control of Thought." Central to the ACT theory is a distinction between two kinds of knowledge, designated as declarative and procedural. *Declarative knowledge* is what we usually call knowledge: propositions that are true. We may think of it as descriptions of the world, or as answers to questions, or as "knowing that." *Procedural knowledge* is the ability to carry out procedures correctly. We may think of it as skill, or as "knowing how."

Procedural knowledge consists of rules of the form "If A, then do B." Simple examples are "If you see a red traffic light, then stop at the edge of the intersection" and "If you want to know the time, then look at your watch." Slightly more complex examples would be "If you are hungry, and if you are far from home, and if you have money, then look for a restaurant" and "If you are adding a series of numbers, and if the sum of the right-hand column is at least 20 but less than 30, then record the last digit of that sum and carry a 2 to the next column."

It is not easy to provide rules that will work for all cases, since the best rule to follow often depends on so many different factors. One way of dealing with this problem is to make rules more and more complex and specific by adding more and more "if" clauses to them. In principle, the process could be carried further and further until there were a large number of specific rules covering every possible situation. This might not, however, be a very efficient production system. It often works better to have both a simple general rule and a few exceptions. For example, so many English words form their plural by adding *s* that the most effective production system is to have the general rule "If you want to make a singular noun plural, then add an *s* at the end," plus a number of more specific rules such as "If you want to form the plural of *man,* write *men.*" The production system for plurals works by using a more specific rule if there is one, and otherwise the general rule.

We should be careful not to define either declarative or procedural knowledge too narrowly. Declarative knowledge does not have to be stated in words; it can also be in the form of spatial images or of expectancies about the sequences in which events happen. Likewise, procedural knowledge is not limited to motor coordinations; the ability to solve an equation involves procedural knowledge just as much as does the ability to drive a nail. A major part of the theory is the relationship between these two kinds of knowledge.

When a person acquires a new ability, the process usually begins with acquiring declarative knowledge. This knowledge may be learned from other people or from observation—or possibly by inference from other things the individual already knows. However acquired, this state of knowledge represents the declarative stage in the learning of a production. In the declarative stage, the knowledge is used to figure out how to do the production. This involves a process of inference by which "knowledge about" (declarative) is converted into the if-then rules of procedural knowledge. Thus, in algebra one may think "I want X alone on the left side of the equation, but there's another term added to the X there; what can I do about it? If I took it away, what would happen to the other side of the equation? Well, I know that equals subtracted from equals are equals, so I guess I could get rid of that term by subtracting that amount from the left side if I also subtracted the same amount from the right side. OK, I'll do that."

As the learner actually practices the production, the nature of the knowledge changes, becoming more procedural. More and more the learner simply uses the procedures, without needing to think about the declarative knowledge. The learner thus gradually moves to the procedural stage, in which the steps in the production are carried out automatically. In the above algebra example, one now simply follows the production rule: "If you want to get rid of a term on one side of the equation, move it to the other side and change the sign." Whereas in the declarative stage one was operating in a cognitive way, now one is showing fairly direct stimulus-response behavior. The process by which this change occurs, from control by declarative knowledge to control by procedural knowledge, is known as *proceduralization.*

Ordinarily the declarative knowledge is not lost; it merely becomes less and less relevant to the production. Sometimes, however, as the procedural knowledge becomes increasingly automatic, the declarative knowledge, not being used, is forgotten. Then one has the case of the person who is very skillful at doing a job but very poor at explaining how she does it, or why what she does works. Another example is a phone number which a person dials often on a touch-tone phone but never writes or tells to anyone else. At first the person knew a sequence of numbers (declarative stage) and had to convert it into a series of presses to carry out the procedure. Eventually the person instead presses the correct sequence of buttons without thinking of the numbers (procedural stage), and if asked the number may need some time to be able to give it.

Combining of Rules

As knowledge is becoming proceduralized, at first it tends to consist of many small units, each accomplishing one specific step in the overall production. However, when two or more of these small steps regularly occur together, they gradually combine into a single unit, a process known as *composition.* In composition, the smaller units do not cease to exist; they are still available as separate units if needed. Instead, the new, composite unit is available in the person's repertoire along with the smaller ones, and is used in place of them when appropriate.

The two processes of proceduralization and composition work together to get from declarative knowledge to smooth, integrated procedural productions. They are therefore grouped together under a single name: *knowledge compilation.* The use of this term reflects Anderson's interest in computers as an analog to human thought. Just as a compiler converts instructions to a computer into the machine language with which the computer actually works, so knowledge compilation converts knowledge about the world into the skills of actual productions.

Both in the declarative stage, when the if-then rules have to be inferred, and in the procedural stage, when they are carried out automatically, there is a problem of conflict among rules. What do you do when the "if" parts of two rules both apply, but the "then" parts are incompatible with one another? One general principle for resolving such conflicts is that the more specific rule takes precedence. In other words, one uses a narrow, specific rule when one is available, and otherwise relies on a more general "rule of thumb." We saw an example of this principle in connection with rules and exceptions for forming plurals. If there is a narrow rule for the specific case (such as "If you want to form the plural of *man,* write *men*), that specific rule is used. Otherwise, one uses the more general rule: "If you want to form the plural of a noun, write the noun plus *s.*"

In addition, a particular production system may have its own hierarchy of rules, indicating which ones take precedence over which others. In a production system for playing chess, for example, the rule "If your king is threatened, protect it" may take precedence over the rule "If you can control the center of the board, do so." Thus only if your king is safe do you worry about the center of the board.

Another general principle for resolving conflicts among rules is the obvious one that the stronger of two conflicting rules is the one that is followed. What is not so obvious is how a rule increases in strength. As we might expect, there will be some sort of reinforcement mechanism. However, ACT has an unusual feature in this regard. The system makes no distinction between rules that lead to success and rules that produce no indication of either success or failure. Whenever a rule is used and nothing happens to indicate that it was wrong, the rule is strengthened; that is, the "if" part of the rule increases its tendency to produce the "then do such and such" part of the rule.

On the other hand, if something happens to indicate that it was a mistake to use the rule in that situation, the rule is weakened; its "if" is less likely to produce the "then do such and such" in the future. The ACT system thus has a mechanism of punishment, or at least of extinction, but no mechanism of reinforcement. This places Anderson in contrast with Thorndike, Hull, and Skinner, all of whom regarded reinforcement as of central importance. In this rejection of simple reinforcement theory he is a little more like Guthrie, though still not at all close. If we reword Anderson by saying that the way to change a cognition is to provide disconfirming evidence, we would find both Tolman and Piaget saying much the same thing as Anderson.

The ACT system is very much goal-oriented. The productions serve to achieve goals, and in the declarative stage the inferences from declarative to procedural knowledge make the productions possible. Getting from declarative to procedural knowledge is a major part of problem solving. The various methods by which this may be done are already familiar from our earlier discussion. ACT emphasizes the process of working backward from the goal, setting up a series of subgoals to get from where one is now to where one wants eventually to be. One then applies a rule to turn one's present situation into a new situation that satisfies the "if" for another rule, so that one can apply that rule to produce another change, and so on toward the goal.

We have noted that some production rules are specific and others general. Specific rules become combined into general ones by a process that Anderson considers the same as generalization. He gives two rules as an example: (1) If you want to show that a coat belongs to you, then say "my coat"; (2) if you want to show that a ball belongs to you, then say "my ball." Just from these two rules, the system can generalize a third rule: If you want to show that any object belongs to you, then say "my [name of object]." In some cases such a new rule will be too general, so discrimination learning will be required before a fully correct rule is developed.

At first Anderson regarded such learning by generalization and discrimination as automatic, as did most of the theorists we discussed earlier in this book. More recently (1987), however, he has decided that these processes depend more on strategies of inductive reasoning. Generalization and discrimination, in his later view, involve the formulating of rules. A person who fails to recognize that a rule might be involved will probably not show generalization. On the other hand, a person who expects some general rule to be involved may generalize from a single case. The learner may reason, for example, that "in German the plural of *Gestalt* is *Gestalten,* so in German plurals are formed by adding *en.*" Since this rule is actually correct for only a minority of German nouns, further discrimination learning would be needed. However, generalization from a single case is a familiar phenomenon, so this new assumption of Anderson's may be good psychology even if it represents poor logic on the part of the learner.

Computers figure in Anderson's thinking, and in that of other theorists with similar interests, in at least three ways. One is as a source of ideas. The analogy between the computer and the human brain has provided many hypotheses about how the brain may work, as well as a vocabulary for discussing human cognition. (Consider the popularity of such words as *input* and *interface* and *networking.*) The second is as a way of testing ideas. If a computer is programmed to do what a theorist thinks the human brain does, and the result is what humans actually do, this supports the view that humans reach that result by the same sorts of processes as the computer did. The view is not necessarily true, but the success of the analogy strengthens that hypothesis.

The third way is as an application to education. To the extent that theories like ACT give an accurate picture of how people learn and think, we should be able to take advantage of that picture in designing teaching devices. Moreover, these devices might best be in the form of computer programs, programs that present material to the learner in just the way that will make learning most efficient. Anderson and his collaborators have developed such teaching programs for geometry and (appropriately) for computer programming. The program infers from a student's answers what rule she is applying, and if it is an inappropriate rule the program provides appropriate remediation (Anderson, Boyle, & Reiser 1985). Thus Anderson shares Skinner's interest in the technology of education. However, the design of his teaching programs puts far more emphasis on the assumed cognitive processes of the student than does the design of Skinner's.

Theories like ACT represent the convergence of ideas from several sources. They combine ideas from the long-established fields of psychology and linguistics with those from such newer fields as computer science, cognitive science, and artificial intelligence. Many psychologists in recent years have felt that such theories were just what was needed—a substitute for outmoded behavioristic theories, an improvement on the older cognitive ones, and at last a truly scientific answer to age-old questions about how the mind works. Not everyone has agreed, of course. Skinner, for example, likes to sneer that one can make any topic sound trendy by putting "cognitive" in front of it. However, not all the objections have come from theorists attached to older positions. New lines of criticism have also appeared, as we will see in the next chapter.

Chapter
14

The New Connectionism

The analyses of problem solving in the previous chapter involved sequences of actions based on rules. The rules might be algorithms or heuristics, they might or might not make explicit use of a knowledge base, and they might be used by either a person or a computer. In any case, however, they were rational, goal-directed, purposeful. They were highly cognitive, the kinds of operations that would be expected to appeal both to Tolman and to Piaget. They, as much as anything in learning theory, gave the cognitive approach its great impetus.

This was the way computers worked, and theorists came to expect that this was also the way humans worked. For a long time the majority of theorists had regarded cognitive approaches as a bit disreputable, threatening to destroy the scientific respectability of connectionist interpretations. Now here was the computer, a basically connectionist "organism" that could nevertheless be programmed to "think" and act in quite cognitive ways. It is understandable that theorists who were sympathetic to the cognitive approach would feel that its time had come and would use this computer model as an analog to human thinking, helping to usher in what came to be considered the cognitive revolution.

PROBLEMS WITH COMPUTER MODELS

Then, in the 1980s, doubts began to appear. Many sources were responsible for them. One was the discovery that human experts do not solve problems simply by following rules. In fact, it is largely the novices who slavishly follow rules, while experts proceed more intuitively, using their great base of experience to select or eliminate courses of action without having to analyze them in any detail. What they do looks more like making learned responses to stimuli than like inferring actions from principles, though perhaps not a great deal like either.

A second source of doubt came from a consideration of the nervous system. Neurons operate a great deal less quickly than transistors, and it seemed increasingly unlikely that humans could think as effectively as they do (perhaps we should say "even as effectively as they do") if they operated in the same step-by-step way as computers. However, the neurons in the brain are organized in complex ways, with each connecting with many others, so that it would be possible for the brain to increase its efficiency considerably by having different sets of neurons working on a problem at the same time in various complex ways. Moreover, as psychologists and physiologists studied those animal nervous systems that were simple enough to analyze in detail, they found evidence that they operated more like a network than like the single central processing unit of a computer. Maybe the difference between a computer's hardware and a person's or animal's "wetware" really does make a difference!

A third factor pushing theorists toward a different point of view came from within computer science itself. Computer scientists are constantly trying to devise more and more powerful machines. The amount of computing power that can be concentrated in a given amount of space has been increased dramatically by several engineering changes during the more than 40 years since the first computer was built. The first computers, made with vacuum tubes, are referred to as the first generation, those with transistors as the second generation, those with transistorized chips as the third, and those with miniaturized chips as the fourth. The next breakthrough, to the fifth generation, involves *parallel processing,* in which different components of the system are working on different parts of a problem at the same time. This, of course, is what we have just suggested that the human brain does. Thus, whereas for some time an attempt has been made to analyze people as if they were computers, now we might say that an effort is being made to design computers to be more like people.

NETWORK MODELS

The combination of these three lines of argument suggested that the nervous system should be analyzed as a network of neurons, multiply interconnected, in which impulses could pass through numerous complex loops, all working together to deal with a situation. Though such ideas were not altogether new, they received a major impetus from the lines of reasoning given above.

Along with this view went another, related one. The earlier computer-oriented views had focused primarily on how a system—human, animal, or computer—operates to solve problems. They had for the most part not concerned themselves with how the system comes to operate that way— that is, with the process of learning. The new approach, however, regarded the process of learning as of central importance. We can see the difference in the way each approach would set up an *expert system*—a computer program designed to do a job as a human expert would (for example, to diagnose illnesses like a medical specialist, or to play chess like a grand master). The older approach would involve discovering the rules a specialist uses for making decisions, and then programming the computer to follow those same rules. The expertness is thus built into the program at the start. The newer approach is to have the program learn from experience, keeping those procedures that work and dropping out those that don't. The system might be very inexpert at the beginning, but since it has perfect memory for its experiences, it would learn fairly rapidly what worked and what didn't. Though it would develop rules of thumb from experience, it would learn by examples rather than be programmed with rules. So, although in some ways it might operate quite cognitively, it would still be a lot like something Thorndike might have imagined.

This new view has only recently been recognized as a special approach, not yet well enough established to be called a theory or a school. A general term for what this approach assumes goes on in the nervous system is *parallel distributed processing*. The kinds of interpretations it uses are often referred to as *network models*, and the approach is generally called *connectionism*.

Though this modern-day connectionism is obviously related to connectionism in the traditional sense of that word, it is nonetheless considerably different. Whereas the older connectionism referred to connections between stimuli and responses, which were assumed to be fairly simple and direct, the new connectionism refers to the whole interconnectedness of the network. The learning processes that are assumed to take place within a network are often more complicated than even Hull supposed, as well as often more cognitive than any of the older connectionist theorists would have considered. This new connectionism thus combines an emphasis on specific connections and on learning by reinforcement that would have appealed to Thorndike or Hull, with an emphasis on the organized operation of whole systems that would have appealed to a gestalt psychologist.

Two Approaches

Theorists within this general framework have followed two considerably different approaches. Some have focused on the real nervous systems of simple organisms. They analyze in detail how the individual neurons in, for example, a sea snail work together to produce conditioning. The advantage of their approach is that they are dealing with a real organism with real neurons. However, the disadvantage is that they are studying organisms that show only simple forms of learning. If many people feel that even rats are too simple to tell us anything interesting about higher mental processes, how much more so must they feel that way about the study of learning in sea snails!

The other approach has been to try to study more complex networks. However, to study humans directly has proved impractical. Although we can study people's behavior, ask them questions, and make inferences about their cognitive intervening variables, we are limited in our opportunity to study their nervous systems. Though a lot has been learned about human brain processes from studying people with brain damage and people undergoing brain surgery, and from recording electrical activities of the brain, researchers cannot do the kinds of thorough studies on people that they can do with lower animals. Partly they are limited by the sheer complexity of the human brain. There are more neurons in one human brain than there are people in the world, and the total number of synapses among all those neurons is hard to imagine; it has been estimated at 1,000,000,000,000,000. Another important limit is the ethical and practical impossibility of doing experimental surgery on humans for purely research purposes. The alternative is to construct physical models to imitate human thinking, and study them.

The connectionist approach assumes that the crucial feature of neural networks is not the biochemistry of the neurons and synapses but rather the patterns in which neurons are interconnected by way of synapses so that they form networks. One can specify the characteristics of such a network, construct a device to act according to those assumptions, and see whether the device shows the expected "learning" (that is, whether its output changes in the predicted way). The logic here is the same as that of constructing and testing any theory or model. The difference is that the model is not just on paper; rather, it is a functioning physical model that goes through the specified operations and then either does or does not show the changes in behavior that are predicted. Like a robot, it provides a technological test of the theoretical model's adequacy.

If the device or working model shows the kind of learning that humans show, one is encouraged to think that the human brain does operate according to the same formal principles as the model, in spite of the many differences between them. However, one never knows for sure. As we noted when looking at Hull's theory, there is always the possibility that the brain and the computer model produce the same results by different processes. What is distinctive about the connectionist approach is not the logic but the particular assumptions of the model.

The principle on which these models operate would seem more familiar to Thorndike or Hull than to the more traditional computer modelers. To begin with, like traditional stimulus-response theories, they are concerned with how we learn to make the appropriate response to a given stimulus. Moreover, the operation by which this learning takes place is in effect reinforcement, since some mechanism is built in to indicate which responses were correct. The tendency of impulses to cross each "synapse" in the network can be set at any initial value, and these values then change as a result of the "reinforcement" mechanism.

An Example: NETtalk

An example of such a system is one called NETtalk. Developed by Terrence J. Sejnowski (b. 1947) of Johns Hopkins University and his collaborators (Sejnowski & Rosenberg 1986; Heppenheimer 1988), it is a system that learns to read aloud. The stimuli are written passages, made up of the 26 letters of the alphabet plus spaces. The responses are sounds that resemble speech, made up of 55 phonemes (speech sounds) in the International Phonetic Alphabet. A linguist decides what sequence of phonemes is the best pronunciation of a written passage. This pronunciation is the "correct" response, which it is the machine's task to try to learn.

At the beginning of a learning session, all the connections in NETtalk are set at random values, unrelated to the correct pronunciations. At first, therefore, the sounds NETtalk makes are gibberish, not only unrelated to the written passage but also quite unlike any understandable speech. After each such effort, some of NETtalk's connections are strengthened and others weakened in an effort to bring its speech closer to a correct oral reading of the written passage. After many "readings" of the passage, the program begins to sound more like real speech, even though it is still incomprehensible. The first step in that direction is the machine's learning that spaces represent periods of silence that divide the passage into words. Once that is learned, NETtalk's speech sounds more like speech in a foreign language, rather than just like gibberish.

Then the output begins to sound more and more like the actual written passage. First NETtalk distinguishes which letters correspond to vowel sounds and which to consonant sounds. Then it learns more and more about the sounds of particular letters. Eventually, after a number of hours, the computer reads the passage quite understandably. It accomplishes this success not by following preprogrammed rules, like most computer programs, but by creating its own rules through trial, error, correction, and changing strengths of connections between letters and sounds.

When NETtalk has achieved this success, has it simply connected each of the 26 letters of the English written alphabet with one or more of the phonemes of the International Phonetic Alphabet? No. We all know that English spelling is far too irregular for that to work. Has NETtalk learned the so-called rules of English spelling, such as to pronounce *c* like *k* when it comes before certain vowels and like *s* when it comes before others? To a considerable extent it has, but such traditional rules are both complex and incomplete. Moreover, NETtalk's responses, whether or not they correspond to any describable rules, keep changing to some extent as they encounter new written passages. Has NETtalk simply learned to do whatever works? Yes, but it was actually far from simple, and the result may fit many familiar rules to varying degrees and perhaps also show other regularities that no one yet has thought of stating as rules.

How Does NETtalk Do It?

Needless to say, building a machine that will show such learning is not easy. There were a number of unsuccessful attempts to build such machines in the late 1950s and the 1960s—so unsuccessful, indeed, that the whole approach was abandoned for over a decade. In the 1980s, however, the approach has been tried again and has achieved some success, as NETtalk demonstrates.

One thing that has made success possible is that the stimulus elements (for NETtalk, the printed letters) are not connected directly to the response elements (the spoken sounds). Instead, the stimulus elements are connected to a set of "hidden units," which in turn are connected to the response elements. Each hidden unit is connected to all the stimuli and the responses. Every one of these units in the machine acts like a neuron in the brain, either firing or not firing when it is stimulated.

When NETtalk reads a particular letter, that letter may or may not fire the connection to each of the hidden units with which it is connected. Each hidden unit, as a result, receives some number of "neural messages" over its various connections with different letters. This stimulation may or may not be enough to get that hidden unit to fire. If a hidden unit does fire, it sends messages to a number of response units (different sounds). The response unit that gets the strongest total message is the one that fires, making that speech sound.

The connections from one unit to another are comparable to synapses between neurons in the actual nervous system. Each of these connections has a certain *weight,* which is the strength with which it fires. If the connection from a given stimulus to a given hidden unit has a high weight, then when the stimulus occurs, the connection fires strongly, whereas if the connection has a low weight, it fires only weakly. Whether or not a given hidden unit fires depends on whether the combined weights of all its connections that are firing are enough to make it fire.

The same arrangement applies to the connections from the hidden units to the responses. When a hidden unit fires, each of its connections to the various responses fires with a certain strength, depending on the weight of that connection. The sum of the weights of all the connections stimulating a given response determines how strongly that response is activated. Whichever is most strongly activated is the sound that will be produced.

Each time NETtalk makes a sound and finds out whether it is correct or wrong, the weights of the various connections change. It is these changes that make learning possible. However, it is not simply that all connections leading to a correct response are strengthened. Instead, throughout the system, the weights of some connections increase and others decrease, according to the learning rules built into the system. Learning is thus a property, not of single connections, but of the whole system.

Another factor that helps NETtalk is that it does not simply read letter by letter. Instead, the actual stimulus is a given letter in the context of the three previous letters in the written passage and of the three following letters. This characteristic of the system makes it possible for NETtalk to deal with such complexities as the difference, mentioned above, in the pronunciation of *c* before *e* and before *o*. It also helps with such peculiarities of English spelling as the special sounds of *ough*.

APPLICATIONS AND EVALUATIONS

These new connectionist models clearly show a resemblance to the older stimulus-response connectionist theories. However, this does not mean that these newer theories are very much like the older ones. Rather than habits connecting a given stimulus directly to a given response, the newer connectionist models specify entire interconnected networks, involving not only input and output units but also the hidden units in between. Moreover, there are not just a number of different pathways being reinforced; rather, reinforcement changes the weights of a number of parallel connections and thus changes the whole pattern of flow within the interconnected network. In this respect, the new connectionist models look like what the classical gestalt theorists would have appreciated. Thus we might say that two characteristics of Hull's theory, learning by reinforcement and the use of intervening variables (the hidden units), result in a total system that Wertheimer, Köhler, and Koffka would have found quite congenial.

One of the most popular applications of the new connectionist models has been to perception. Even though computers can solve many problems faster and more accurately than humans, they are notoriously poor at dealing with complex patterns. Most people are inferior to computers at playing chess or evaluating mathematical functions, but they are way ahead of computers in their ability to recognize individual faces. They are also much better than computers at recognizing a particular object even when it is surrounded and partly hidden by other objects. This fact makes it difficult to design "smart missiles" that will use computers to home in on tanks but not on other large battlefield objects.

To traditional computer experts, the poor performance of computers at recognizing patterns is an embarrassment. To the new connectionist theorists, however, it is a sign that their approach is needed. The sorts of patterns that develop spontaneously in distributed networks seem just right for analyzing perceptual patterns. Whether the problem is how to recognize an object whichever way it is turned, or how to find a hidden picture within a larger picture, or how to distinguish one face from another, connectionists have worked enthusiastically at applying their methods to it.

What makes the connectionists' machines more effective for these purposes than are ordinary computer programs is that they work on the patterning of elements. As many of us know from painful experience, computers are exceedingly literal. Misspell a word or misplace a comma and the computer is baffled. This means that in order to match a picture to the computer's template for a certain person's face, there must be exact point-by-point correspondence between the two. Differences so small that a person would barely notice them will prevent the computer from detecting that the two are the same. Computers have ways around this problem, but they are still rather literal-minded ways, such as counting the number of features (long nose, closely spaced eyes, and so on) that the two faces have in common. The connectionists' networks, however, can react to the overall similarities in pattern between two faces, just as a human would, even though there is no point-by-point correspondence. Again we see why, of all the classical learning theorists, the ones who might sympathize most with this new approach are the gestaltists.

The connectionist network models illustrate in fairly extreme degree the use of modeling as an approach to the study of learning. Models such as NETtalk are not theories of learning; rather, they are models illustrating one particular way that a certain kind of learning could possibly occur. The general theory is that learning occurs through changes in the strength of connections in a network with many distributed connections. A specific model is just one example, illustrating how such learning could occur, not necessarily how it does occur in any particular organism or any particular situation. The model itself is a set of rules about how to change the weights of connections depending on the nature of the input (the stimuli) and on the success of the output (which corresponds to reinforcement). If following those rules leads to changes that resemble actual learning in real organisms, this suggests two things: that the model is an accurate representation of how learning occurs in some situation, and that the whole approach is a useful one.

At present these models are still in the early stages of development. Their supporters see at least two values in them. One is practical. A machine designed to learn through connectionist networks has the potential to become the ultimate expert system. Whereas an expert system constructed by people can never be better than the knowledge that is built into it, a self-teaching system has the potential to go beyond existing knowledge, learn by experience, and become more expert than any system that could have been produced in any other way. The implications for computerized problem solving are enormous.

The other potential value of this approach is in finding out how learning occurs in humans and other organisms. Obviously these models do not tell us how learning occurs at the biochemical level—the connectionist machines are not made of living cells. However, they do show us how the neurons in a real brain could work together to produce learning. Of all the ways that real nervous systems might work, these models represent the most plausible guess as to how they actually do work, say their supporters.

Critics are more skeptical. The models are still only in a preliminary stage of development. None of them has yet done as good a job as the best of the competing models, which are computer programs designed to reason logically about information given to them by their creators. Quite possibly, for a variety of reasons, the connectionist models never will. At present they represent an interesting new approach, a set of high hopes, and the possibility of combining the best of connectionist and cognitive approaches more effectively than ever before. To what extent the hopes will be realized remains to be seen.

Chapter
15

Issues in Motivation

Why do we want what we want, seek what we seek? Why are we sometimes relaxed, sometimes working busily but quietly, and occasionally wildly excited? These are the questions of motivation, and to many people they are the most central issues in psychology. Attempts to answer them are part of nearly all the major theories of learning, since these topics are not only important but also closely related to the processes of learning. However, there have also been a number of contributions to the analysis of motivation that were not closely associated with any of the major theories we have considered. In this chapter we will examine some of them.

INTERPRETATIONS OF REINFORCEMENT AND DRIVE

One topic on which there have been important recent developments is the nature of reinforcement. No theorist questions that the effects of our actions influence whether we will repeat these actions (which is the basic principle of reinforcement), but theorists disagree widely on how this influence should be interpreted. What, if anything, do all reinforcers have in common that makes them reinforcing? Guthrie, though he avoids the term "reinforcement," says in effect that all reinforcement involves is stimulus change. Skinner and Estes for the most part ignore the question, saying simply that whatever reinforces behavior is a reinforcer. Hull, Mowrer (as regards solution learning, even when it is reinterpreted as another kind of sign learning), Lewin, and Tolman all interpret reinforcement as some kind of drive reduction, even though some of them do not

183

speak either of drive or of reinforcement. Thus the drive-reinforcement interpretation, in whatever words, is a widely recognized one.

New Descriptions of Drives

There are currently three trends in the interpretation of reinforcement, two that work within a drive-reduction framework and one that does not. Within the drive-reduction framework, there has been a concentration on what drives are innate. In the past, connectionist psychologists who used the concept of drive have tended to treat as primary, or innate, only a few drives (such as hunger, thirst, sex, and pain) that are clearly physiological. Cognitive psychologists, on the other hand, have been more likely to discuss such motivational tendencies as pride, ambition, and affection, which have no apparent physiological basis. These latter motivational tendencies are regarded by connectionist theorists as the result of complex learning processes, including the acquisition of learned drives. There is not necessarily any disagreement between these two points of view, since cognitive theorists have tended to take little interest in the origins of the tensions or demands they discuss. The chief importance of these interpretations is that the connectionist theorists have had to make assumptions about the learning of motives that are extremely difficult to support by experiments. Although Miller was quite successful in demonstrating a learned drive of fear, other learned drives that are predicted by theory have proved very difficult to demonstrate in the laboratory. As a result, there has been increasing interest in the possibility that there may be far more primary drives than have previously been recognized.

One such drive (or perhaps category of drives) that has received much attention is that which is satisfied by new experience. It is known variously as a drive of curiosity or exploration or manipulation or novelty seeking. Its existence is supported by many lines of evidence. Harlow (whom we discussed earlier in connection with learning sets) showed that monkeys would work to unfasten a clasp device over and over again, even though neither food, escape, nor any other obvious reward was given for doing so. Butler (1953) showed that monkeys in a closed cage would press a lever to open a window so they could look out. If the monkeys were kept in the closed cage for several hours before the lever was made available, they would press more (indicating higher drive following deprivation). If the lever no longer opened the window, their rate of pressing would drop (indicating extinction). Such novelty-seeking behavior is found not only in monkeys, which have long been famous for their curiosity, but also in rats. Montgomery and Welker have made extensive studies of rats exploring new places and of the responses they will learn in order to be able to do such exploring. These and other related studies are discussed by Berlyne (1960) and by Welker (1961).

A second kind of drive that has been investigated is satisfied by activity. This is different from the kind of drive we have just discussed in that the activity does not have to produce any novel stimulation. Such activity occurs when a rat runs in an activity wheel, which is a sort of voluntary treadmill. A rat in such a wheel can, if it chooses, get exercise by running, but no exploration is involved, since the wheel just goes around without getting anywhere. Kagan and Berkun (1954) have shown that a chance to run in such a wheel will reinforce lever pressing, and Hill (1956) has shown that rats do more running in the wheel when they have been deprived of activity for a long time.

A third kind of drive has been referred to as contact comfort. It was first analyzed in detail, as were so many interesting phenomena, by Harry Harlow. Contact comfort is a drive which is satisfied by certain kinds of physical contact. Harlow (1958) originally studied it by rearing baby monkeys with *surrogate mothers*, wire models that gave milk like real mothers. He found that monkeys not only preferred a "mother" covered with terry cloth to one made of bare wire, but ran to the terry cloth "mother" when frightened. They did so even if the wire "mother" supplied milk and the cloth "mother" did not. These and other findings in his experiments suggested to Harlow that contact comfort, exemplified by the baby monkeys' attraction to the cloth surrogate mother, is an important factor in personality development. It may well play a major part in personality development, not only in the attachment of infants to their mothers, but also in other aspects of love, in sexual behavior, and in the development of social relationships.

The importance of these various drives is not simply in the recognition that people and animals seek new experience, activity, and pleasant sensations of touch. All these tendencies have long been known. Rather, their importance is in the recognition, supported by experimental evidence, that they may well be just as much a part of our innate, biological nature as hunger, sex, or pain. This recognition does not by any means answer all our questions about why we seek companionship, achievement, or glory. (Why it doesn't is discussed in Hill 1968.) Nevertheless, it helps to bridge the gap between the drives usually employed in laboratory studies of learning and the motives we all recognize in ourselves and others.

Optimal Arousal

The second trend involves a modification of drive theory—the theory of *optimal arousal.* Different versions of this theory have been presented by several writers; one good collection of ideas about it is Berlyne and Madsen (1973). The optimal-arousal theory holds that reinforcement consists not necessarily of a decrease in drive but rather a change in drive toward some optimal level. The term *arousal* is preferred to *drive* in discussing this interpretation, so as to avoid confusion with more conventional drive theory. If the present level of arousal is higher than the optimal level, a decrease will be reinforcing, as in the ordinary drive interpretation. However, if the present level is below the optimum, an increase rather than a decrease will be reinforcing. When the level of arousal is exactly at the optimum, reinforcement is presumably not possible for the moment. However, both the level and the optimum are constantly changing, so any such limitation is quite temporary.

Optimal-arousal theory allows for the often observed fact that people frequently seek more stimulation rather than less. Conventional drive interpretations, such as Dollard and Miller's (1950), have not been very successful in explaining such behaviors as riding on roller coasters, reading exciting stories, or just complaining of boredom and expressing a wish that something would happen to break the monotony. Since optimal-arousal theory states that increases as well as decreases in arousal can be reinforcing, it has less trouble with such occurrences. However, the recognition that either kind of change in arousal, up or down, can sometimes be reinforcing carries with it a responsibility to indicate when one will be reinforcing and when the other. This responsibility in turn requires knowing a lot about the determinants both of the present level of arousal and of the optimal level.

One additional assumption (or postulate, in Hull's terms) about the relationship between stimulation and arousal represents a start toward making the theory more specific. This assumption states that the level of arousal is an increasing function of the intensity, the complexity, and the novelty of the stimulation. More intense stimuli, more complex ones, and more novel ones are more arousing than those that are weaker or more familiar. This assumption, along with the one we have already mentioned—that moderate levels of arousal are more reinforcing than either high or low levels—forms the basis of optimal-arousal theory.

Several predictions follow from these two assumptions. If novelty and complexity remain constant, moderate stimuli should be reinforcing as compared with either weak or intense stimuli. If intensity and complexity remain constant, stimuli that are somewhat different from those we are used to should be preferred both to thoroughly familiar ones (which would be judged uninteresting) and to highly unfamiliar ones (which would be judged incomprehensible). If intensity and novelty remain constant, stimuli that are moderately complex should prove more reinforcing than those that are either dully simple or overwhelmingly complex. Finally, if more than one aspect of the stimulus varies, then the higher the stimulus is on intensity, novelty, or complexity, the lower the optimal value of the other variables should be. Thus a highly novel stimulus should be more reinforcing if it is mild and simple, whereas among very familiar stimuli the more intense and complex ones should be preferred.

The assumption that arousal is an increasing function of intensity, novelty, and complexity fits in well with a concept that has been quite popular among theorists in the Soviet Union—the *orienting reflex*. Although the term implies that individuals tend to orient themselves in varying degrees toward stimuli as they appear, what is actually measured in the orienting reflex is primarily the general arousal produced by a stimulus. The greater the galvanic skin response, the change in heart rate, or the increase in muscle tension produced by a stimulus, the greater the orienting reflex to that stimulus is said to be. Measures of central-nervous-system activity, such as the electroencephalogram (EEG), also give indications of the strength of the orienting reflex. The orienting reflex is greater for more intense stimuli than for milder ones and shows some tendency to be greater for more complex stimuli than for simpler ones. If the same stimulus is presented repeatedly (thus making it more familiar), the orienting reflex progressively decreases. However, it can be restored a good part of the way to its original strength in either of two ways—by changing it in some way or by just waiting for a while—either of which has the effect of making it more novel. Thus the orienting reflex serves as evidence that the level of arousal is affected by various aspects of stimuli in the way that optimal-arousal theory says it should be.

The reader will have noted that optimal-arousal theory attempts to deal with some of the same phenomena that drive theory has tried to deal with by postulating such drives as exploration and activity. To say that there are drives which can be reduced by exploring new things or by becoming more active is to say that sometimes an increase in stimulation produces a decrease in drive. Thus both drive theory and optimal-arousal theory are getting away from the older version of drive theory—particularly closely associated with Hull—that what is reinforcing is a reduction in the level of stimulation. Drive theory makes the shift by looking at each drive separately without worrying about whether it conforms to any general notion about drives as states of high stimulation. Optimal-arousal theory, however, keeps the idea of an overall level of arousal that is closely related to reinforcement, but broadens its interpretation of just what the relationship to reinforcement is.

Responses as Reinforcers

The third trend in the interpretation of reinforcement, outside the drive-reduction framework, relates reinforcement to the learner's own responses to a goal. Reinforcement depends not on what happens to the individual (drive reduction, for example) but on what the person does. This wording sounds like something Guthrie might say—and indeed, one of the psychologists who developed this idea, Fred Sheffield at Yale (b. 1914), drew his inspiration from Guthrie. Sheffield maintained that the act of consuming a goal object, rather than any form of drive reduction, is the essential factor in reinforcement. Will a response that leads to some goal object be reinforced by the goal object and learned? This depends, says Sheffield, on whether the goal object is consumed. Food, for example, is reinforcing to the extent that we eat it. Our own activity of eating provides the reinforcement for whatever response brings us to the food.

Sheffield did several experiments to support this position. For the most part, however, they were inconclusive. He showed, for example, that drinking a saccharine solution is reinforcing for rats, even though saccharine is completely nonnutritive (Sheffield & Roby 1950). This finding certainly argues against the view that all reinforcers involve reduction in a body need, since saccharine does nothing to reduce the body's need for food. The study does not show, however, that the drinking activity was what produced the reinforcement. One could just as well say that the sweet taste of saccharine is the critical reinforcing factor.

Sheffield's point of view can be elaborated by noting that every species of animal has some stereotyped responses by which it consumes rewards. In the case of food rewards, these include not only such obvious responses as chewing and swallowing, but also such related behaviors as the raccoon's "washing" of its food. Whereas the behaviors by which animals obtain food are fairly variable and subject to learning, the eating responses are much more stereotyped and less subject to learning. Because they involve consuming a reward and also because they consummate the whole process of food getting, they are called consummatory responses. All sorts of motivated behavior sequences end with consummatory responses: not only eating but also drinking, chewing (especially in rodents), copulation, elimination, and in various aggressive species, attacking. It is the opportunity to engage in these species-specific consummatory responses that serves to reinforce the whole chain of instrumental behavior leading to them. This biologically oriented extension of Sheffield's theory has been developed in considerable detail by Glickman and Schiff (1967).

A more general formulation of the idea that responses are reinforcing has been presented by David Premack (b. 1925), currently at the University of Pennsylvania. He simply states that of any two responses, the one that occurs more often when both are available can reinforce the one that occurs less often, but not vice versa. This relationship is illustrated by an experiment with children (Premack 1959). The children were given an opportunity to engage in two activities, eating candy and playing a pinball machine. Some did one of these two more often, some the other. Premack then arranged the apparatus so that for half the children the candy dispenser would work only if the child first operated the pinball machine. To the children who preferred playing, the new arrangement made little difference—they just went on happily playing the machine. To the children who preferred eating to playing, however, this change did make a difference—their rate of playing went up, indicating that candy was reinforcing the playing. So far this is a familiar relationship—food reinforcing an instrumental activity. For the other half of the children, the arrangement was reversed, so that the pinball machine would work only if the child first took candy from the dispenser. To the children who preferred candy, this change made no difference. The children who preferred playing, however, ate more candy under this arrangement than before. In this case, playing reinforced eating.

In this experiment, for any one child only one of the two activities could function as a reinforcer. This is not, however, a necessary restriction.

For example, Premack (1962) also studied the reinforcement relationships between running and drinking in rats. If a rat has spent a day without water, but with continuous access to an activity wheel, it will run for the reinforcement of a chance to drink, as we would expect. If, instead, the wheel is locked so that the rat cannot run unless it first drinks, this relationship will have no effect on how much the rat drinks—running will not reinforce drinking.

However, the situation can be reversed by having the same rat live for a day with water always available but with no chance to run. Now the tendency to run will be high and to drink will be low. Consequently, running can be used to reinforce drinking—if the rat has to drink in order to unlock the wheel and run, its drinking will increase. On the other hand, requiring the rat to run in order to be able to drink will now have no effect on the amount of running. Thus the same animal can be in either a state where drinking reinforces running or a state where running reinforces drinking, and in each case the reverse does not apply. All that is necessary to change the animal from one state to the other is to do something (in this case, deprive it of drinking or of running) that will change its relative tendency to engage in these two activities.

In a conventional schoolroom, where one of the most difficult demands on pupils is to sit still for long periods of time, we would expect from Premack's analysis that it would often be possible to use access to the playground as a reinforcer for a certain amount of quiet work, but rarely possible to do the reverse. However, in a strenuous program of physical education, it might be possible to reinforce a student's putting forth her last ounce of athletic effort by rewarding her with the chance to sit quietly and read a book. This latter arrangement would of course be expected to work better for the less athletic and more bookish students. Both individual differences and situational differences determine what activities can reinforce what other activities for a given individual at a given time.

In Premack's interpretation, then, there is no special class of consummatory responses that act as reinforcers. Any kind of response can reinforce any other kind of response, says Premack. All that is necessary is for the reinforcing response to be one that the learner makes more frequently than the response being reinforced. Actually, the relationship is more complex than that. We must consider not only whether, for example, a rat chooses to spend more time running or drinking, but also how much drinking it has to do to earn a given amount of running, or vice versa. Under some such "work requirements," the less frequent activity could actually reinforce the more frequent activity (Timberlake & Allison 1974). Consider, for example, a boy whose free choice would be to spend four times as many hours playing baseball as painting fences. We might (inspired by Tom Sawyer) make fence painting a scarce opportunity that had to be earned: eight hours of baseball playing for every hour of fence painting. Under those conditions, the boy would probably do even more baseball playing than otherwise, reinforced by the less frequent activity, fence painting. Thus a more general statement of Premack's principle is that in order for one kind of response (such as painting) to reinforce another (such as playing), opportunities for the reinforcing one must be scarcer relative to what the person would freely choose.

With these ideas, the view of reinforcement as response becomes less a theory of reinforcement and more a theory of behavioral control. For every possible activity there is an amount of time that the individual will freely choose to spend doing it. This amount of time is called the *bliss point*. The higher the bliss point, the more a person likes or values that activity. The bliss points of different activities thus provide an objective scale of liking or of value.

If it were possible for us to perform every activity exactly at its bliss point, we would be in a sort of Garden of Eden (Allison 1979). However, in the real world this is rarely possible. In order to do something we want to do, we typically first have to do something else we like less, whether it is as minor as walking upstairs or as major as working enough to earn thousands of dollars. More generally, in order to maintain the bliss point of one activity, we have to do either more or less than the bliss point of some other activity.

One way of dealing with this necessity is by doing more than the bliss point of the less preferred activity (which means, in Premack's terms, that the more preferred activity is reinforcing the less preferred). Alternatively, one can deal with the problem by doing less than the bliss point of the more preferred, or by some compromise in which both activities change away from their bliss points to some degree. Usually the result is such a compromise, and selecting the particular compromise is a complex process of behavior regulation. Various mathematical models have been developed to describe this process of regulation (e.g., Hanson & Timberlake 1983). These models can become rather complicated, especially when more than two activities are considered, and we will not explore them here.

Psychologists have noted that there is some similarity between these models of behavior regulation, typically studied with rats, and the kinds of models developed by economists. Suppose a rat's bliss point involves eating six pellets of food per minute and pressing a lever once per minute, but the rat is required to press the lever five times for every pellet. A psychologist says that in that situation eating will reinforce lever pressing. An economist, commenting on the same situation, might say that the rat must buy the food at a price of five presses per pellet. One could then ask how the amount the rat "buys" varies with the "price" (in economists' terms, how elastic the demand curve is), and what difference it makes how hungry the rat is, how good the food tastes, and how available other kinds of food are. Mathematical models developed by psychologists to describe what rats do in such situations turn out to agree well with models developed by economists to describe the behavior of human consumers as prices change. This and other convergences suggest that the models deal correctly with important general aspects of behavioral regulation (Allison 1983).

This way of looking at behavior and the effects of reinforcement suggests that much of life consists of trying to maintain as nearly as possible the bliss points of many different activities. We do more of some activities and less of others as necessary, but keep departures from all the bliss points as small as possible. The bliss-point view of behavior sounds surprisingly like another that came originally from a quite different source. It is to this related view that we now turn.

CYBERNETICS

At least since the Industrial Revolution, some theorists have thought of animals and sometimes even people as just glorified machines. Until quite recently, however, it has been evident that the emphasis in that suggestion would have to be on "glorified," since no machine could come close to the performance of humans or even of the higher animals. Now the suggestion is beginning to look more realistic, though it is still a long way from accurate. Two characteristics have seemed to separate humans and at least some animals on the one hand from machines on the other: intelligence and purpose. We have already seen how computers can be programmed to behave in seemingly quite intelligent ways. As for purpose, there are various devices, called control mechanisms or servomechanisms, that show at least rudimentary forms of purpose. The study of such mechanisms is called *control theory* or *cybernetics*.

The term *cybernetics* was coined by Norbert Wiener (1948). The word is derived from the Greek for "steersman," since it is concerned with devices that keep some operation, like the sailing of a ship, on its proper course. In order to keep an operation on course, it is necessary to compensate for any deviation in either direction. If a ship drifts off course, either to port or to starboard, the helmsman must move the rudder the proper amount and direction to bring the ship back on course. This illustration presents the general concept of *negative feedback*. Negative feedback involves adjustments in a system to keep it in a steady state by compensating for any deflections from that state.

Negative Feedback

The concepts of cybernetics emerged from the branch of engineering concerned with control mechanisms. Such mechanisms operate by negative feedback. The thermostat is a simple familiar example. The purpose of a thermostat is to regulate a particular variable, temperature. In the terminology of control systems, temperature is the *controlled quantity*. At any given time the thermostat is set to maintain the temperature in a room at a given constant level, the *set point*. When the room temperature drops below the set point, the thermostat turns on the furnace so that the temperature will rise. Then when the temperature rises above the set point, the thermostat turns the furnace off and lets the temperature fall. In such a system, the output (a change in temperature) is fed back to the thermostat as input—hence the term feedback. The effect of the feedback is to produce a change in the opposite direction (warmer if it is too cool, cooler if it is too warm), which is why it is called negative feedback. Thus negative in this case does not imply anything bad; on the contrary, negative feedback is the stabilizing factor that permits systems to keep operating effectively.

When a person performs any skilled act, he is constantly guided by sensations from his muscles, usually also from his eyes, and often from other sources. These sensations warn him whenever he is starting to make a mistake and thus enable him to return to the proper procedure. This response often happens so quickly and automatically that he is unaware of it, but it occurs nonetheless. This behavior is an example of negative feedback, with the output being fed back to control the operation and keep it on course.

A similar process operates in the body's physiological regulation. Body temperature, blood sugar level, alkalinity of the blood, and a great variety of other physiological variables must be maintained within some range in order for the body to function properly. They are, then, controlled quantities, and the optimal level for each of them is its set point. Negative feedback operates at the physiological level to correct deviations either up or down from the set point. These automatic regulatory processes are known collectively as *homeostasis.*

To maintain all these physiological controlled quantities close to their set points over long periods of time, it is not enough to have homeostatic mechanisms at the physiological level. To make homeostasis possible, we must eat, drink, and in most environments also move around, change clothes, and engage in many other activities. When we discuss these more molar activities, we are clearly in the realm of motivation. Just as there is a set point for level of blood sugar at a given time, so is there also a set point for amount of food intake over a period of time. We are aware of deviations from this set point—sometimes being hungry, at other times uncomfortably stuffed—and eat or stop eating to correct them. Over a period of time this negative feedback is often remarkably effective in maintaining the set point. When people eat whatever amount they wish, neither dieting nor under social pressure to eat more than they want, their weight often stays quite stable for months or even years. It may not be the weight they would most like to be at, but it is the level that their free food consumption maintains, and therefore a set point.

As we noted earlier in this chapter, hunger is only one of many drives or motives that have been observed, even in animals. Among humans there is an even greater variety. For a great many of them, the most desirable level is neither the maximum nor the minimum possible, but somewhere in between. We want a certain amount, but not too much, of exercise and rest and company and privacy and adventure and security. Each of these motives, then, can be considered a controlled quantity. When we get too little of any controlled quantity, we seek more, and when we get too much, we try to cut down. Whereas optimal-arousal theory says that this is true of general arousal, a cybernetic theory of motivation says that it is also true of most of the things we desire.

When we proceed to more complex purposive behaviors, the same principle applies. A student going through college may discover that she is getting failing grades. If the discovery leads her to work harder and thus bring up her grades, she affords an example of negative feedback. In the unlikely event that the student studies so hard as to affect her health, she can cut down her studying. In both cases she discovers a deviation from her progress through college, one that threatens the success of her education, and she corrects the deviation so as to continue on her progress toward the degree.

The Place of Cybernetics in Learning Theory

Cybernetics as the answer to questions discussed in the two previous sections of this chapter is clear. Reinforcement is a change in a controlled quantity, bringing it closer to its set point. All the theories of reinforcement we have discussed so far can be incorporated within this framework. Drives, for example, involve controlled quantities with low set points. Our set point for pain, for instance, is very low, so it is nearly always a reduction in pain rather than an increase that brings that particular controlled quantity closer to its set point. The theory of optimal arousal reflects the fact that the set point for general arousal is typically neither very high nor very low, so decreases from high to medium arousal and increases from low to medium are both reinforcing. The basis of behavioral regulation is the rate at which we make any given response when free to respond as much or as little as we like. That rate is the set point for that response, and we do what we have to in order to keep the rate of responding as close as possible to its set point. If the response is restricted to a rate below its set point, any other response that moves it up toward its set point will be reinforced. Cybernetics is thus a very broad theory of motivation and reinforcement.

The great strength of feedback theory in psychology is the range of topics to which it applies. It is a method of analysis that applies to units as small as a flick of the hand or as large as a person's aim in life. It shows that the coordination of a movement, the pursuit of a goal, the regulation of a physiological function, and the operation of a motive can be viewed as basically the same thing: maintenance of a set point through the process of negative feedback. Moreover, the various levels at which this process operates are interrelated. For example, a coordinated movement, which has set points for speed and direction, may be the means of bringing some other controlled quantity back to its set point (as by getting a glass of water to the mouth and thus reducing thirst). It is possible to think of all our activities as arranged in a hierarchy, interrelated in such a way that maintaining the set point of each one serves to correct a deviation from the set point of the next higher one. This idea is too complicated and speculative to pursue here, but the interested reader can find discussions of it in Powers (1973).

The great weakness of feedback theory in psychology, at least for the purposes of this book, is that it is not a theory of learning. Like Lewin's theory, it tells us how a system operates but not how its operation changes as a result of learning. Presumably one learns what techniques are successful in bringing any given controlled quantity back toward its set point, but cybernetics tells us nothing about how that learning occurs. Thus, although it is a theory of motivated behavior within which learning can be studied, cybernetics is still tangential to the study of learning itself.

OPPONENT-PROCESS THEORY

During the 1950s and 1960s, Richard L. Solomon (b. 1918), currently of the University of Pennsylvania, was involved in various experiments that involved giving electric shocks to dogs. His initial interest was in how the dogs learned a response that permitted them to avoid the shock, but later he became increasingly interested in the dogs' emotional responses to the shocks, including the response to shocks that could not be avoided. He and his collaborators observed that when dogs were first exposed to electric shocks, they appeared terrified by the experience. For a few minutes after the shocks were over, the dogs acted unfriendly and stealthy, before returning to their more typical active, friendly behavior. After a number of days of being shocked, their reactions were considerably different. The reaction to the shocks was much less extreme, more one of anxiety or annoyance than terror. More striking was the change in behavior just after the shocks ended: the dogs were even more active and friendly than usual; they seemed to be expressing their joy that the shock was over.

At about the time Solomon was making these observations, he learned about a study of skydivers (Epstein 1967) and noticed a marked resemblance between their reactions and those of the dogs. Before their first few jumps, the skydivers were highly anxious, and afterward they experienced first a sort of emotionally drained numbness and then a few minutes of pleasant liveliness. After a number of jumps, their reactions were quite different. Before the jump their arousal was in the form of nervous eagerness rather than anxiety, and afterward they spent a couple of hours in a state of exhilaration. For both dogs and skydivers, one thing remained the same: the period just after the frightening experience was (not surprisingly) more pleasant than just before the experience. The whole level, however, had changed, from frightened before and fairly unemotional after to less emotional before and pleasantly excited afterward.

Thinking about these changes in the ways dogs and people react to situations that are originally frightening, Solomon wondered whether there might be similar changes in an experience that was originally pleasant. A striking example came to mind: morphine addiction. Early in the addict's experience with morphine (before becoming an addict), the initial reaction to taking the drug is highly pleasant, whereas the effect of its wearing off is fairly neutral. After many exposures, the person (whom we can now call an addict) gets less pleasure from the administration of the drug, but finds its wearing off very unpleasant (withdrawal symptoms). Though the directions are reversed, the kinds of changes are the same as with the dogs and the skydivers: the emotional reaction at the beginning of the experience becomes weaker, whereas at the end of the experience there is an opposite reaction that gets larger and larger.

The Theory

Eventually Solomon and J. D. Corbit collected a number of such examples and stated a theory to explain them (Solomon & Corbit 1974) known as the *opponent-process* theory. First, this is a *hedonic* theory; that is, it refers to pleasure and displeasure. Second, it might be summarized by saying that for every feeling there is an opposite (but not exactly equal) reaction. The original feeling and the opposite reaction are the opponent processes that give the theory its name. Third, the opposite reaction increases with repeated exposures, producing the changes noted in the examples above. Thus there are opponent processes that counteract both pleasure and displeasure, weakly so at first, but more and more strongly with repeated presentations of the pleasant or unpleasant experience.

Figure 15.1 makes these ideas more explicit. The graphs in panel A of the figure show what happens when a pleasant stimulus (such as an addictive drug) is first presented. When the stimulus is presented (top), the immediate effect is hedonically positive, as shown in the middle graph. This positive (pleasant) effect (called the *a* process) increases rapidly to a maximum, remains at that high level as long as the stimulus is on, and then drops rapidly back to zero when the stimulus is turned off. (In the case of a drug, the "stimulus on" period is the time that the drug remains active in the body.) This simple sequence of the *a* process is represented by the solid line. Shortly after the stimulus goes on, its opponent *b* process also begins, as represented by the broken line. Compared with the *a* process, the *b* process not only begins later but also increases more slowly and to a lower level. When the stimulus goes off, the *b* process again lags behind the *a* process: it continues for a short time after the stimulus is gone and then drops slowly toward zero. Since the *b* process tends to counteract the *a* process, we can determine the net effect of combining them by adding them algebraically (that is, taking account of sign), as shown in the bottom graph. As long as the stimulus is on, the *a* is much stronger, so the *b*

Figure 15.1 *Hedonic opponent processes.* Each panel shows the time that a stimulus is on (top), the *a* process with its opponent *b* process (middle), and the resulting manifest hedonic reaction (bottom). From Solomon (1980). Copyright © 1980 by the American Psychological Association. Adapted by permission of the author.

process has only a slight counteracting effect. However, since the *b* process is still going on after the *a* process has returned to zero, the net effect at the end will be negative. Thus the ending of a pleasant experience is not just neutral but slightly unpleasant.

Panel B of the graph shows the situation for the same stimulus after it has been presented many times. The *a* remains the same, but the *b* process has now increased in strength. Thus when we combine the two there is still a pleasant period just after the stimulus goes on and an unpleasant period just after the stimulus goes off. The relative sizes of these two, however, are much different than before. Whereas at first the initial pleasure was strong and the displeasure at the end mild, now it is just the reverse. As for the period in between, while the stimulus remains on, whereas before it was quite pleasant (though not as much as the initial few moments), now it is barely pleasant at all. The *b* process has not completely counteracted the *a* process during that period of time, but it has come very close to doing so.

If we were graphing an unpleasant primary process, as with the shocked dogs or the skydivers, we would get exactly the same graphs except that the up and down directions would be reversed. The *a* process would now be in the negative direction and the *b* process in the positive direction, but the *b* process would still lag behind the *a*. Moreover, the *b* process would still increase with repeated presentations of the stimulus until it almost but not quite counteracted the unpleasant *a* process.

Some Implications

The most interesting examples of opponent processes are not necessarily the most practical on which to do research. One that lends itself well to quantitative research is *imprinting* in ducklings. The attachment of ducklings to their mother appears to be learned rather than innate, and the process by which it is learned is called imprinting (Lorenz 1952). What most students of imprinting have studied is the duckling's response of following the mother, which can be considered to involve a pleasant *a* process. Solomon and his collaborators chose instead to study the distress calls that the duckling makes when separated from the mother—the opponent *b* process. The number of distress cries in the first minute after separation from the mother makes a good quantitative measure of the strength of the *b* process. In one study (Hoffman et al. 1974) ducklings received 12 exposures of 30 seconds each to the mother with intervals of separation between. For different groups of ducklings, the lengths of the separation periods were different. When these intervals were 1 minute each, the number of distress calls increased from one interval to the next. This change indicates that, as the theory predicts, repeated presentations were strengthening the *b* process. Where the separation intervals were 5 minutes long, however, no such increase occurred. This difference led the researchers to conclude that repetition increases the strength of the *b* process only if the repetitions are close enough together. How close is close enough would vary from one situation to another, but for any particular *b* process there would be a *critical delay duration*, the period within which the stimulus must be presented again in order for the repetition to strengthen the *b* process. With intervals between presentations that are longer than the critical delay duration, the increase in strength of the *b* process would not occur.

It should be noted that the increase with repetition in the *b* process, provided the repetitions come within the critical delay duration, results only from the fact that they occur. This is not a matter of conditioning or even of learning, as that term is often used. Nothing else has to be paired with the *b* process in order to produce the change. It is the repetition of the *b* process itself which strengthens it, as in the repeated use of a muscle. Of all the forms of learning we have considered so far, the only one resembling it in this respect is the habituation of the orienting reflex. This kind of change resulting simply from exposure, has, however, received increasing attention relative to more traditional changes through conditioning (e.g., Hill 1978).

Why should there be such opponent processes? We may note that *b* processes, by counteracting *a* processes, tend to move hedonic states back toward zero. Thus neither pleasure nor displeasure is able to become very powerful without being counteracted by negative feedback. This tendency would suggest that affective neutrality is a more adaptive state than either strong pleasure or strong displeasure. Perhaps either kind of strong affective state is too much of a strain on the organism, and homeostasis must be restored to keep us from being emotionally worn out. In any case, opponent-process theory resembles traditional drive theory in one respect: both regard a reduction in arousal as the standard tendency of the motivational system.

Although the b process can thus be seen as a negative feedback mechanism correcting a deviation from a set point of affective neutrality, it is not a very efficient one. It undercorrects while the stimulus is on and then overcorrects after the stimulus goes off, pushing the controlled quantity in the opposite direction. As the b process becomes stronger, its undercorrection during the stimulus becomes less, but its overcorrection at the end becomes greater. Using the steersman analogy from cybernetics, it is as though the boat is constantly buffeted by strong and rapidly shifting currents, so that the steersman can never completely compensate for them while they are flowing, but then shoots off in the other direction when the current for which he was correcting suddenly stops. Presumably it would be a wild ride indeed if the steersman were not there to exert at least some degree of control.

At a more philosophical level, the theory suggests that the pursuit of pleasure is bound to be less successful than one might hope, since a pleasant a process not only often carries an unpleasant b process along with it but also keeps strengthening that b process. On the other hand, the theory also suggests that life's misfortunes are not as bad as they might be, since so many unpleasant a processes have opponent b processes that not only blunt the displeasure but provide a "sweet aftertaste." (Neither Solomon nor anyone else claims to know just how many a processes have opponent b processes strong enough to be important, only that a great many of them do.) As Solomon (1980) comments, it is a puritan's theory. Ralph Waldo Emerson would probably feel that it captures much of the spirit of his essay on compensation.

Chapter
16

Some Interpretations of Memory

*T*he theories we have discussed so far in this book for the most part have not had much to say about memory. This silence may well seem strange, since remembering what we have learned is such an important aspect of learning, while forgetting what we have learned is so often a problem. To a considerable extent, however, learning theorists have tended either to take both remembering and forgetting for granted or (like Guthrie and Estes) to explain them in general terms without looking at them in much detail.

A CONNECTIONIST APPROACH TO MEMORY

In spite of this relative lack of interest in the topic, learning theorists have not entirely neglected memory. In particular, there has long been a moderate degree of interest among connectionist theorists in verbal learning and memory. Though we remember (or forget) all sorts of things—events, faces, scenes, skills, feelings—the remembering of words and other verbal materials is particularly prominent, especially for those of us who are either students or teachers. Moreover, both words and trigrams are the sorts of simple units that can easily be analyzed as stimuli and responses. It is therefore not surprising that until recently the study of memory focused mainly on memory for verbal material and was done largely by connectionist psychologists (though also, as we have seen, by gestalt psychologists). Hull and collaborators, for example, wrote an impressively elaborate deductive analysis of the process of serial memorization. The greatest interest in the topic was not among the theorists we have mentioned, however, but among other psychologists who, though connection-ist in their biases, were less inclined to the building of grand theories. They preferred, instead, to construct smaller theories dealing with specific top-ics in verbal learning and memory—sometimes called miniature theories. This approach began with the early German psychologist Hermann Eb-binghaus, whose classic experiments on memory (using himself as subject) began the experimental study of the topic (Ebbinghaus 1964). In America, the most prominent examplar of this tradition is Benton J. Underwood (b. 1915) of Northwestern University.

Interference as a Source of Forgetting

Underwood should certainly be classified as a connectionist psychologist, for most of his analyses are in terms of verbal responses and the stimuli, usually also verbal, that elicit them. Many of his experiments are simply concerned with finding the relationships between independent and de-pendent variables, with little interest in theoretical interpretations. In this respect he resembles Skinner. When he does act as a theorist, however, his interpretations are relatively formal: though he does not put them in the Hullian form of postulates and theorems, he does make them specific enough to be clearly testable with experiments. He uses the term *rein-forcement,* but without much concern as to what the nature of reinforce-ment is. A cautious, step-by-step approach, with great emphasis on proper research methods, characterizes all of his work.

One of Underwood's many interests in verbal learning has been the question of why we forget. Once something has been memorized, why do we not remember it forever? Of the various explanations that have been offered, by far the most influential has been the *interference* interpreta-tion, that we forget because our retention of any given item is interfered with by all the other items we have learned that resemble it in some way. Though we have mentioned only Guthrie as having such an interpreta-tion, actually a number of the theorists discussed in this book agree that forgetting is caused primarily, if not exclusively, by such interference.

Underwood agrees on the importance of interference in forgetting, but raises a question as to which of two sources of interference is the more important. If we forget any given thing because of interference from something else that we learned afterward, this effect is known as *retroac-tive interference.* The second thing we learned has in some sense replaced the first in memory, so that it is harder to retrieve the first. Traditionally, retroactive interference has been regarded as the major form of interfer-ence (again, think of Guthrie's explanation of forgetting). However, it is also possible that the interference with any given material could come from other material that had been learned before. This effect is known as *proactive interference.*

These two possible forms of interference are shown in Table 16.1. By comparing retention of one list in the table (called the key list) by groups with different experiences of learning another list, we can measure the

Table 16.1 RETROACTIVE AND PROACTIVE INTERFERENCE

Group	Period 1	Period 2	Period 3	Period 4[a]
A	Nothing	Learn key list	Learn other list	Test on key list
B	Learn other list	Learn key list	Nothing	Test on key list
C	Nothing	Learn key list	Nothing	Test on key list

[a]Comparisons of key-list scores on the retention test in period 4:
    C − A = amount of retroactive interference
    C − B = amount of proactive interference
    B − A = extent to which retroactive interference is greater than proactive (if negative, proactive is
        greater)

amounts of proactive and retroactive interference. Note that the retention interval between learning the key list in period 2 and testing in period 4 is the same for all three groups, so differences in performance on the test cannot be attributed to any differences in elapsed time.

At first glance, proactive interference seems like a less plausible cause of forgetting than does retroactive interference. Once the new material has been learned, and the old material therefore supposedly unlearned, or at least pushed into the background, why should it interfere with retention of the new? Underwood points out that what happens to the first material when the second is being learned is comparable to extinction. But what happens to an extinguished response with the passage of time? Very often it shows spontaneous recovery. Why should we not expect that the material which was learned first would remain only temporarily extinguished, and then return through spontaneous recovery to interfere with the material learned second? If this process does indeed take place, the passage of time should serve not only to increase the effect of proactive interference but also to decrease the effect of retroactive interference through the recovery of the material to be remembered. Underwood (1948) found that this expectation is indeed what occurs. With the amount and difficulty of the interfering materials held constant, retroactive interference produced much more interference with retention five hours after learning than did proactive, but after a two-day interval there was practically no difference between them.

Which Kind Is More Important?

This experiment of Underwood's demonstrates that proactive interference is just as plausible an explanation of forgetting as is retroactive. It does not, however, give us much basis for deciding how much each of these processes actually contributes to everyday forgetting. Underwood's impression about the relative importance of these two processes came from another line of evidence. He noted that when college students memorized a list of words or trigrams, the amount that they remembered from the list a day later depended greatly on how much prior experience they had had in memorization. We might expect that the more experienced memorizers would show an advantage, and indeed they do if we look at the rate of original learning. However, if both experienced and inexperienced memorizers keep on working until they have mastered the list, and then stop, it is the inexperienced memorizers who retain more after an interval of time (Underwood 1957). This difference does not seem so surprising when we consider that all the previous lists learned by the experienced group were building up proactive interference with retention of the final list. If there are many previous lists to produce proactive interference, the effect can be huge. In one experiment (Keppel, Postman, & Zavortink 1968), subjects learned a series of paired-associate lists at two-day intervals and were tested for retention of each before learning the next. On the average, they remembered 70 percent of the items on the first list and only 5 percent of the items on the thirty-sixth list, even though the lists were equally difficult and were tested the same length of time after being learned. Clearly, differences in proactive interference alone can make remarkable differences in the amount of forgetting.

Does it follow that proactive interference from things we have learned previously is the major cause of our ordinary forgetting? Not necessarily, since experiments that vary only the proactive interference do not tell us about the effects of the retroactive interference or of other possible causes of forgetting. However, if we are concerned with forgetting over periods of days or weeks, there is likely to be much more other material that can interfere proactively (given the previous years we have had to learn such material) than retroactively (which would have to be learned during the days or weeks of the retention interval). It thus seems highly plausible that proactive interference is the most important cause of forgetting.

Though the above line of argument with its supporting data represents a major contribution to our understanding of forgetting, Underwood was not satisfied to leave it at that. He went on to gather new data, and not all of what he found fits well into his explanation of forgetting. Because Underwood's theory of forgetting is fairly simple and quite close to data, it has the sort of self-correcting character that Hull sought but did not always achieve. Through his application of simple learning principles to more complex forms of learning and through his constant checking of predictions against data, Underwood has provided not only an interpretation of forgetting but also an impressive example of careful, small-scale theory building.

COGNITIVE APPROACHES TO MEMORY

Although the approach to memory that we have considered so far has not been closely associated with any of the major schools of learning theory, it has been very much a connectionist approach. Responses to stimuli are learned; they compete with one another; and they undergo extinction and spontaneous recovery. Increasingly, however, a different approach has become popular. Rather than focusing on the responses, it focuses on the information that makes the responses possible. Though it differs substantially from the cognitive theories we have looked at so far in this book, it is still more a cognitive than a connectionist approach. It has led to substantial changes both in the ways memory is studied and in the ways it is talked about by theorists.

In the connectionist view of memory, what is remembered or forgotten is responses, and the main reason for some responses being forgotten is competition from other responses to similar stimuli. The alternative point of view, popular through much of the 1960s and 1970s, regarded the units as items of information and memory as a matter of storing and then retrieving those items. For the connectionist view, the appropriate analogies are telephone switchboards or mazes through which to find one's way. For the newer view, the appropriate analogy is a library where information is stored. These items of information are cognitive units, even though they may still be measured by the making of a response. If this approach is not as cognitive as Tolman's cognitive maps, it is at least in a class with Bolles's S-S* and R-S* expectancies.

Three Memory Stores

Perhaps the best-known version of this approach was presented by Richard C. Atkinson (b. 1929) and Richard M. Shiffrin (b. 1942), both then of Stanford University (Atkinson & Shiffrin 1968, 1971; Shiffrin & Atkinson 1969). It regarded memory as made up of three *stores,* that is, locations where information can be stored for some period of time. We do not need to take the concept of location literally. If information is received via the senses and can then affect behavior at a later time, it must have been stored in some form during the interval. There seem to be three different forms of storage, in terms of how long it lasts, how it is retrieved, and why it cannot stay stored longer than it does. These differences make it natural to think of three different stores located in three different places, but we do not have to look at it that way. The three stores are intervening variables, and whether we accept them depends on whether we can use them as a basis for predicting the laws of memory, not on knowing where they are located or even whether they have any specific location at all.

The first of the three stores is the *sensory register.* It is first in the sense that all information arising via the senses is registered there first; hence the name. Actually it may be misleading to speak of it in the singular, since in a way there are as many sensory registers as there are senses. All information that we receive, whether by vision, by hearing, or in any other way, goes at once into a sensory register. It remains there for less than a second (for vision) or slightly longer (for hearing and perhaps other senses) and is then lost. Moreover, it is stored in just the form that it is received, like a copy of the image from the retina of the eye or of the sound from the inner ear.

We can demonstrate this very short storage of information in its original form by showing someone an array of 12 letters for one-twentieth of a second and then, as soon as the display is turned off, giving her a signal to report the top, middle, or bottom row of letters. People average about three out of four correct, and since they did not know which row they would be asked to report until after the display was gone, we can presume that some image of the array lasted long enough for them to "read" the letters from it (Sperling 1960). (If we had simply asked them to read all 12, they would still have gotten only four or five right, indicating that the image is very short lived.) The sensory register is thus rather like a television picture: it contains a lot of information, but only for a very short time.

The sensory register holds information too briefly to be of much interest to students of learning. The second store holds information considerably longer, and not necessarily in its original form. This is the *short-term store,* also known as *short-term memory* or as *working memory.* The most common example of information in the short-term store is a phone number one has looked up and wants to remember just long enough to dial it. It is not remembered in any permanent sense; in fact, it is often forgotten in a matter of seconds. Still, as contrasted with the sensory register, it is held long enough to be used in fairly complex ways. If dialing a number does not seem very complex, consider the information one holds while doing arithmetic in one's head. You may, for example, remember a number long enough to multiply it by another number, but as soon as you have the product, you start to forget it. This example helps to show why the short-term store is also called working memory.

Only a limited number of items can be kept at any one time in this short-term store or working memory. As soon as additional items are added, some of those already there have to go. This means that items can be kept in short-term memory almost indefinitely as long as one concentrates on those particular items. If for some reason you had to look up a phone number in one place and then spend some time going to the phone without being able to write the number down, you could still remember it. However, if getting to the phone required remembering other new information or making calculations, these other uses of working memory might take over the limited space and make you forget the number you intended to dial. This interference between the old and the new material may seem a lot like retroactive interference, but the interpretation is rather different. The interference is not between two responses to the same stimulus, one of which will be retained over a long period, but between two items, one of which will be retained in working memory when there is not room enough for both.

The capacity of the short-term store is about seven items. This capacity is about the same regardless of the kinds of items one is remembering, as long as they are familiar enough to function as units. Thus, the letter sequence c-a-t, being a familiar word, would be a unit, and one could expect to hold about seven such units in working memory at a time. However, the same sequence rearranged as t-c-a might be only a meaningless sequence of three letters and therefore represent three units in working memory. The capacity of the short-term store is not always exactly seven units, but it is rarely fewer than five or more than nine. This regularity, consistent across both different individuals and different kinds of items, is one manifestation of what George Miller (1956) (not to be confused with Neal Miller) referred to as "The Magical Number Seven, Plus or Minus Two."

Although rehearsal is a good way of keeping an item in working memory, it is not always necessary. Items do not drop out of the short-term store just because they are not rehearsed; they drop out because they are replaced by other items. Suppose you read a short series of letters and are tested a number of seconds later to see how well you remember it. If you spent the intervening seconds doing mental arithmetic, you are likely to have forgotten the letters, since the arithmetic required using working memory for numbers, which crowded out the letters. If, on the other hand, you spent the time listening intently to try to detect a faint signal, you would remember the letters much better, even though you had not had a chance to rehearse them. There would have been nothing to crowd the letters out of the short-term store, so they would still be remembered.

Finally, the *long-term store* is closer to what we considered in the previous two sections, though still substantially different. Whereas in the previous section we asked how responses are memorized and what determines how they are retained, now we ask how items enter the long-term store and how they are later retrieved from that store. Although there is no way to be sure, the assumption is that the long-term store has unlimited capacity and that nothing is lost from it. When we forget something that was once in the long-term store, the reason is that we can no longer find it, but it is still there, available to be found if we can select the right search strategy for retrieving it.

Although the long-term store corresponds to what Underwood analyzed, the nature of the analysis is rather different. We might think of the long-term store as a filing system of a library, where a great deal of information is stored on a permanent basis for use when needed. Each item of information is filed under a number of headings and may be retrieved whenever there is a call for any of these headings. The headings may be of various sorts: by topic (e.g., everything I know about magnetism), or by occasion (e.g., everything that happened to me during the winter of 1987–1988), or by place (e.g., the locations of the major public buildings in Philadelphia), or a number of other possibilities. Some items of information carry many such tags and thus are fairly often retrieved from the long-term store, while others have few such labels and are rarely retrieved. Hence an item that seems to be completely forgotten may still be retrieved if one hits on the right search label.

When an item is retrieved from the long-term store, it goes into the short-term store, which again justifies the latter's alternative title of working memory. As with any other item, it stays there for some period of time and then is crowded out by other items. When that happens, however, it is not lost, but returns to (or remains in) the long-term store. Atkinson and Shiffrin suggest the metaphor of a photocopier: when an item is in the long-term store, a copy is put in the short-term store when needed, used there, and then discarded as a new item would be, while the original item remains unchanged in the long-term store.

The relationship between the long-term and short-term stores is illustrated by what happens when we hear a long series of words or other items and then try to remember them in any order—a test of retention known as *free recall*. We usually remember more items both from the first part of the list and from the last part than from the middle. The better retention of the early part is called a *primacy effect* and the better retention of the late part, a *recency effect*. Why do they occur? We can get a partial answer by doing the experiment slightly differently: waiting a number of seconds after the list is presented before trying to recall it, while keeping occupied with some other task so that there is no chance to rehearse the list. If we do this, the recency effect disappears, but the primacy effect is still found. It seems, therefore, that the items near the end of the list were better retained in the immediate test because they were still in the short-term store. In the delayed test, they had been lost from the short-term store, so the last part of the list was no better remembered than the middle.

The primacy effect, however, must be due to some other factor, since more items from the first part of the list have evidently got into the long-term store, so that they were not lost during the interval between the list and the test. Perhaps this happened because they were studied more carefully than the later items, or because they were rehearsed during presentation of the rest of the list. Whatever the reason, it seems clear that the primacy and recency effects occur for different reasons. The primacy effect reflects a difference in the number of items that get into the long-term store, whereas the recency effect is indeed due to recency, since it lasts only as long as the items near the end of the list remain in the short-term store.

If nothing is ever lost from the long-term store, why is it typically harder to retrieve items the longer they have been in the long-term store? The answer is that the older items have more items that can be confused with them; and it is harder to find the correct item among all the incorrect ones. Again, this sounds a good deal like proactive and retroactive interference. However, the ways of thinking about the process are still rather different. The interference is a matter, not of competing responses that show extinction and spontaneous recovery, but rather of a more or less organized clutter in which it gets harder and harder to find what you want when there are more items to be searched through. The age of a memory is not a crucial factor in itself; what matters is whether the way it is labeled matches the search device you are currently using. This approach thus puts less emphasis on what happens to items after they are learned and more emphasis on the ways one goes about looking for them. A good memory therefore depends on the relationship between the way items are labeled as they go into the long-term store and the way they are searched for when the time comes to retrieve them.

How, then, do items get into the long-term store? The basic answer is by rehearsal. The more an item is rehearsed in the short-term store, the greater the probability that it will move into the long-term store. However, what is rehearsed, and perhaps stored, is a particular version of the item—that is, the item *encoded* in a certain way. Encoding is a major determinant of whether an item is stored in a form that can later be retrieved, and so has been studied by a number of psychologists in ways that go beyond Atkinson and Shiffrin's theory.

The Process of Encoding

What does encoding consist of? There are many possibilities, and the applied psychology of memory is largely the study of devices for effective encoding. At the theoretical level, we will consider two approaches that have received a good deal of attention in recent years.

One approach was presented by F. I. M. Craik and R. S. Lockhart (1972). This approach maintains that how well something is remembered depends on how deeply it is processed. What is meant by depth of processing is best indicated by an example. People were given a list of words and asked to make one of three decisions about each word: (1) whether it was in capital or lowercase letters, (2) whether it would rhyme with *right*, or (3) whether it referred to something commonly found in the home. There were no instructions to remember the words, but afterward the people were in fact asked to try to remember them. Memory was least good for (1), better for (2), and best for (3). Craik and Lockhart explained these differences by saying that question (1), dealing only with the form of the word, required little processing; question (2), dealing with its sound, required more; and question (3), dealing with meaning, required the deepest processing. The deeper the processing, in turn, the better the memory for the words.

Obviously the three questions call for different *kinds* of processing, but what does it mean to say that they require different *depths* of processing? Though deeper processing often takes longer, which would automatically give it an advantage in memory, that is not the main answer. Primarily, deeper processing involves those aspects of a word that are most relevant to remembering it. The letters in which it is printed make up a superficial aspect of the word, one unrelated to what is essential about that word. The sound with which the word ends is a slightly more distinctive characteristic of the word but still not as distinctive or basic as the meaning. Processing that involves the meaning is the deepest kind, the kind involving what is essential about the word to be remembered. This, as well as simply the time involved, makes it the most efficient kind of processing.

This emphasis on different depths of processing leading to different lengths of retention can be seen as an alternative to the distinction between short-term and long-term stores. Perhaps, rather than having two different places that items are stored, we have some items that are processed shallowly and are quickly lost and others that are processed more deeply and therefore retained longer. However, we can also use the two sets of ideas together, with the depth of processing determining whether or not an item moves from the short-term into the long-term store. In any case, the idea of different depths of processing offers one answer to the question of why some items are remembered for a long time and others are not.

A different approach to the questions of encoding has been developed by Allan Paivio (1971). He suggests that information is stored in memory in two forms, verbal and imaginal. Verbal representation of information is, of course, in words, whether isolated words, single statements, or complex sequences of related statements. Imaginal representation is in terms of images, which can be of any form (e.g., the sound of a tune or the smell of fresh-ground coffee), but is primarily in the form of visual images, or mental pictures. Some items of information are stored in one form, some in the other, and some in both.

What determines how an item will be represented in memory? In general, it will be stored in any form that it can be. Anything that can readily be expressed in words will be represented verbally in memory and anything that can be coded as a picture will be represented imaginally in memory. Many items, therefore, will be represented in both ways. Pictures that can readily be described, and words or statements referring to something that can readily be pictured, would lend themselves to double representation, both verbal and imaginal. Other items, however, are so much easier to represent one way than the other that they are likely to be stored in only one form. A picture of some complex design for which there is no easy description in words would probably be represented only imaginally in memory, whereas a word like *truth*, which is hard to picture, would probably be represented only verbally. Paivio assumes we are so experienced in applying words to all sorts of things that most stimuli get stored verbally, whereas quite a number of more abstract stimuli do not get stored imaginally. Most items therefore are stored either in both verbal and imaginal form, or only in verbal form.

A key assumption of Paivio's theory is that it is easier to retrieve an item from memory storage if it is represented there in two ways than if it is represented in only one way. There are, so to speak, twice as many ways that one can find the item if it is stored in two forms. It follows from this that concrete words, such as *house* and *dog*, that can easily be pictured should be better remembered than abstract words, such as *truth* and *eternity*. This prediction has been confirmed.

Psychologists are used to analyzing variables as matters of degree rather than simply as present or absent, so Paivio does not stop with saying that an item can easily be coded in one way or in two—he goes on to ask how easily. He gave people a series of words and asked them to form a visual image of each and signal as soon as they had done so. He then used these data to give each word an imagery score: the faster an image could be formed, the higher the score. If the theory is correct, words with high imagery scores should be easier to remember than words with low imagery scores. This prediction has been tested and confirmed in several different forms of memory experiments.

If instead of words a person is given pictures to remember, it should be very easy to represent them imaginally, even more so than for concrete words. At the same time, given our tendency to label the things we see with words, pictures should also be at least moderately well represented verbally. Memory for pictures should thus be especially good—better than for words. This prediction too has been confirmed.

Paivio's theory helps us to understand why certain tricks for remembering things (*mnemonic devices,* as such tricks are called) work as well as they do. One such mnemonic device, useful when learning pairs of items, is to form a mental image of the two items interacting in some way. Thus, to remember that *hat* and *train* go together, one might imagine a train racing along the tracks with a hat perched on top of the locomotive. (If the image looks silly, so much the better, say some experts.) When a whole series of items is to be remembered, one suggestion (dating back to ancient Greece) is to imagine a building one knows well and picture each item at some particular place in the building. One can then mentally "walk" through the building, retrieving one item from the living room sofa, another from the kitchen sink, and so forth. The reader will readily recognize that both of these methods are useful mainly for concrete items, those with high imagery scores. Given that kind of item, there is evidence to indicate that both of these mnemonic devices are quite helpful in increasing the number of items one can commit to memory in a given amount of time (Bower 1972).

Schemata in Memory

These various approaches to memory, in terms of stores and encoding, dominated the study of memory through much of the 1960s and 1970s. Quite recently another even more cognitive approach has become prominent. It is not, however, a new approach; it goes back both to the gestalt psychologists and to the early British psychologist Frederic C. Bartlett (1932). It is also closely related to Piaget's work. This approach treats memory neither as responses to be retained nor as items to be stored but as a pattern of understanding. When we are exposed to new material, we incorporate it into the existing structure of our knowledge and beliefs. In this process, the original material may be distorted to fit better with the existing structure. Perhaps it would be more appropriate to say not that the material is distorted but that what is remembered is a new construction, one which depends both on the presented material and on the existing cognitive structure. When we are asked to recall the new material, what we come up with is this new construction, which reflects the original material but may differ from it in any of various ways.

As with Piaget, this cognitive approach makes heavy use of the concept of *schema*. As used here, a schema may be thought of as a basic pattern or prototype on which specific experiences represent variations. When we have an experience and afterward try to remember it, we first remember the schema and then work on the details. If some of the details are inconsistent with the schema, we may remember them incorrectly, not as they actually happened but as the schema suggests that they should have happened. On the other hand, a detail that could not have been remembered in isolation can, if consistent with the schema, be given correctly by a mixture of memory and of inference from the schema. Details are not remembered in isolation, therefore, but rather are incorporated into existing schemata. Even an item that is not consistent with the schema is still linked to it, either remembered incorrectly or remembered correctly as a strange (and perhaps, therefore, especially memorable) anomaly.

This gestalt-oriented view of memory helps to make a number of social phenomena easier to understand. Hence it has been popular with social psychologists. They have noted a number of kinds of schemata that affect not only our memory but our perception and understanding of the world around us. For example, there are schemata about people that lead us to organize the things we see other people do under a particular heading, such as "intelligent" or "athletic" or "generous." Once we have decided that someone shows one of these traits, it serves as a schema leading us to expect certain behaviors from the person but not to expect others and to remember some better than others. Another example is our understanding of stories. We expect a story to start somewhere and go somewhere, with one event leading to another and with the characters motivated in normal ways. Items in the story that fit our story schema are usually easier to remember than ones that don't, which we say "don't make sense." Moreover, we may "remember" details that were not a part of the story at all, but that are consistent with it and fill in gaps in the original presentation (e.g., Mandler 1978; Spiro 1976). This process reduces the distinction between "true memory" on the one hand and inference from schemata on the other. Our social world can be seen as made up of schemata that give the world order and make the world easier both to remember and to deal with effectively, but that also sometimes lead us to inaccurate memories and mistaken conclusions.

One kind of schema that has received considerable attention is a *script* (Schank & Abelson 1977). This is a typical sequence of events that would occur in a given setting. We have schemata about what normally happens at a baseball game, a cocktail party, or an evening at the theater. Each of these schemata constitutes a script that helps us to make sense out of the sequence of events. Thus, if we read in a story that "with three balls and two strikes on the batter, he hit a home run," we know that there were at least six pitches to that batter. If we later try to recall the story as completely as possible, we may give the incident as "The batter sent the sixth pitch into the stands for a home run." Because we have such scripts for familiar situations, we can reconstruct and elaborate stories from minimal information, whereas people unfamiliar with the situation (i.e., lacking the script) would find the same minimal version of the story quite difficult both to understand and to remember.

An example of this last point is what happens when we read and try to remember a passage like the following:

> The procedure is actually quite simple. First you arrange things into different groups. Of course, one pile may be sufficient depending on how much there is to do. If you have to go somewhere else due to lack of facilities, that is the next step; otherwise you are pretty well set. It is important not to overdo things. That is, it is better to do too few things at once than too many. . . . After the procedure is completed one arranges the materials into different groups again. Then they can be put into their appropriate places. Eventually they will be used once more and the whole cycle will have to be repeated. However, that is part of life [Bransford & Johnson 1973, p. 400].

Even though the words are familiar and the writing is grammatical, the passage as a whole does not seem to make much sense, and it is hard to memorize. The problem is that the specific points in the passage require a script to give them a clear and coherent meaning, but we do not know what script to apply. If we knew in advance that the passage referred to washing clothes, the elliptical meanings of its various parts would become clear. We would then be able not only to understand what these various parts meant but also to recall the passage much better than if we lacked the script for interpreting it.

If our goal is to remember the main points in the passage, having the script is clearly an advantage. If our goal, instead, is to memorize it verbatim, the script is still helpful, but it does raise problems. Without the script, we have trouble remembering the main points, because we have no framework to help. With the script, we instead have trouble remembering whether something was actually said in the passage or whether we inferred it. Given the script and a few details to fill it in, our inferences are often so clear that we cannot distinguish them from items that were specifically mentioned, as has been shown in various experiments (e.g., Bransford, Barclay, & Franks 1972).

Just as classical gestalt theory treated perception and thought as much the same process, so this gestaltish approach to memory treats memory and inference as, if not the same thing, at least almost inextricably interwoven. Other people might ask, "Do we actually remember a given item, or do we infer that it must have been there and then act accordingly?"

People using the analysis in terms of schemata, however, are likely to conclude that the two cannot be distinguished. Our cognitions about a given event may be formed in any of various ways, but once formed they usually influence our behavior in much the same way regardless of how they were formed. To say that some cognitions represent "real memories" and others do not is pointless.

A Parting Thought   Of the various topics we consider in this book, memory is probably the one that most illustrates the recent upswing in cognitive theorizing. The approach discussed in the second section of this chapter has largely (though by no means entirely) replaced that from the first section as the dominant approach to memory. That is, the view of memory as a system of storing and retrieving information has become more popular than the view of memory as facilitation and inhibition of responses. One might say that a "library" model of memory ("Do we have that item in our library collection and how can we find it there?") has to a considerable degree replaced a "switchboard" model ("Do our wires still have the connections so that each incoming signal will activate the correct mechanism?"). It is a change that Tolman would have applauded.

Moreover, even within cognitive theory, the use of the concept of schema seems to be gaining in popularity. Memory is regarded less as a collection of items in a library and more as a total view of some topic. Information is incorporated into an existing schema and in some cases modifies the schema. Since an item of information cannot be analyzed apart from the whole pattern of which it comes to form a part, this is distinctly a gestalt view of memory. Thus in the area of memory, as in numerous others, cognitive theory has come very much into its own.

Chapter
17

Evolution and Learning

Development refers not only to the changes within an individual from conception to death, but also to the changes in a lineage over generations—in other words, evolution. Biologists and physical anthropologists have taken a strong interest in these evolutionary changes, but psychologists have for the most part been little interested in them. Though learning theorists have done research on a variety of species, they have seldom focused on the differences between species, differences which are products of evolution. Rather, they have been mainly interested in the similarities between species, with the differences commonly being dismissed as inconvenient irrelevancies.

Skinner's attitude may be taken as representative. He recognizes that species differ in their responsiveness to different stimuli (e.g., dogs are color-blind, while pigeons have excellent color vision); in the responses they can easily make (e.g., grasping by monkeys but not by dolphins); and in the reinforcers that affect their behavior (e.g., raw worms as positive reinforcers for robins but not for humans). To study learning in different species effectively, therefore, it is necessary to find the right stimuli, responses, and reinforcers for each species. When that is done, however, different species will react to the same independent variable in the same way. A thirsty rat pressing a lever for drops of water, a hungry pigeon pecking a key for access to a hopper of grain, and a human pulling a vending-machine-type plunger for chewing gum will show the same reactions to their schedules of reinforcement. Put all three on a fixed-ratio 5, for example, and their response patterns will be indistinguishable.

This view that the basic laws of learning are the same for different species has been a fundamental tenet of most learning theories. It serves to justify the fact that out of all the species in the world, learning theorists have made greatest use of rats; moderate use of pigeons, monkeys, dogs, and humans; and only slight use of all the rest. It also serves to justify applications of learning theory based largely on rats or pigeons to complex human clinical and social issues, as in the publications of Skinner and of Dollard and Miller. Without this assumption, learning theory would be a substantially different enterprise.

Along with this assumption has gone another: that stimuli, responses, and reinforcers can be paired up in any way, and all ways are equally effective. In other words, how much one learns from a given series of experiences depends on the distinctiveness of the stimuli, the ease of making the required responses, and the effectiveness of the reinforcers, but it does not depend on which stimuli are used with which reinforcers to teach which responses. For example, if lever pressing and jumping are equally easy responses to learn, and if food and escape from shock are equally powerful reinforcers, it does not matter whether the lever pressing is reinforced with food and the jumping with escape from shock or vice versa; either will be learned equally well. This assumption makes it possible to state laws of learning in general terms, referring only to stimuli, responses, and reinforcers, without having to specify what particular ones are to be paired.

SPECIES-SPECIFIC BEHAVIOR

Although the two assumptions above have been basic articles of faith for many if not most learning theorists, evidence has increasingly been accumulating over the past quarter century or so that they are not altogether valid. Perhaps the first widely noticed sign that all was not well with the assumptions was an article by Keller and Marian Breland. This husband-wife team had been leaders in the use of Skinnerian techniques of animal training, preparing animals to perform on television, at fairs, and in many kinds of exhibits. As such, they were dedicated believers in the power of reinforcement. To their surprise, however, they found their animals sometimes behaving in ways that seemed quite un-Skinnerian. For example, a raccoon that was supposed to put two coins in a slot machine in exchange for food would instead keep rubbing the coins together—as in the raccoon's familiar "food washing" pattern. A pig in a similar situation would drop the coins and root for them in the ground in typical pig fashion. The common problem was that the food-related consummatory responses characteristic of a species often interfered with the response that the experimenter was trying to shape with food reinforcement. Parodying Skinner's book *The Behavior of Organisms* (1938), the Brelands said that they were observing the "misbehavior of organisms" (Breland & Breland 1961).

The "misbehavior" that the Brelands observed consisted of the responses that animals typically make in the presence of food. They are not learned food-getting responses, but innate responses that tend to occur when food is present or is anticipated. Since they vary from species to species, but are relatively fixed and stereotyped for the members of any given species, they are known as *species-specific responses.* Though there are many kinds of species-specific responses, those connected with food are among the most conspicuous to psychologists, since psychologists so often use food as a reinforcer. Since the psychologist arbitrarily selects some response to reinforce, there is always the chance that species-specific responses relevant to the reinforcer will interfere with the animal's making that response.

Species-specific responses do not always interfere with learning, however. In some cases they may make learning easier. Consider, for example, that Skinnerian favorite, a pigeon reinforced with food for pecking a lighted key on the wall of its cage. To Skinner it is obvious that the pigeon pecks because it is reinforced for pecking. However, we can show that things are not always as obvious as they seem. Suppose we vary the experiment by leaving the key dark most of the time, but every now and then lighting it briefly, followed immediately by presenting food. Since the light is always followed by the food, we might expect some form of classical conditioning to occur but we would not expect any operant behavior to be learned, since the food comes regardless of what the pigeon does. Nevertheless, pigeons exposed to this series of events show an increasing tendency to peck the key whenever the light goes on. Skinner might call the pecking a superstition, since anything the pigeon does is followed by food, but the interesting thing is that what pigeons almost universally come to do is that one response—pecking. This process of acquisition, in which pigeons come to peck the lighted key even though there is no systematic connection between the pecking and the food, is called *autoshaping* (Brown & Jenkins 1968).

Once we know that autoshaping will occur, we see the traditional learning to peck a key in a new way. Why do pigeons learn so readily to peck a key when they are reinforced with food? Perhaps it is not so much because pecking is reinforced as because food and a conspicuously peckable target (the key) occur close together. This possibility is strengthened by the fact that autoshaping can occur even when pecking *prevents* the food from appearing on that trial. With that arrangement, pecking is never reinforced; in fact it is punished by loss of food. Nevertheless, most pigeons peck the key often enough under these conditions to lose a substantial proportion of the reinforcers they could have obtained by simply waiting without pecking (Williams & Williams 1969). Apparently, in the presence of food, pecking at the most conspicuous object in the vicinity is a species-specific behavior of pigeons—fortunately so, for this is exactly the behavior that the experimenter wants the pigeon to learn. So, whereas the Brelands kept finding that species-specific behaviors were interfering with what they wanted to teach their animals, here species-specific behavior makes the learning exceptionally easy.

Not all species-specific behaviors involve reward situations. There are also species-specific responses to danger—responses that an organism makes under conditions of pain or fear. In general, such responses to danger involve either fleeing, freezing, or in some cases fighting, but the detailed form they take varies considerably with the species. They are the responses that members of the species tend to make automatically, without the need for any special learning, when confronted with indications of danger.

Just as with species-specific responses to reward, those to danger can either facilitate or interfere with new learning. If an animal can escape or avoid shock by doing something that resembles its species-specific fleeing or freezing behavior, that response will be learned very quickly. If, on the other hand, it can escape or avoid the shock only by doing something very different from its innate reactions to danger, that response will be quite difficult to learn. Bolles (1970) has shown that a number of findings about the way rats learn to escape and to avoid shock, ranging from responses that are often learned in one trial to responses that are nearly impossible for a rat to learn as a way of dealing with shock, can be explained by noting how similar a given response is to the species-specific behavior in situations of danger.

A similar example of a species-specific response giving rise to rapid learning is seen in the experiment by Guthrie and Horton (1946) that was mentioned in Chapter 4. The cats in that study escaped from a puzzle box by bending a flexible pole in the middle of the box. A large proportion of the cats made this response in a stereotyped way, by rubbing their sides against it, rather than moving it in the many other ways that would have been possible. Guthrie saw this stereotyping as evidence that they continued to make the response in whatever way they had made it before. (To Skinner it might be an example of superstition.) It now appears, however, that the cats were actually making a species-specific "greeting" response. Normally cats will rub up against people in that way as a form of greeting. When in the box they cannot rub against people, so they rub against what is available—the pole. The response need not produce escape from the box, or food, or any other obvious reinforcer. However, if there are no humans in the room, the cats do not make the response. This combination of facts suggests that the rubbing was not acquired, as Guthrie believed, by being the last thing done in the situation, but rather that it was an innate species-specific social reaction (Moore & Stuttard 1979).

PREPAREDNESS

What we have seen so far of the misbehavior of organisms is to some extent only an extension of what was already known: that some responses are easier to learn than others, and that those which are easiest for one species may be quite different from those which are easiest for another species. It is, however, a considerable extension. Whether a given response is easy or hard for a given individual to learn depends not only on whether the individual is pigeon, pig, or person, but also on the relevant drives and reinforcers. It is not simply that pecking is an easy and natural response for a pigeon, but that it is particularly natural for a hungry pigeon in an environment where there is or has been food. We thus see foreshadowed a new kind of specificity—that certain responses may be easy to learn for one reinforcer but not for another. And indeed that suspicion is quite correct, for pigeons are almost as bad at learning to peck a key to avoid shock as they are good at learning to peck to get food.

Moreover, it turns out that the relationship between responses and reinforcers is only part of the issue. Not only are certain responses easy to learn for some reinforcers and hard for others, but certain stimuli are effective cues for some responses but not for others. One example is what happens when sounds are used as discriminative stimuli for dogs. If the discrimination to be learned is whether to turn right or left for reinforcement, it works well to have a tone coming from above the dog as the cue to turn right and a tone from below the dog as the cue to turn left. If the tones come from the same place, with a high-pitched tone signaling that the food is on the right and a low-pitched tone signaling that it is on the left, learning is much more difficult. Suppose, instead, that the discrimination is whether to go to get the food or to stay put. In that case just the opposite relationship applies. It is easy for the dog to learn that a high-pitched tone means "go" and a low-pitched tone means "stay," but hard to learn that a tone coming from above means "go" and one coming from below means "stay." In short, location of the tone is a good cue for location of the food, and pitch of the tone is a good cue as to whether going for the food will be reinforced, but not vice versa (Lawicka 1964).

So far we have seen that the specific pairing is important both for stimuli with responses and for responses with reinforcers. How about the pairing of stimuli with reinforcers? This too turns out to be important, particularly with negative reinforcers. Suppose you want to teach a rat not to drink a certain liquid by following the drinking with some unpleasant consequence. You might (like many psychologists) use electric shock as the unpleasant consequence. Or you might instead make the rat sick, which can be done by (among other ways) subjecting it to a heavy dose of X rays. Garcia and Koelling (1966) compared these two methods, but they also varied the characteristics of the liquid. In one case what made it distinctive was its sweet taste, in the other case the fact that it was accompanied by a light and a noise. By now the reader may be able to guess the outcome, even though it came as a surprise to a great many psychologists. If drinking was followed by shock, the rats learned to avoid lighted and noisy liquid, but not to avoid sweet liquid. If drinking was followed by illness, they learned to avoid sweet liquid but not liquid accompanied by light and noise. In this case, therefore, whether or not a negative reinforcer would lead the rat to avoid a stimulus depended not merely on what stimulus and what negative reinforcer, but on which pairing of the two.

Seligman (1970) has concluded from findings such as these that any given organism may be *prepared, unprepared,* or *contraprepared* to learn any particular response to any particular stimulus for any particular reinforcer. Prepared responses are especially easy to learn because they reflect species-specific tendencies; pigeons pecking a lighted key for food are an example. Contraprepared responses are exceptionally difficult to learn because they run counter to species-specific tendencies, as with dogs using the pitch of a tone as the cue for a left-right discrimination. Unprepared responses are those that are neither prepared nor contraprepared, those that can be learned with moderate effort, such as lever-pressing for food by a rat. Learning theorists have tended to think of all responses as unprepared, as neutral with regard to stimuli and reinforcers, capable of being learned but with no special advantage. It is this assumption that Seligman rejects.

We implied above that preparedness is a characteristic of the species—that learning a particular combination of stimulus, response, and reinforcer may have a different degree of preparedness for one species than for another. There is not yet very much evidence for this claim, but there is some. For example, we noted above that rats did not learn to avoid a liquid on the basis of its appearance if drinking the liquid was followed by illness, even though they did when drinking was followed by electric shock. Quail, however, for which vision is more important in seeking food, *will* learn to avoid the appearance of a liquid that has been followed by illness (Wilcoxon, Dragoin, & Kral 1971). Thus belongingness involves not only species-specific behavior but also species-specific patterns of learning.

Do humans, like rats, pigs, and pigeons, have species-specific tendencies? Humans sometimes seem to be so adaptable, capable of such varied learning, that we might suspect they lack such tendencies. One striking piece of evidence to the contrary is the existence of language. Although many species communicate with sound, and chimps have been taught to carry on conversations in sign language (Gardner & Gardner 1969, 1980; Linden 1974), no species except *Homo sapiens* (at least so far as we know) uses vocal sound as the basis of a complex, grammatical language. Most humans, by the age of 3 and usually without any deliberate training, have learned to speak in sentences, with an extensive vocabulary, and make reasonably correct use of a complexity of grammatical rules that they would be quite unable to explain. In fact, children under the age of 3 often use the rules more consistently than do adults. For example, they may follow the general rule for plurals by saying "two mans" or the general rule for past tenses by saying "bunny runned away," rather than using the correct irregular forms "men" and "ran." The use of vocal language thus appears to be an example of human species-specific behavior, and the learning of regular grammatical rules a form of prepared behavior.

IMPLICATIONS FOR LEARNING THEORY

At first glance, the notions of species-specific behavior and preparedness seem rather disconcerting for learning theory. The great beauty of learning theory has seemed to be that it offered some hope of reducing all the complexities of learning (and possibly motivation, thinking, or perception as well) to a manageable list of general laws. These laws would not depend on the particular stimuli, responses, and reinforcers being learned or on the species being studied. Thus experiments on rats pressing levers would be relevant to the training of seeing-eye dogs, and experiments on pigeons pecking keys would be relevant to humans working on a production line. But if the laws of learning depend on what particular stimulus, response, or reinforcer are being paired, and for what species, can there be any such generality? Must the simplicity and generality of theory which psychologists of learning have sought be replaced by a bewildering complexity of highly specific laws?

Although the recent findings we have discussed are discouraging for the more optimistic hopes of learning theorists, they are by no means disastrous. For one thing, the degree of generality of any given law is a matter to be determined by research. It remains to be seen how many of the laws of learning are specific to the stimulus, response, reinforcer, and species, and how many have instead the degree of generality for which learning theorists hope.

For another thing, it has always been the role of theory to organize laws in some more general way. Perhaps the situation now seems confused only because we have no good way to predict what particular combinations of stimuli, responses, and reinforcers will be easily learned by which species. What is needed is a theory that can tell us under what conditions a response is prepared, unprepared, or contraprepared. Finding the right bases of classification for independent and dependent variables and finding intervening variables to link them meaningfully is what theories are all about. The task of learning theory may be even more challenging than had previously been realized, but that does not mean that theorists cannot rise to the challenge. If the world of variables and laws relevant to learning seems to be in a state of confusion, there is all the more need for theories to bring order out of that confusion.

Moreover, there is already a basis for starting to find that order. Species-specific behavior and preparedness are part of the biological heritage of a given species. This heritage, however, is by no means random. The characteristics of any species have come about through the process of evolution, according to the principle of natural selection. Presumably, therefore, the characteristics of any species are those which have helped that species to survive. If we want to find order in the patterns of learning, we need to ask what patterns are likely to have had survival value in the environment where the ancestors of a given species lived.

Let us consider the case of a rat learning what to avoid in its environment. (For the present purpose it does not matter whether we assume it is learning a habit of avoidance or a cognition about what is dangerous.) If it gets sick, it is probably because of something it ate, and the best way of recognizing that food again is by taste or smell. Whether the dangerous food was in a place that was light or dark or noisy or quiet probably had nothing to do with whether the food would make it sick. It would therefore be to the rat's advantage to learn to avoid any food that tasted like what it ate before it became ill, but it would not be to the rat's advantage to avoid eating in places that looked or sounded like the place where it ate the tainted food. Suppose, however, that it suffered an injury. In that case, the taste or smell of anything it ate just before would probably be irrelevant, but what the place looked or sounded like would be much more likely to serve as a warning of traps or predators or other dangers. It would thus be to its advantage to avoid places that looked or sounded like the place where it was hurt, but of no advantage to avoid foods that tasted like what it ate before it was hurt. The reader will note that this is exactly the learning pattern that Garcia and Koelling (1966) found.

For other species, what it is most adaptive for the individual to learn might be different. A bird preparing to swoop down and capture its dinner cannot afford to follow the rat's strategy of carefully tasting a bit of food to see if it has the same flavor as something that once made the animal sick. The bird is much better off deciding on the basis of what it can see whether to snap up an insect that may or may not be edible. One would predict, therefore, that when a bird eats something that makes it sick, the bird will learn to avoid other foods that look the same, to a much greater extent than do rats. As already noted for quail, that is what has been found.

To find such evidence that organisms learn in ways that are adaptive for their lifestyle, we do not need to compare organisms as different as rats and quail. Cowan (1977) studied a different form of avoidance learning—the tendency to avoid an unfamiliar object that suddenly appears in a familiar place. He compared this kind of learning among several kinds of rats. Some were lab rats, whose ancestors had lived in lab rat colonies for numerous generations. Others were members of the same species, but their recent ancestors were wild rats, living close to humans in houses and alleys, but not domesticated. Still others were members of two different species of rat, one living in the desert and the other in the forest, far from humans.

All three of these kinds of rats were kept in a maze until they were familiar with it, at which point two white aluminum cubes were put in one of the arms. One of the three kinds of rat showed a strong tendency to avoid that arm for all of the next day; the other two did not. Which of the three might we expect it to be?

If we simply try to guess which group would be most distinctive from the others in general, we would probably predict that it would be the desert and forest rats, since they were of different species from the others. They were also the ones whose ancestors had lived for the shortest time in captivity; indeed, some of these rat subjects had themselves been born in the wild. If, instead, we focus on wildness versus domestication, we might expect the lab rats to be most distinctive from the others, since their ancestors had been domesticated by humans for many generations. Both of these predictions, however, would be wrong.

If we ask for what kind of rat such an avoidance response would be adaptive, we might predict instead that the most cautious around the new objects would be the wild rats whose ancestors had lived near humans but not been domesticated by them. Why? One of the great risks their ancestors faced was being trapped by humans, and only those rats that avoided the risk at least long enough to have offspring ever got to pass their genes on to subsequent generations. Since a rat trap generally appears as an unfamiliar object in a familiar place, rats that avoided such objects would be the ones most likely to become ancestors and to pass that form of caution on to their descendents. As predicted, it was this group that avoided the unfamiliar objects in the familiar maze. Again, therefore, we see an example of differences in the pattern of learning (or, in this case, motivated behavior resulting from learning of familiarity) that fit predictions from the principle of evolutionary adaptation.

Organic evolution and learning have a good deal in common, at least if one takes a reinforcement view of learning. In natural selection those behaviors (as well as structures) that work for a species are passed on to subsequent generations. In learning, those behaviors that work for an individual are continued by that individual. In learning, the mechanism is reinforcement of some behaviors and not of others. In evolution the mechanism is selective survival and procreation: those organisms that tend to behave in certain ways because of their genes are more likely to survive and pass those genes on to their offspring. In spite of their differences, both evolution and learning are adaptive mechanisms that increase the effectiveness of organisms in dealing with their environment.

Given that both processes are forms of adaptation to the environment, it remains only to look at their connection. The capacity to learn in certain ways is one of the characteristics that increases (or decreases) through evolution. Or, to put it another way, evolution determines the ways in which learning will occur for a given species. In trying to predict an organism's preparedness for given patterns of stimuli, responses, and reinforcers, it therefore seems reasonable to ask, "What pattern would be most likely to have survival value in the environment in which this species evolved?" What this means is that a theory of learning is most likely to be complete and accurate if it is a theory of evolution as well—or, most generally, a theory of overall adaptation to the environment.

Chapter
18

Learning Theory Past, Present, and Future

*I*n any survey of an area of knowledge, such as that attempted in this book, there is a great danger that the reader will come away with a kaleidoscope of impressions—some, we may hope, interesting and enlightening—but with no overall picture of the field. To a cognitive theorist, at least, such an outcome would seem most regrettable. In hopes of avoiding this, let us consider what the various interpretations we have examined can contribute to our understanding of learning.

ISSUES ON WHICH LEARNING THEORIES DIVIDE

The theories we have considered in this book can be grouped according to the ways they answer certain basic questions, including questions about both the nature of learning and the process of theory building (Hillner 1978). The answers to these questions indicate not the details of the theory but in broad outline what it tries to do and how it tries to do it. Eight such questions (differing somewhat from Hillner's) are given below.

Eight Controversial Questions

The first question a learning theorist needs to answer is whether or not to use intervening variables. Tolman, who introduced the idea of intervening variables into psychology, and Hull, who developed the most elaborate system, are the two theorists who have given the most emphatically positive answers to this question. Skinner, with his rejection of theories of learning, has given the clearest negative answer. Most theorists have included elements in their theories that could reasonably be called intervening variables, but often without labeling them as such. The most common answer to this question might therefore be given as "yes, but . . ."

The second question is whether the intervening variables, or whatever else plays a similar role in the theory, should be connectionist or cognitive. This is the question that has caused more argument than any other in the history of learning theory, and around which more than any other this book has been organized. The majority of theories through most of the history of the field have been connectionist, though with various concessions to the cognitive position.

More recently, however, cognitive approaches have come to dominate the scene. We have seen something of this change in the importance of Bolles's approach, in the newer formulations of memory, in the increasing respect accorded to Piaget, and in the increasingly cognitive tone of Bandura's writings. Even so, the extent of the change may not have been evident from reading this book, in view of the continuing importance of the Skinnerian approach for many of the topics considered here. Psychologists who focus more on other aspects of psychology have labeled this change the "cognitive revolution."

The third question deals with reinforcement: Is reinforcement a basic and central principle of learning, or is it a sloppy way of talking about certain phenomena that could more appropriately be explained in other ways? Thorndike, Hull, and Skinner have been among the strongest supporters of the former answer, and Watson and Guthrie the strongest supporters of the latter, with other theorists taking weaker intermediate positions. However, it has become increasingly evident that this is not an either-or question, that there are a number of possible positions about the way in which the consequences of actions affect subsequent behavior.

The fourth question, not as strongly argued but nonetheless significant, is whether learning should be analyzed at a molar or a molecular level. All theorists work at least partly at the molar level, that is, at the level of everyday acts, but they differ as to whether these acts should be explained by analysis at a more molecular level. Though Tolman was most explicit about staying at the molar level, the majority of the theorists we have considered also took a predominantly molar position. Two striking exceptions were Guthrie and Estes, both of whom saw the learning of molar acts as resulting from a more basic kind of learning at the molecular level, a conditioning of tiny elements that combine to produce the molar acts. Hull's theory and Estes' stimulus-sampling model provide a sharp contrast in this respect, given their similarities in various other respects.

The fifth question is whether the theory should be presented formally or casually. The majority of the earlier systems were closer to the casual end of the scale: even when there was the suggestion of a strong logical structure to the theory (as, for example, with Guthrie), it was not worked out with the formal trappings of logic and philosophy of science. Hull and Estes represent theorists, in contrast, who did have those formal trappings, who presented the logical structure of their theories explicitly. Tolman was fairly formal at times, but had trouble sticking to any one particular structure. More recently, a number of mathematical model builders have been formal. Computer approaches have had to be formal in the sense of giving precise instructions to the computer, since computers don't respond to (understand) any other kind. However, it is not always clear how to relate these formal computer programs to more general formulations about the nature of learning.

The sixth question is one of breadth: How wide a range of topics should a theory try to deal with? There is some tendency for those theories that answer the fifth question in favor of formality to answer this one in favor of narrowness. Almost inevitably, the more formally a theory is stated, the more rigorous and precise it will have to be, which in turn makes it harder for the theory to deal effectively with a wide range of topics. A more casually stated theory, on the other hand, can deal with a wider range of topics with less danger of being caught in inconsistencies or ambiguities. Nevertheless, a theory that would combine formal precision with great breadth is such a desirable goal that its challenge has continued to lure theorists. Hull tried hard to achieve such a theory, and while part of his failure can be attributed to his invalidism and premature death, part of it also reflects the enormous difficulty of the challenge. Though Hull's impressive failure may have led a number of other theorists to stick to narrower theories, some have continued to try to combine formal rigor with breadth. Estes and Anderson are two examples.

The seventh question is how much emphasis to give to the innate aspects of behavior and to the biological constraints on learning. This has become an issue only in the last 25 years, and for most of the theories we have considered the answer has been "not much emphasis." American learning theory, from Watson and Thorndike on, has emphasized the acquired over the innate; although Watson's rejection of hereditary factors was extreme, it nevertheless set the tone for the field. Increasingly, however, theorists are considering this issue. Bolles has emphasized it, and the Skinnerians are increasingly making concessions to it. The question is how far those concessions should go. Are we now in a phase that overemphasizes the innate, as the earlier phase probably overestimated the acquired, or are we only beginning to discover the actual extent of biological constraints on learning and behavior? It is a question for which theorists have only recently begun to stand up and be counted.

Finally, there is the question of practicality. Is a theory of learning a creation of the laboratory and the armchair, an intellectual exercise in understanding the world, or is it a device for dealing with and perhaps changing that world? Though at times theorists have demanded the right to do pure science, undistracted by any pressures toward practical usefulness, that attitude has been distinctly the exception. The question is not so much whether theories of learning should be useful but rather who should do the applying. Some theorists, like Thorndike and Skinner, have jumped directly into applications. Others, like Dollard and Miller and Tolman, have written about possible applications but played relatively little part in putting them into practice. Still others, like Hull, have been themselves pure scientists but had substantial influence on others of a more applied bent. Even these examples are debatable; the distinction is a hard one to maintain, given the generally applied nature of American learning theory.

Positions of the Right, Left, and Center

Although all of the above issues have to some extent divided learning theories, the two that dominated much of the history of the field were the second and third, as can be inferred from the table of contents of this book. If we look at the positions various theorists took on these two issues, we can see the history of American learning theory through the greater part of the twentieth century as consisting of a mainstream that dominated the field, withstood challenges from different directions, incorporated some of those challenges within the mainstream, and continued on its way. This is the connectionist-reinforcement tradition that began with Thorndike, reached its greatest theoretical flowering in Hull, and has recently been dominated by Skinner. It may seem odd, given the sharp disagreements between Hull and Skinner about both theory construction and research technique, to group them together in this way, especially since Skinner is not a connectionist in the narrow sense of talking about habits or stimulus-response bonds as something inside the organism. Nevertheless, they stand together in contrast to two other traditions that have challenged the mainstream.

Perhaps it would be best at this point to change the metaphor to a political one and speak of the mainstream instead as a party of the center whose basic principle is that what is learned is the tendency to make various responses, and that an essential feature in that learning is reinforcement. This party of the center was challenged both from the right and from the left by smaller though vocal parties. The party of the right agreed enthusiastically with the center that what was learned was responses, and focused even more consistently than the center on the stimulus-response bond as the unit of learning. It disagreed with the center, however, in rejecting the central role of reinforcement in favor of simple contiguity as the basic principle of learning. It is the most mechanistic of the approaches, and it focuses particularly on the importance of practice and of learning by doing. The outstanding figures in this party of the right were Watson and Guthrie. Its challenge to the center was thus most dominant in the earlier part of the century, though its influence continues to be felt.

The challenge from the left, in contrast, has to a considerable degree ignored the reinforcement issue and instead concentrated on rejecting the idea that responses are what is learned. Instead, they argue that we learn knowledge, beliefs, expectancies, understanding—in other words, cognitions. Among actual learning theorists, the outstanding early exponent of this position was Tolman. Although Tolman himself never succeeded in founding a school of psychology, his point of view remained influential. For a number of years, as we have seen, the dominant theme in learning theory was the attempt by the center to incorporate cognitive ideas like Tolman's into its theories while still maintaining a basically connectionist orientation. More recently, the cognitive approach has become increasingly strong, so that many would argue that it has now replaced connectionism in the center.

What is the present situation? Although the old right no longer represents a strong position, in a limited sense it made its point. Few theorists now regard reinforcement in the Thorndikian way, as stamping in stimulus-response bonds. Rather, the majority see learning as taking place by contiguity, as the right claimed, and reinforcement as affecting only the performance of what has already been learned. However, this learning by contiguity is seen as involving contiguity of stimuli with other stimuli rather than of stimuli with responses, so this view contains more of Tolman, Bolles, Bandura, and the later Mowrer than of Guthrie or Watson. Indeed, the main question is to what extent the left has now become the center, crowding the former center off to the right. Some would argue that it has done so completely, and that the former center is not only crowded off to the side but even moribund. Others would argue that the left, though far stronger than in earlier times, is not really dominant over the former center, but that the two are still competing for dominance on fairly equal terms.

The argument focuses partly on Skinner's place in the current scene. On the one hand, he more than anyone else represents learning theory to those outside the field. This is ironic, in view of his claim not to be a theorist, yet it is just as an exemplar of the traditional ideals of learning theory—straightforward, wide-ranging, practical—that Skinner stands. He does not represent the psychology of learning as a whole, which is now too cognitive for his taste, but the traditional connectionist-reinforcement mainstream of learning theory, a direct descendent of Thorndike. Does he represent the last flickering popularization of a dying tradition, or does he represent those aspects of learning theory that will have the most lasting influence on psychology and on other fields?

The argument also focuses partly on interpretations of the new connectionism of network models and parallel distributed processing. To its supporters, this approach combines the best features of other approaches and resolves the disagreements between the older connectionist and cognitive positions. It demonstrates, they claim, that learning distributed through many specific connections can combine to produce a quite gestaltish cognitive outcome. Its opponents claim, however, that it has serious problems and so far represents much more of high hopes than of real achievement. With this approach, as with the Skinnerian, only time will tell.

CRITERIA FOR AN IDEAL THEORY

The arguments among theorists of learning are not as strident as they were in the "golden age" of learning theory, when Hull and Spence traded barbs with Guthrie on the right and Tolman on the left, while Skinner in effect said, "A plague on all your houses." More of the theorizing is in the form of models for predicting a narrower range of phenomena, with each theorist trying to see how far a given model can go in predicting data. Thus the person who developed a model may also be the one who reveals its inadequacies, as suggested in the title of an article by Frank Restle (1966): "Run Structure and Probability Learning: Disproof of Restle's Model." Nevertheless, more general disagreements do remain, and we can reasonably ask to what extent the questions raised in the previous section can now be resolved. To put it another way, can we now see what the criteria for an ideal theory of learning would be?

The ideal kind of theory toward which the most ambitious theorists strive is much like the ideal that Hull set up but failed to realize: formal, precise, internally consistent, yet at the same time broad enough to cover the whole range of topics in learning and motivation. It would have postulates and theorems and would be so constructed that it could be changed to deal with new evidence as one or another theorem failed to be confirmed by experiments. Given this combination of breadth and precision, it inevitably would be useful in the solution of practical problems.

This ideal theory would undoubtedly include intervening variables, and being a formal theory it would be quite explicit about what they were. The variables would be much more cognitive than those of the earlier theories of the center; they would deal with the acquisition, storage, and use of information, with beliefs and the evidence on which they are based, with both logical and illogical thinking. The theory would thus have a very cognitive sound—not only more so than any of the connectionist theories we have considered, but perhaps even more so than some of the cognitive ones. However, there would be postulates linking the cognitions both to behavior and to the processes by which cognitions are acquired and changed, thus making the theory more behavioristic than such highly cognitive theories as Lewin's. So, while its format would be most like Hull's and also bear some resemblance to Estes', its content would be more like Tolman's. It might be quite close to Anderson's ACT.

Such a cognitive theory would be less disturbing to connectionist theorists than would be the case if we were not familiar with computers. Since the computer, which is physically a connectionist device, can be programmed to behave in such cognitive ways, a connectionist theorist might argue that he was right all along, that this is really a connectionist theory which deals effectively with the behaviors, including internal ones, of reasoning, imagining, remembering, and planning. It could thus be considered either an updating of Tolman or an outstanding example of a connectionist move in cognitive directions. It might turn out to be much like the new connectionist network theories currently being developed—but that remains to be seen.

Moreover, the theory would need to be somewhat connectionist in another sense. It would have to explain not only our knowledge and understanding but also the responses we make automatically without thinking and the skills we are able to perform without being able to explain just how we do them. Even Tolman (1949) conceded that there is noncognitive learning of what he called motor patterns. Again the computer analogy is helpful, since computers can just as easily be programmed to make certain specific responses under certain conditions as to behave in more cognitive ways. So, while the details of the theory will be very complex, there should be no problem for the theorist in having some of those details appear straightforwardly connectionist and others highly cognitive.

The complexity of the theory would be of a developmental sort. In other words, it would explain how humans and animals get programmed to function in the way they do. "Programmed," of course, reflects again the computer analogy. A computer system consists basically of certain "hardware," comparable to the physique, perceptual and learning capacities, and innate motivational tendencies of an organism. To be useful, it must also have "software," the programs to determine what it will do. Whereas computer programs are written by people, the programs of people and animals are developed through experience. Learning can thus be regarded as the process that corresponds to program writing. We might say either that a computer is like an animal that has been carefully trained, or that an animal (or person) is like a computer with a very open-ended program that in effect keeps rewriting itself on the basis of its experience. Again, the new connectionist network models may have a lot to offer here.

The hardware, of course, corresponds to those species-specific characteristics that set constraints on behavior and learning. Some computers can do jobs that others cannot. Of two that can both do a job, one can often do it faster than the other, or the procedure that is fastest for one computer to do may be different from that which is fastest for the other. These are the same sorts of differences that are found among species of animals, and to a lesser extent among individuals within a species. They are the constraints within which learning has to work, but within which it can still produce enormous individual differences in behavior depending on differences in experience.

The results of this long-term programming would have a hierarchical structure, as suggested by Gagné and numerous other people. As indicated above, the hierarchy would include both knowledge that can be expressed in words or other symbols and skills that to a considerable degree cannot, as noted by Anderson. These skills would very likely be analyzed in cybernetic terms, with each unit of skill in the hierarchy dependent on lower-level units that would serve to maintain the set point of the higher-level unit. The process by which all of these hierarchies would develop would be one of accommodation, as described by Piaget, in which the structure would gradually change in response to experiences that were inconsistent with it. However, in most cases these accommodations would not be simply changes but rather the incorporation of less adequate patterns of skill and understanding into higher-level patterns that would include their good points while at the same time improving on them. Though this process includes the possibility of mistaken or maladaptive learning, such as that discussed by Dollard and Miller, for the most part it would represent a continuing increase both in complexity and in effectiveness.

How would reinforcement and motivation be treated? This may be the hardest question for which to provide even the outline of an answer. On the one hand, as we have noted, there is fairly wide support for the view that much learning depends only on contiguity, without the need for reinforcement. This includes not only learning by doing but also learning by observation, as emphasized particularly by Bandura. In this view, we acquire knowledge and skills by a mixture of observation and practice. Among the things we learn are what activities toward what objects are rewarding or punishing. We then use our knowledge and skills to obtain access to the rewards and to avoid the punishments. When we speak of a motive, what we mean is a certain class of rewards (such as food, or sex, or prestige), along with the knowledge and skills connected with obtaining those rewards.

On the other hand, there seem clearly to be some cases that do not fit this interpretation. When we gradually master a skill without being able to explain completely what we are now doing differently, the best explanation seems to be that the precise responses that work are being acquired and those that don't work are dropping out. Though Guthrie would say that "work" means "change the situation into something else," most people would insist that it means "change the situation into something *better.*" This latter meaning sounds like traditional Thorndikian reinforcement: stamping in the rewarded stimulus-response bonds. So, although the simple, old-fashioned notion of reinforcement is a good deal less popular than it used to be, it doesn't look as though we can entirely get rid of it.

Perhaps the ideas of cybernetics can help here. They suggest that all the stimuli which Skinner would call positive reinforcers are signals that a deviation is being corrected, that one is moving closer to a set point. With higher-level set points, we can describe accurately what is happening, and in those cases we may speak of the set point as an incentive toward which behavior is directed. With lower-level set points we are only hazily able to describe what is happening, or perhaps not at all able, making the term *incentive* seem inappropriate. However, what is actually going on is the same at all levels: a set point, deviations from it, behavior that serves to reduce the deviations, and "reinforcement" by getting closer to the set point. The principles are the same; only the degree of our conscious awareness is different. This is one direction from which a resolution of the question about reinforcement might eventually come. It would be ironic if cybernetics, which has very little to say directly about learning, should nevertheless provide the answer to such a persistent issue in learning theory as the nature and significance of reinforcement!

Two other aspects of learning need to be considered, though they were not referred to in the questions in the preceding section. One is the nature of memory. To the extent that we focus on knowledge and on learning by observation, it seems more consistent to treat memory as a matter of information stored and retrieved than as a matter of competing responses. On the other hand, for highly practiced skills, including verbal ones, interference theory seems more appropriate. To what extent these models lead to different predictions is not altogether clear. Moreover, no complete theory can afford to ignore the way that new experiences get assimilated into schemata. Though we considered this process as it is usually considered, in terms of information, it operates at the level of muscular coordinations as well. For example, a speaker of English assimilates foreign speech sounds to the sounds in English that they most nearly resemble, thus achieving an adequate approximation to the foreign language, but still with an English accent. Though such assimilation to schemata needs to be included in any complete theory of learning, it also needs to be developed in more precise detail than has so far been done.

The other aspect of learning that needs to be considered is perception. Most learning theorists have taken perception for granted, while the gestaltists, who focused on perception, were only secondarily theorists of learning. However, learning can be no better than the perceptual input on which it is based, so that the topic cannot be ignored by any complete theory. Atkinson and Shiffrin's reference to the sensory register is one example of a perceptual concept in a theory of learning (or of memory). Theories dealing with how we interpret what we see and hear have become increasingly prominent in psychology, so much so, in fact, that to have included them in this book would have carried us too far afield. Nevertheless, they represent an important part of any complete theory— if not of learning, at least of learned behavior.

Along with perception goes the related topic of attention. Though theorists differ as to whether it is possible to learn about something without paying any attention to it, we can at least say with confidence that one usually learns more about something to which one is paying attention than about something to which one is not. Such concepts as "observing response," "acquired distinctiveness of cues," and "blocking" all refer to the selectivity of attention, to our learning (not always correctly) which aspects of a situation are worth noticing and which are not. Though the selectivity of attention is itself receiving a lot more attention than in the golden age of learning theory, it is not yet fully integrated into most theories of learning. To what extent special principles are needed to deal with it remains to be seen.

THE PRESENT-DAY VALUE OF LEARNING THEORY

Whatever form the theory of the future may take, most of us have to make the best of the theories we have today. Granted that all of them fall short of the ideals we have set for a truly adequate theory, what use can we make of them? For the most part, whatever exact predictions they make are applicable only to carefully controlled laboratory conditions. They can rarely predict directly to the complex, uncontrolled conditions of everyday life. Even with the most precise of scientific theories, engineers are needed who can use their ingenuity and experience to apply the theory to practical ends. Since theories of learning are not among the most precise, this "psychological engineering" is perhaps even more challenging than in other areas of science. Such "engineering" enters into many jobs, from animal training to psychological warfare, but above all it is the province of the educator.

Hilgard (1964) has argued that a single category of behavioral engineers or applied psychologists, in contrast to pure research psychologists, is much too simple. He suggests that we can distinguish six steps along the scale from the "purest" of researchers on learning at one extreme to the "purest" of educational appliers at the other. The first three steps all fall under the heading of "pure-science research," but vary in the extent to which the learners and the learned materials resemble those in ordinary educational practice. The remaining three steps, which he groups under "technological research and development," are of more specific interest here. These are step 4—"research conducted in special laboratory classrooms, with selected teachers"; step 5—"a tryout of the results of prior research in a 'normal' classroom with a typical teacher"; step 6—"developmental steps related to advocacy and adoption" (1964, p. 409). Here the research and development proceed from asking "Will it work under the best of conditions?" in step 4, to "Will it work under typical conditions?" in step 5, to "Will it be generally adopted by educators?" in step 6.

The applied psychology of learning is important not only as a way of putting theories to practical use but also as a way of improving theories. Along with their other contributions, applied studies help to determine the boundary conditions of theories. If a theory based on laboratory data is used to make predictions to an applied situation, and the predictions are not confirmed, this event shows that the theory is not appropriate for that situation. It may still, however, be a perfectly good theory for predicting in other situations. In addition, applied studies reveal new laws that may then be used in the modification of old theories or the construction of new ones. For example, as we noted earlier, Gagné developed his ideas about the hierarchical organization of tasks largely as a result of an unsuccessful attempt to apply more traditional laws of learning to the problems of military training. The ideas about learning that emerged from that applied work served as the basis for new theoretical developments in the pure psychology of learning.

For most of us, the various learning theories have two chief values. One is in providing us with a vocabulary and a conceptual framework for interpreting the examples of learning that we observe. These are valuable for anyone who is alert to the world. The other, closely related, is in suggesting where to look for solutions to practical problems. The theories do not give us solutions, but they do direct our attention to those variables that are crucial in finding solutions.

Let us consider the ways in which various theoretical interpreters do these two things for us. Guthrie directs our attention to the importance of practicing the particular responses to be learned under the particular conditions in which they will be used, and also to the value of practicing them under varied conditions if they are to be firmly established. Skinner advises us always to find out what reinforces a given act, so that we can present that reinforcer if we want the act to occur or remove it if we want to extinguish the act. Dollard and Miller warn us to consider the drives that may be learned in a situation and may then serve as the basis of new, often undesired, learning. Wertheimer and Köhler point out the importance of arranging learning situations so as to foster real, creative understanding rather than blind rote memorization. Lewin suggests that we try to reconstruct the learner's life space, with the tensions and goals and the paths and barriers that the learner perceives. Bandura reminds us how much of our learning involves observation of other people's behavior and its outcomes. Piaget and Gagné emphasize the extent to which present learning develops out of earlier learning. Tolman, Hull, Estes, and Anderson offer many of these same suggestions in more technical form. All of these suggestions require ingenuity if they are to be put to practical use. Each, however, serves to emphasize some aspect of the learning process that we would be wise to consider. Thus each serves both to enrich our understanding of the learning situations we observe and to help us find solutions to the practical learning problems with which we have to deal. Although many theorists aspire to make a greater contribution than this, and to some extent succeed in doing so, this contribution alone is enough to make their theories invaluable to the study of learning.

Summary List of Theorists

Most of the theorists discussed in the text are listed here in the order in which they are considered. With each theorist are one or more key terms or summary comments to serve as mnemonic devices.

Ivan P. Pavlov (1849–1936) Classical conditioning; excitation; inhibition.
John B. Watson (1878–1958) Founder of behaviorism; laws of frequency and recency.
Edward L. Thorndike (1874–1949) Law of effect; satisfiers and annoyers; cats in a puzzle box.
Edwin R. Guthrie (1886–1959) Single principle of learning by contiguity of a stimulus and a movement; maintaining stimuli; movement-produced stimuli; three methods of changing habits.
Clark L. Hull (1884–1952) Postulates and theorems; $_sE_R = {}_sH_R \times D \times K - I_R$; oscillations; r_G.
Kenneth W. Spence (1907–1967) Boundary conditions of theories; updating of Hull's theory.
Neal E. Miller (b. 1909) and John Dollard (1900–1980) Learned drives; imitation; personality; psychotherapy.
B. F. Skinner (b. 1904) Rejection of intervening variables; emphasis on reinforcement; respondent and operant behavior; shaping; behavior modification and other applications.
Max Wertheimer (1880–1943) Founder of gestalt psychology; emphasis on insight; laws of proximity and closure.
Wolfgang Köhler (1887–1967) Gestalt psychologist; research on problem solving in chimpanzees.
Kurt Koffka (1886–1941) Gestalt psychologist.
Kurt Lewin (1890–1947) Topological psychology; life space; valences; vectors.

Jean Piaget (1896–1980) Development of schemata; accommodation and assimilation; four stages of development; conservation.

Edward C. Tolman (1886–1959) Purposive behaviorism; originator of intervening variables; sign-gestalt expectations; cognitive maps; latent learning.

Robert C. Bolles (b. 1928) S-S* expectancies and R-S* expectancies.

Harry F. Harlow (1905–1981) Learning sets; manipulation drive; contact hunger.

O. Hobart Mowrer (1907–1982) Sign and solution learning; learning of hope, fear, relief, and disappointment.

Albert Bandura (b. 1925) Imitation; modeling; self-efficacy.

Robert M. Gagné (b. 1916) Development of hierarchical organization.

William K. Estes (b. 1919) Stimulus-sampling model; probability matching.

John R. Anderson (b. 1947) ACT theory; declarative and procedural knowledge.

Terrence J. Sejnowski (b. 1947) NETtalk.

David Premack (b. 1925) Response interpretation of reinforcement; reversibility of reinforcement relationship.

Norbert Wiener (1894–1964) Cybernetics; negative feedback.

Richard L. Solomon (b. 1918) Opponent-process theory of motivation.

Benton J. Underwood (b. 1915) Forgetting through proactive and retroactive inhibition.

Richard C. Atkinson (b. 1929) and Richard M. Shiffrin (b. 1942) Three memory stores.

Martin E. P. Seligman (b. 1942) Biological constraints on learning; species-specific behavior; preparedness.

Glossary

A1 and A2 (*Estes*) The two possible response classes to which a stimulus element may be conditioned.

***a* process** (*Solomon*) The hedonic effect produced immediately by a stimulus, lasting as long as the stimulus lasts.

accommodation (*Piaget*) A change in a schema to incorporate new experience.

assimilation (*Piaget*) Interpretation of new experiences in terms of an existing schema.

asymptote The limit that a curve approaches and can never go beyond.

autoshaping The learning of what appears to be an instrumental response (such as key pecking in pigeons) through the procedures of classical rather than instrumental conditioning.

***b* process** (*Solomon*) The hedonic opponent process that lags behind and serves to counteract an *a* process.

behavior modification (*Skinner*) The process of changing behavior in practical situations, such as education or psychotherapy, by appropriately changing the contingencies of reinforcement.

behavioral contrast (*Skinner*) A higher rate of responding on a given schedule of reinforcement if it alternates with another schedule that provides fewer reinforcers.

behaviorism Any learning theory that focuses on observable behaviors and the stimuli that control them.

bliss point The amount of time an individual would spend on an activity if there were no requirements or restrictions.

boundary conditions (*Spence*) Those conditions that must apply in order for a theory to be valid in a given situation.

chain (*Skinner*) A series of responses, leading to a reinforcer, that comes to function much like a single operant.

cognition A belief (including expectancies, items of knowledge, and the like).

cognitive Explaining behavior and learning in terms of cognitions.

cognitive map (*Tolman*) A cognition about where various things are located.

composition (*Anderson*) The combining of smaller units of procedural knowledge into larger ones.

compound Two or more stimuli presented simultaneously.

conditioned stimulus See *conditioning, classical.*

conditioning, classical A form of learning in which two stimuli are presented together and the response originally elicited by one of them, the unconditioned stimulus, comes to be elicited also by the other, the conditioned stimulus.

connectionism The view that learning is the forming and changing of connections, now especially those interpretations based on models of neural networks.

connectionist Dealing with the connections between stimuli and responses, especially as assumed to represent connections in the nervous system.

conservation (*Piaget*) A person's understanding that certain characteristics of things, such as their length or number, remain the same when other characteristics are changed.

consummatory response A response by which one takes in or uses a reward.

contiguity The occurrence of two or more events together.

contingencies of reinforcement (*Skinner*) Specific relationships of reinforcers to the responses and stimuli that precede them; determinants of when reinforcement occurs.

contraprepared (*Seligman*) Especially difficult to learn; applied to a response in relation to particular stimuli or reinforcers with which that response is hard to learn.

controlled quantity (*cybernetics*) A variable maintained at a set point by the operation of negative feedback.

critical delay duration (*Solomon*) The longest delay between successive presentations of a stimulus that will still permit the b process to increase with repetition.

cue A stimulus that serves to guide behavior.

cybernetics (*Wiener*) The study of control mechanisms.

D (*Hull*) Abbreviation for *drive.*

declarative knowledge (*Anderson*) Knowledge in the form of propositions about what is true; "knowing that" (as opposed to *procedural knowledge*).

demand (*Tolman*) A motive or desire for a given goal object.

discrimination Learning to make different responses to similar stimuli.

disinhibition Removal of inhibition.

drive An aroused state which motivates action in an organism, and the reduction of which often functions as a reinforcer.

encode To convert (information) into a specific form, especially for entering into memory.

error factor (*Harlow*) A systematic wrong way of responding in a problem situation.

excitation (*Pavlov and others*) The activation of a response tendency, as opposed to *inhibition.*

excitatory potential (*Hull*) The strength of the tendency for a given response to occur.

experiment   A research study in which one or more independent variables are manipulated and the effects on one or more dependent variables are measured.

extinction   A weakening of the tendency to make a response when the response is not followed by a reinforcer.

fading (*Skinner*)   Gradually removing a prompt, so that the behavior supported by the prompt still continues.

feedback (*cybernetics*)   The process by which the effects of a response control that response.

> **negative**   The form of feedback that compensates for deviations so as to maintain a steady state.

> **positive**   The form of feedback that enhances deviations so as to produce larger and larger changes.

fixed-interval schedule (*Skinner*)   An arrangement in which reinforcement follows the first response after a fixed period of time since the previous reinforcement.

fixed-ratio schedule (*Skinner*)   An arrangement in which reinforcement follows a given number of responses since the previous reinforcement.

fixed-time schedule (*Skinner*)   A schedule of reinforcement in which reinforcers are delivered at a fixed rate regardless of what the individual does.

generalization   The tendency for a response to occur to a new stimulus that is similar to one present during original learning.

gestalt   A form or pattern perceived as a whole.

habit   A learned tendency for a certain stimulus to elicit a certain response.

habit strength (*Hull*)   The strength of the bond connecting a stimulus with a response.

hedonic   Pertaining to pleasure and displeasure.

homeostasis   The process by which various physiological processes are regulated automatically at set points.

hypothesizing   Assuming for theoretical purposes that something is true although it has not been shown to be definitely true.

imprinting   The formation of attachments early in life, especially attachments of young birds to their parents.

incentive motivation (*Hull*)   The strength of the tendency to approach a given goal object.

inhibition   Suppression of a response by any active process within the organism (cf., various kinds of inhibition).

insight   A sudden understanding of the solution to a problem.

I$_R$ (*Hull*)   Abbreviation for *reactive inhibition*.

irradiation (*Pavlov*)   A spreading out of excitation or inhibition on the surface of the cortex.

K (*Hull*)   Abbreviation for *incentive motivation*.

key   A disk that when pressed closes an electrical circuit to activate a recording and/or reinforcing device, especially one designed to be pecked by pigeons.

knowledge compilation (*Anderson*)   The combination of proceduralization and composition, making behavior increasingly efficient as learning progresses.

latent learning (*Tolman*)   Learning that is not immediately evident in behavior.

law of effect (*Thorndike and other reinforcement theorists*)   The principle that a tendency to make a response depends on the reinforcing consequences of making it.

law of exercise (*Thorndike*)   The principle that simply making a response to a stimulus increases the likelihood that one will do so again; regarded as a much weaker principle than the law of effect.

law of frequency (*Watson*)   The principle that the more often one has made a certain response to a particular stimulus, the more likely one is to do so again.

law of recency (*Watson and Guthrie*)   The principle that the more recently one has made a certain response to a particular stimulus, the more likely one is to do so again.

law, scientific   A statement about the conditions under which certain kinds of events occur.

learning curve   A graph showing how much has been learned at each stage of practice.

learning set (*Harlow*)   Systematic improvement in solving a series of different discrimination problems that have a principle in common.

life space (*Lewin*)   The world as it affects a person's behavior, as distinguished from the objective world.

long-term store (or **memory**) (*Atkinson & Shiffrin, and others*)   The place or process in which material is stored permanently in memory.

maintaining stimuli (*Guthrie*)   Strong stimuli that keep an organism active; their removal contributes to learning.

mand (*Skinner*)   An utterance that instructs someone to do something.

manipulandum   A device that an organism can manipulate.

mediating responses   Responses whose main function is the stimulation they produce, so that they serve as intermediate steps in a sequence running from an initial stimulus to a final response.

mnemonic device   Any technique helpful in memorizing specific items.

modeling (*Bandura*)   Trying to make oneself more like someone else (the model), either in specific behavior (equaling imitation) or in more general characteristics.

molar (*esp. Tolman*)   Analyzed at the level of everyday acts, as opposed to molecular.

molecular   Analyzed in terms of small units, such as stimulus elements (*Estes*) or muscle contractions (*Guthrie*), as opposed to molar.

movement-produced stimuli (*Guthrie*)   Stimuli produced by one's own responses that serve to direct further behavior.

observing response   A response whose main function is to provide information.

operant (*Skinner*)   A unit of behavior emitted by the organism without being elicited by a specific stimulus, as opposed to *respondent.*

orienting reflex   An aroused reaction to a novel stimulus.

oscillation (*Hull*)   Momentary random fluctuations in excitatory potential.

parallel (distributed) processing   Carrying out different mental or computer operations at the same time in different parts of a system, rather than one at a time.

postulates (*Hull*)   The basic statements in a theory assumed to be true without proof and then used to deduce theorems.

prepared (*Seligman*)   Especially easy to learn; applied to a response in relation to particular stimuli or reinforcers that go well with it for rapid learning.

proactive interference (*Underwood*)   Forgetting that results from interference by something else previously learned.

procedural knowledge (*Anderson*)   The ability to carry out procedures; "knowing how" (as opposed to *declarative knowledge*).

proceduralization (*Anderson*) The change from control of behavior by declarative knowledge to its control by procedural knowledge.

production theory (*Anderson and others*) A theory of how knowledge gives rise to behavior.

program A series of instructions, as for a computer or for a student using a teaching machine.

prompt (*Skinner*) Any stimulus that makes a given operant more likely to occur.

psychotics People who are mentally ill.

reactive inhibition (*Hull*) The tendency not to repeat a response immediately after it has been made.

reinforcement The strengthening of the tendency to make a response that occurs when the response is followed by a reinforcer.

  continuous Occurring after every response.

  intermittent Occurring after only some of the responses, according to any schedule of reinforcement.

  vicarious Resulting from reinforcement to someone else (the model) rather than to the learner.

reinforcer One of a class of events that, when they follow a response, increase the tendency for that response to occur.

  conditioned One that is effective because of previous pairing with a primary reinforcer.

  negative One whose removal strengthens the tendency for the response to occur.

  positive (Understood when neither positive nor negative is specified.) One whose presentation strengthens the tendency for the response to occur.

  primary One which is effective without prior learning.

respondent (*Skinner*) A response elicited by a specific stimulus, as opposed to *operant.*

response Any item of behavior (usually analyzed in relation to a stimulus).

  consummatory One that takes in or uses a reward.

  instrumental One that leads toward a goal.

retroactive interference (*Underwood*) Forgetting that results from interference by something else learned more recently.

R-S* expectancy (*Bolles*) Cognition that a certain response will lead to a certain biologically important stimulus.

S (*Estes*) The set of all stimulus elements available for sampling on a given occasion.

S′ (*Estes*) The set of all stimulus elements not available for sampling on a given occasion but potentially available on another occasion.

scalloping (*Skinner*) A pattern of response in which the rate is lowest immediately after reinforcement and then gradually increases.

schedule of reinforcement (*Skinner*) The relationship of responses emitted to reinforcers received; the systematic pattern according to which reinforcers are delivered.

schema (*Piaget and others*) A fairly generalized cognition; an element of cognitive structure.

self-efficacy (*Bandura*) A person's sense of being able to deal effectively with the environment.

sensory register (*Atkinson & Shiffrin*)   The very brief recording of information as received by the senses before it either enters the short-term store or is lost.

$_sE_R$ (*Hull*)   Abbreviation for excitatory potential.

set point (*cybernetics*)   The particular level at which a controlled quantity is maintained by negative feedback.

shaping (*Skinner*)   Teaching a novel response by reinforcing closer and closer approximations to that behavior.

short-term store (or **memory**) (*Atkinson & Shiffrin, and others*)   The place or process in which information is stored temporarily in memory after being transferred there either from the sensory register (new information) or from the long-term store (old information).

$_sH_R$ (*Hull*)   Abbreviation for habit strength.

sign learning (*Mowrer*)   Classical conditioning of stimuli to emotional responses, so that those stimuli become signals for coming events.

Skinner box   An experimental chamber in which an organism can be placed for measuring the rate at which some operant occurs under various conditions.

solution learning (*Mowrer*)   The learning of responses that reduce drives.

species-specific behavior   Behavior particularly characteristic of a given species of animal that will tend to appear in that species under a wide variety of conditions and without any special training.

spontaneous recovery   The tendency for a response that has been extinguished to recover in strength with the passage of time without further training.

S-S* expectancy (*Bolles*)   A cognition that a certain stimulus will be followed by another biologically important stimulus.

stimulus   Any input of energy to the organism that tends to affect behavior.

stimulus control (*Skinner*)   The capacity of a stimulus to determine whether and when a particular operant will occur.

subject   A person or animal studied in an experiment.

tact (*Skinner*)   An utterance that conveys information, as opposed to *mand.*

theorem   A statement deduced logically from a set of postulates.

theory   A systematic way of describing and analyzing regularities in the way events occur, organizing scientific laws in a broader framework.

θ **(theta)** (*Estes*)   The proportion of elements in S (see above) sampled on a given trial.

threshold   The weakest stimulus that will elicit a response.

token economy (*Skinner*)   A form of behavior modification in which the desired behavior is reinforced with some form of symbolic reward (functioning as a conditioned reinforcer) that can be traded for primary reinforcers.

topology (*Lewin*)   The form of geometry that deals only with boundaries, not with distances or specific directions.

trigram   A sequence of three letters, usually not spelling a word, used as a stimulus or response in studies of verbal learning.

valence (*Lewin*)   The positive or negative value of a given place or situation for a given person.

variable   A characteristic that can vary from one situation to another.

> **dependent**   One that changes in response to changes in other (independent) variables.

> **independent**   One whose changes produce or predict changes in other (dependent) variables.

   intervening   Concepts hypothesized by a theorist to explain the connection between independent and dependent variables.

variable-interval schedule (*Skinner*)   An arrangement in which reinforcement follows the first response after a predetermined time since the previous reinforcement, a time that varies randomly with a specified average.

variable-ratio schedule (*Skinner*)   An arrangement in which reinforcement follows a predetermined number of responses since the previous reinforcement, a number which varies randomly with a specified average.

vector (*Lewin*)   A line representing the strength of the tendency to move in a given direction in the life space.

   identification performance (*Tolman*)   Vector referring to a tendency to observe something.

   pragmatic performance (*Tolman*)   Vector referring to a tendency to go somewhere or otherwise act on the environment.

working memory   A synonym for short-term memory (or store).

References

Allison, J. 1979. Demand economics and experimental psychology. *Behavioral Science* 24: 403–415.

———. 1983. *Behavioral economics.* New York: Praeger.

Anderson, J. R. 1982. Acquisition of cognitive skill. *Psychological Review* 89: 369–406.

———. 1983. *The architecture of cognition.* Cambridge, MA: Harvard University Press.

———. 1987. Skill acquisition: Compilation of weak-method problem solutions. *Psychological Review* 94: 192–210.

Anderson, J. R., Boyle, C. F., & Reiser, B. J. 1985. Intelligent tutoring systems. *Science* 228: 456–462.

Atkinson, R. C. 1974. Teaching children to read using a computer. *American Psychologist* 29: 169–178.

Atkinson, R. C., & Shiffrin, R. M. 1968. Human memory: A proposed system and its control processes. In *The psychology of learning and motivation: Advances in research and theory,* eds. K. W. Spence & J. T. Spence, vol. 2. New York: Academic Press.

———. 1971. The control of short-term memory. *Scientific American* 224: 82–90.

Bandura, A., ed. 1971. *Psychological modeling: Conflicting theories.* Chicago: Aldine-Atherton.

———. 1973. *Aggression.* Englewood Cliffs, NJ: Prentice-Hall.

———. 1977. *Social learning theory.* Englewood Cliffs, NJ: Prentice-Hall.

———. 1982. Self-efficacy mechanism in human agency. *American Psychologist* 37: 122–147.

————. 1986. *Social foundations of thought and action: A social cognitive theory.* Englewood Cliffs, NJ: Prentice-Hall.

Bandura, A., Adams, N. E., & Beyer, J. 1977. Cognitive processes mediating behavioral change. *Journal of Personality and Social Psychology* 35: 125–139.

Bandura, A., & Walters, R. H. 1963. *Social learning and personality development.* New York: Holt, Rinehart and Winston.

Bartlett, F.C. 1932. *Remembering.* London: Cambridge University Press.

Berlyne, D. E. 1960. *Conflict, arousal, and curiosity.* New York: McGraw-Hill.

Berlyne, D. E., & Madsen, K. B., eds. 1973. *Pleasure, reward, preference: Their nature, determinants, and role in behavior.* New York: Academic Press.

Bolles, R. C. 1970. Species-specific defense reactions and avoidance learning. *Psychological Review* 77: 32–48.

————. 1972. Reinforcement, expectancy, and learning. *Psychological Review* 79: 394–409.

Bolles, R. C., Holtz, R., Dunn, T., & Hill, W. 1980. Comparisons of stimulus learning and response learning in a punishment situation. *Learning and Motivation* 11: 78–96.

Boneau, C. A. 1974. Paradigm regained? Cognitive behaviorism restated. *American Psychologist* 29: 297–309.

Bootzin, R. R. 1975. *Behavior modification and therapy.* Cambridge, MA: Winthrop.

Bower, G. H. 1972. Mental imagery and associative learning. In *Cognition in learning and memory,* ed. L. G. Gregg. New York: Wiley.

Bransford, J. D., & Johnson, M. K. 1973. Consideration of some problems of comprehension. In *Visual information processing,* ed. W. G. Chase. New York: Academic Press.

Bransford, J. D., Barclay, J. R., & Franks, J. J. 1972. Sentence memory: A constructive versus interpretive approach. *Cognitive Psychology* 3: 193–209.

Breland, K., & Breland, M. 1961. The misbehavior of organisms. *American Psychologist* 16: 681–684.

Brown, P. L., & Jenkins, H. M. 1968. Auto-shaping of the pigeon's key peck. *Journal of the Experimental Analysis of Behavior* 11: 1–8.

Buxton, C. E. 1940. Latent learning and the goal gradient hypothesis. *Contributions to Psychological Theory* 2: 6.

Campbell, D. T., & Krantz, D. L. "Tolman's failure as a tribal leader: An essay in the social psychology of science." Paper read at 82nd annual convention of the American Psychological Association, 1 September 1974, New Orleans. Mimeographed.

Chambers, J. A., & Sprecher, J. W. 1983. *Computer-assisted instruction: Its use in the classroom.* Englewood Cliffs, NJ: Prentice-Hall.

Cowan, P. E. 1977. Neophobia and neophilia: New-object and new-place reactions of three Rattus species. *Journal of Comparative and Physiological Psychology* 91: 63–71.

Cowan, P. A., Langer, J., Heavenrich, J., & Nathanson, M. 1969. Social learning and Piaget's cognitive theory of moral development. *Journal of Personality and Social Psychology* 11: 261–274.

Craik, F. I. M., & Lockhart, R. S. 1972. Levels of processing: A framework for memory research. *Journal of Verbal Learning and Verbal Behavior* 11: 671–684.

Dollard, J. C., & Miller, N. E. 1950. *Personality and psychotherapy.* New York: McGraw-Hill.

Ebbinghaus, H. 1913. *Memory: A contribution to experimental psychology.* Trans. by H. A. Ruger & C. E. Bussenius. New York: Teachers College, Columbia University. Reprint. New York: Dover, 1964.

Elms, A. C. 1981. Skinner's dark year and *Walden Two. American Psychologist* 36: 470–479.

Epstein, S. 1967. Toward a unified theory of anxiety. In *Progress in experimental personality research,* ed. B. A. Maher, vol. 4. New York: Academic Press.

Ernst, G., & Newell, A. 1969. *GPS: A case study in generality and problem solving.* New York: Academic Press.

Eron, L. D., Huesmann, L. R., Lefkowitz, M. M., & Walder, L. O. 1972. Does television violence cause aggression? *American Psychologist* 27: 253–263.

Estes, W. K. 1959. The statistical approach to learning theory. In *Psychology: A study of a science,* ed. S. Koch. Vol. 2. New York: McGraw-Hill.

———. 1976. The cognitive side of probability learning. *Psychological Review* 83: 37–64.

Feigenbaum, E. A., & Feldman, J., eds. 1963. *Computers and thought.* New York: McGraw-Hill.

Ferster, C. B., & Skinner, B. F. 1957. *Schedules of reinforcement.* New York: Appleton-Century-Crofts.

Flavell, J. H. 1963. *The developmental psychology of Jean Piaget.* New York: Van Nostrand.

Fleming, R. A., Grant, D. A., North, J. A., & Levy, C. M. 1968. Arithmetic correctness as the discriminandum in classical and differential eyelid conditioning. *Journal of Experimental Psychology* 77: 286–294.

Frey, P. 1983. *Chess skill in man and machine.* 2nd ed. New York: Springer-Verlag.

Gagné, R. M. 1962*a*. The acquisition of knowledge. *Psychological Review* 69: 355–365.

———. 1962*b*. Military training and principles of learning. *American Psychologist* 17: 83–91.

Garcia, J., & Koelling, R. 1966. Relation of cue to consequence in avoidance learning. *Psychonomic Science* 4: 123–124.

Gardner, B. T., & Gardner, R. A. 1980. Two comparative psychologists look at language acquisition. In *Children's language,* ed. K. E. Nelson, vol. 2. New York: Halsted.

Gardner, R. A., & Gardner, B. T. 1969. Teaching sign language to a chimpanzee. *Science* 165: 664–672.

Glickman, S. E., & Schiff, B. B. 1967. A biological theory of reinforcement. *Psychological Review* 74: 81–109.

Goss, A. E., & Greenfeld, N. 1958. Transfer to a motor task as influenced by conditions and degree of prior discrimination training. *Journal of Experimental Psychology* 55: 258–269.

Greenspoon, J. 1955. The reinforcing effect of two spoken sounds on the frequency of two responses. *American Journal of Psychology* 68: 409–416.

Guthrie, E. R. 1960. *The psychology of learning.* Rev. ed. Gloucester, MA: Smith.

Guthrie, E. R., & Horton, G. P. 1946. *Cats in a puzzle box.* New York: Rinehart.

Haggbloom, S. J. 1981. Blocking in successive differential conditioning: Prior acquisition of control by internal cues blocks the acquisition of control by brightness. *Learning and Motivation* 12: 485–508.

Hanson, H. M. 1959. Effects of discrimination training on stimulus generalization. *Journal of Experimental Psychology* 58: 321–334.

Hanson, S. J., & Timberlake, W. 1983. Regulation during challenge: A general model of learned performance under schedule constraint. *Psychological Review* 90: 261–282.

Harlow, H. F. 1958. The nature of love. *American Psychologist* 18: 673–685.

———. 1959. Learning set and error factor theory. In *Psychology: A study of a science,* ed. S. Koch, vol. 2. New York: McGraw-Hill.

Hart, B. M., Allen, K. E., Buell, J. S., Harris, F. R., & Wolf, M. M. 1964. Effects of social reinforcement on operant crying. *Journal of Experimental Child Psychology* 1: 145–153.

Hebb, D. O. 1949. *The organization of behavior.* New York: Wiley.

Heppenheimer, T. A. 1988. Nerves of silicon. *Discover* 9, no. 2: 70–79.

Hilgard, E. R. 1964. A perspective on the relationship between learning theory and educational practices. In *Theories of learning and instruction. Sixty-third yearbook of the National Society for the Study of Education. Part I,* ed. E. R. Hilgard. Chicago: University of Chicago Press.

Hilgard, E. R., & Marquis, D. G. 1940. *Conditioning and learning.* New York: Appleton-Century-Crofts.

Hill, W. F. 1956. Activity as an autonomous drive. *Journal of Comparative and Physiological Psychology* 49: 15–19.

———. 1968. Sources of evaluative reinforcement. *Psychological Bulletin* 69: 132–146.

———. 1978. Effects of mere exposure on preferences in nonhuman mammals. *Psychological Bulletin* 85: 1177–1198.

Hillner, K. P. 1978. *Psychology of Learning: A conceptual analysis.* New York: Pergamon.

Hoffman, H. S., Eiserer, L. A., Ratner, A. M., & Pickering, V. L. 1974. Development of distress vocalization during withdrawal of an imprinting stimulus. *Journal of Comparative and Physiological Psychology* 86: 563–568.

Hull, C. L. 1943. *Principles of behavior.* New York: Appleton-Century-Crofts.

———. 1952. *A behavior system.* New Haven: Yale University Press.

Huxley, A. L. 1932. *Brave new world*. London: Chatto & Windus.

Kagan, J., & Berkun, M. 1954. The reward value of running activity. *Journal of Comparative and Physiological Psychology* 47: 108.

Kamin, L. J. 1968. Attention-like processes in classical conditioning. In *Miami symposium on the prediction of behavior: Aversive stimulation*, ed. M. R. Jones. Miami: University of Miami Press.

Kazdin, A. E. 1984. *Behavior modification in applied settings*. 3rd ed. Chicago: Dorsey.

Keppel, G., Postman, L., & Zavortink, B. 1968. Studies of learning to learn: 8. The influence of massive amounts of training upon the learning and retention of paired-associate lists. *Journal of Verbal Learning and Verbal Behavior* 7: 790–796.

Kinkade, K. 1973. *A Walden Two experiment: The first five years of Twin Oaks Community*. New York: Morrow.

Koffka, K. 1925. *The growth of the mind*. Trans. by R. M. Ogden. New York: Harcourt Brace Jovanovich.

———. 1935. *Principles of gestalt psychology*. New York: Harcourt Brace Jovanovich.

Kohlberg, L. 1964. The development of moral character and ideology. In *Review of child developmental research*, M. L. Hoffman & L. W. Hoffman. Vol. 1. New York: Russell Sage.

Köhler, W. 1925. *The mentality of apes*. Trans. from 2nd rev. ed. by Ella Winter. New York: Harcourt Brace Jovanovich.

Komar, I. 1983. *Living the dream: A documentary study of the Twin Oaks community*. Norwood, PA: Norwood.

Lawicka, W. 1964. The role of stimuli modality in successive discrimination and differentiation learning. *Bulletin of the Polish Academy of Sciences* 12: 35–38.

Lawrence, D. H. 1949. Acquired distinctiveness of cues: I. Transfer between discriminations on the basis of familiarity with the stimulus. *Journal of Experimental Psychology* 39: 770–784.

———. 1950. Acquired distinctiveness of cues: II. Selective association in a constant stimulus situation. *Journal of Experimental Psychology* 40: 175–188.

Lewin, K. 1935. *Dynamic theory of personality*. Trans. by D. K. Adams and K. E. Zener. New York: McGraw-Hill.

———. 1936. *Principles of topological psychology*. Trans. by F. Heider and G. M. Heider. New York: McGraw-Hill.

Linden, E. 1974. *Apes, men, and language*. New York: Saturday Review Press, E. P. Dutton.

Loftus, E. F. 1975. Leading questions and the eyewitness report. *Cognitive Psychology* 7: 560–572.

Loftus, E. F., Miller, D. G., & Burns, H. J. 1978. Semantic integration of verbal information into a visual memory. *Journal of Experimental Psychology: Human Learning and Memory* 4: 19–31.

Lorenz, K. Z. 1952. *King Solomon's ring*. New York: Crowell.

Mandler, J. M. 1978. A code in the node: The use of a story schema in retrieval. *Discourse Processes* 1: 14–35.

Meichenbaum, D. H. 1971. Examination of model characteristics in reducing avoidance behavior. *Journal of Personality and Social Psychology* 17: 298–307.

Miller, G. A. 1956. The magical number seven, plus or minus two: Some limits on our capacity for processing information. *Psychological Review* 63: 81–97.

Miller, N. E. 1963. Some reflections on the law of effect produce a new alternative to drive reduction. In *Nebraska symposium on motivation,* ed. M. R. Jones. Vol. 11. Lincoln: University of Nebraska Press.

Miller, N. E., & Dollard, J. C. 1941. *Social learning and imitation.* New Haven: Yale University Press.

Moore, B. R., & Stuttard, S. 1979. Dr. Guthrie and *Felis domesticus:* On tripping over the cat. *Science* 205: 1031–1033.

Mowrer, O. H. 1947. On the dual nature of learning: A reinterpretation of "conditioning" and "problem solving." *Harvard Educational Review* 17: 102–148.

———. 1960. *Learning theory and behavior.* New York: Wiley.

Orwell, G. 1949. *1984.* New York: Harcourt Brace Jovanovich.

Paivio, A. 1971. *Imagery and verbal processes.* New York: Holt, Rinehart & Winston.

Pavlov, I. P. 1960. *Conditioned reflexes.* Trans. & ed. by G. V. Anrep. New York: Dover (orig. trans. Oxford University Press, 1927).

Phillips, J. L., Jr. 1969. *The origins of intellect: Piaget's theory.* San Francisco: Freeman.

Piaget, J. 1926. *The language and thought of the child.* Trans. by M. Worden. New York: Harcourt Brace Jovanovich.

———. 1932. *The moral development of the child.* New York: Harcourt Brace Jovanovich.

Powers, W. T. 1973. *Behavior: The control of perception.* Chicago: Aldine.

Premack, D. 1959. Toward empirical behavior laws: I. Positive reinforcement. *Psychological Review* 66: 219–233.

———. 1962. Reversibility of the reinforcement relation. *Science* 136: 255–257.

Razran, G. 1961. The observable unconscious and the inferable conscious in current Soviet psychophysiology: Interoceptive conditioning, semantic conditioning, and the orienting reflex. *Psychological Review* 68: 81–147.

Restle, F. 1966. Run structure and probability learning: Disproof of Restle's model. *Journal of Experimental Psychology* 72: 382–389.

Rosenfeld, H. M., & Baer, D. M. 1969. Unnoticed verbal conditioning of an aware experimenter by a more aware subject: The double-agent effect. *Psychological Review* 76: 425–432.

Schank, R. C., & Abelson, R., 1977. *Scripts, plans, goals, and understanding.* Hillsdale, NJ: Erlbaum.

Schank, R. C., & Colby, K. M., eds. 1973. *Computer models of thought and language.* San Francisco: Freeman.

Schwartz, A. 1982. *The behavior therapies: Theories and application.* New York: Free Press.

Sejnowski, T. J., & Rosenberg, C. R. 1986. NETtalk: A parallel network that learns to read aloud. Electrical Engineering and Computer Science Department, Johns Hopkins University, Tech Report JHU/EECS-86/01.

Seligman, M. E. P. 1970. On the generality of the laws of learning. *Psychological Review* 77: 406–418.

Seligman, M. E. P., & Johnston, J. C. 1973. A cognitive theory of avoidance learning. In *Contemporary approaches to conditioning and learning,* eds. F. J. McGuigan & D. B. Lumsden. Washington, D.C.: V. H. Winston.

Seward, J. P. 1942. An experimental study of Guthrie's theory of reinforcement. *Journal of Experimental Psychology* 30: 247–256.

Sheffield, F. D., & Roby, T. B. 1950. Reward value of a nonnutritive sweet taste. *Journal of Comparative and Physiological Psychology* 43: 471–481.

Shiffrin, R. M., & Atkinson, R. C. 1969. Storage and retrieval processes in long-term memory. *Psychological Review* 76: 179–193.

Simon, H. A., & Newell, A. 1971. Human problem solving: The state of the theory in 1970. *American Psychologist* 26: 145–159.

Skinner, B. F. 1938. *The behavior of organisms: An experimental analysis.* New York: Appleton-Century-Crofts.

———. 1948. *Walden Two.* New York: Macmillan.

———. 1953. *Science and human behavior.* New York: Macmillan.

———. 1957a. The experimental analysis of behavior. *American Scientist* 45: 343–371.

———. 1957b. *Verbal behavior.* New York: Appleton-Century-Crofts.

———. 1958. Reinforcement today. *American Psychologist* 13: 94–99.

———. 1968. *The technology of teaching.* New York: Appleton-Century-Crofts.

———. 1971. *Beyond freedom and dignity.* New York: Knopf.

———. 1979. *The shaping of a behaviorist: Part two of an autobiography.* New York: Knopf.

Smith, K. U., & Smith, M. F. 1966. *Cybernetic principles of learning and educational design.* New York: Holt, Rinehart & Winston.

Smith, M. L., Glass, G. V., & Miller, T. I. 1980. *The benefits of psychotherapy.* Baltimore: Johns Hopkins Press.

Solomon, R. L. 1980. The opponent-process theory of acquired motivation: The costs of pleasure and the benefits of pain. *American Psychologist* 35: 691–712.

Solomon, R. L., & Corbit, J. D. 1974. An opponent-process theory of motivation: I. Temporal dynamics of affect. *Psychological Review* 81: 119–145.

Spence, K. W. 1956. *Behavior theory and conditioning.* New Haven: Yale University Press.

Sperling, G. 1960. The information available in high visual presentations. *Psychological Monographs* 74, no. 11.

Spielberger, C. D., & DeNike, L. D. 1966. Descriptive behaviorism versus cognitive theory in verbal operant conditioning. *Psychological Review* 73: 306–326.

Spiro, R. J. 1976. Remembering information from text: The "state of schema" approach. In *Schooling and the acquisition of knowledge*, eds. R. C. Anderson, R. J. Spiro, & W. F. Montague. Hillsdale, NJ: Erlbaum.

Stanfill, C., & Waltz, D. 1986. Toward memory-based reasoning. *Communications of the ACM* 29: 1213–1228.

Sullivan, E. V. 1967. The acquisition of conservation of substance through film-mediated models. In *Recent research on the acquisition of conservation of substance*, eds. D. W. Brison & E. V. Sullivan. Education Monograph. Toronto: Ontario Institute for Studies in Education.

Terrace, H. S. 1963. Discrimination learning with and without "errors." *Journal of the Experimental Analysis of Behavior* 6: 1–27.

———. 1971. Escape from S−. *Learning and Motivation* 2: 148–163.

Thorndike, E. L. 1898. Animal intelligence: An experimental study of the associative processes in animals. *Psychological Review Monograph Supplements* 2, no. 8.

———. 1913. *The psychology of learning.* New York: Teachers College, Columbia University.

Timberlake, W., & Allison, J. 1974. Response deprivation: An empirical approach to instrumental performance. *Psychological Review* 81: 146–164.

Tolman, E. C. 1932. *Purposive behavior in animals and men.* New York: Appleton-Century-Crofts.

———. 1938. The determinants of behavior at a choice point. *Psychological Review* 45: 1–41.

———. 1942. *Drives toward war.* New York: Appleton-Century-Crofts.

———. 1959. Principles of purposive behavior. In *Psychology: A study of a science*, ed. S. Koch, vol. 2. New York: McGraw-Hill.

Tolman, E. C., Ritchie, B. F., & Kalish, D. 1946. Studies in spatial learning: I. Orientation and the shortcut. *Journal of Experimental Psychology* 36: 13–24.

Underwood, B. J. 1948. Retroactive and proactive inhibition after five and forty-eight hours. *Journal of Experimental Psychology* 38: 29–38.

———. 1957. Interference and forgetting. *Psychological Review* 64: 49–60.

Verplanck, W. S. 1955. The control of the content of conversation: Reinforcement of statements of opinion. *Journal of Abnormal and Social Psychology* 51: 668–676.

Waldrop, M. M. 1988a. Toward a unified theory of cognition. *Science* 241: 27–29.

———. 1988b. Soar: A unified theory of cognition? *Science* 241: 296–298.

Walter, W. G. 1953. *The living brain.* New York: Norton.

Watson, J. B. 1913. Psychology as the behaviorist views it. *Psychological Review* 20: 158–177.

———. 1930. *Behaviorism.* Rev. ed. Chicago: University of Chicago Press. (6th printing, 1966.)

Welker, W. I. 1961. An analysis of exploratory and play behavior in animals. In *Functions of varied experience,* eds. D. W. Fiske & S. R. Maddi. Homewood, Ill.: Dorsey.

Wertheimer, M. 1945. *Productive thinking.* New York: Harper & Row.

Wiener, N. 1948. *Cybernetics.* New York: Wiley.

Wilcoxon, H. C., Dragoin, W. B., & Kral, P. A. 1971. Illness-induced aversions in rat and quail: Relative salience of visual and gustatory cues. *Science* 171: 826–828.

Williams, D. R., & Williams, H. 1969. Auto-maintenance in the pigeon: Sustained pecking despite contingent nonreinforcement. *Journal of the Experimental Analysis of Behavior* 12: 511–520.

Wulf, F. 1922. Uber die Veranderung von Vorstellungen (Gedachtnis und Gestalt). *Psychologische Forschung* 1: 333–373. [Translated and condensed by W. D. Ellis as "Tendencies in figural variation" in *A sourcebook of gestalt psychology.* London: Kegan Paul, 1938.]

Wyckoff, L. B. 1952. The role of observing responses in discrimination learning. *Psychological Review* 59: 431–442.

SUPPLEMENTAL REFERENCES

Readers wanting to study more thoroughly the topics covered in this book will find the following references helpful.

Bower, G. H., & Hilgard, E. R. 1981. *Theories of learning.* 5th ed. Englewood Cliffs, NJ: Prentice-Hall. The standard secondary reference on contemporary theories of learning, providing both authoritative descriptions and critical evaluations. The chapters vary in ease of reading; some are rather technical.

Koch, S., ed. 1959. *Psychology: A study of a science.* Vol. 2. New York: McGraw-Hill. A collection of 12 readings on various modern learning theories, most of them written by the theorists themselves. The study, of which this volume forms a part, emphasizes certain topics in the philosophy of science, with the result that the distinctive styles of some of the authors are partly lost. However, this is the most complete source book available for the classic learning theories.

Mazur, J. E. 1986. *Learning and behavior.* Englewood Cliffs, NJ: Prentice-Hall. A presentation of current psychology of learning organized by topics rather than by theories and with a good deal of experimental data on the various issues that concern psychologists of learning.

Index